D0880852

GUIDE TO ANALYSING COMPANIES

OTHER ECONOMIST BOOKS

Guide to Business Modelling
Guide to Business Planning
Guide to Economic Indicators
Guide to the European Union
Guide to Financial Management
Guide to Financial Markets
Guide to Investment Strategy
Guide to Management Ideas
Guide to Organisation Design
Guide to Project Management
Guide to Supply Chain Management
Numbers Guide
Style Guide

Brands and Branding
Business Consulting
Business Miscellany
Business Strategy
Coaching and Mentoring
Dealing with Financial Risk
Economics
Emerging Markets
The Future of Technology
Headhunters and How to Use Them
Mapping the Markets
Marketing
Successful Strategy Execution
The City

Directors: an A–Z Guide
Economics: an A–Z Guide
Investment: an A–Z Guide
Negotiation: an A–Z Guide

Pocket World in Figures

GUIDE TO ANALYSING COMPANIES

Bob Vause

THE ECONOMIST IN ASSOCIATION WITH
PROFILE BOOKS LTD

Published by Profile Books Ltd
3A Exmouth House, Pine Street, London EC1R OJH
www.profilebooks.com

Typeset in EcoType by MacGuru Ltd
info@macguru.org.uk

Printed and bound in Great Britain by
Clays, Bungay, Suffolk

A CIP catalogue record for this book is available
from the British Library

ISBN 978 1 84668 121 9

The paper this book is printed on is certified by the © 1996 Forest Stewardship
Council A.C. (FSC). It is ancient-forest friendly. The printer holds FSC chain of
custody SGS-COC-2061

FSC
Mixed Sources
Product group from well-managed
forests and other controlled sources
Cert no. SGS-COC-2061
www.fsc.org
© 1996 Forest Stewardship Council

Contents

Introduction

THE AIM OF THIS BOOK is to provide an understanding of how to analyse and assess the performance and financial position of a company from the various sources of information available. Financial analysis is as much an art as it is a science. Combine any two figures from an annual report and a ratio is produced; the real skill is in deciding which figures to use, where to find them and how to judge the result.

Before attempting to analyse a company, a sound grasp of financial terminology and presentation is required. Part 1 of this book explains the content and intent of the main financial statements appearing in a company's annual report: the balance sheet; the income statement (profit and loss account); and the cash flow statement.

All countries and companies share the basic accounting framework used in the preparation of financial statements, but their presentation is not yet completely standard. Adjustments may have to be made, but the outline in Part 1 is applicable to most companies and countries. Reference is made to the appropriate International Financial Reporting Standards (IFRS), but there is no attempt at a detailed interpretation of their application. This is an area of study you may move on to after this book.

As far as possible, the examples given have been kept simple in order to emphasise or reinforce the subject matter; once the fundamental theory and practice are grasped there should be no problem in moving to more detailed and sophisticated analysis. In general, the book's examples focus on retail, service and manufacturing companies rather than banks and other financial services companies, which are subject to a different set of legal and reporting requirements (as this fifth edition was prepared at the height of the 2008 financial crisis this proved an unexpected benefit).

Part 2 deals with the analysis of the different aspects of corporate performance and position. Three important ground rules apply:

1 Never judge a company on the basis of one year's figures. Always look at three, or, ideally, five years' figures.
2 Never judge a company in isolation. Always compare its performance with others of the same size and/or in the same business sector and/or country.
3 When comparing companies always make sure, as far as you can,

that you are comparing like with like – in other words, that the basis of the data being analysed is consistent.

Profit and finance are the two broad strands interwoven in the overall management of successful business organisations today. They also provide the basis for the analysis of a company. Each strand is equally important and both must be followed. Analysing a company's profitability without any reference to its financial position is of little value. Similarly, there is little point in completing a detailed financial analysis of a company's financial structure without reference to its performance. Profit is not sufficient on its own; a company must have the resources to allow it to continue in business and flourish.

A common corporate objective is to achieve a level of profit necessary to satisfy shareholders' requirements – to add value to their investment. Without profit there can be no dividend or share value improvements, or reinvestment for future growth and development. A substantial part of this book focuses on various ways of identifying and measuring profitability. Shareholder value is more than just annual profit, and not everything is capable of quantification. Future expectations of a company's performance outweigh its historic track record in determining its share price – which probably offers as good an indicator as any of shareholder satisfaction. Chapter 5 offers some general guidelines for undertaking practical analysis.

When the analysis of a company is completed, the tables in Part 3 offer some benchmarks against which the ratios explained in Part 2 can be tested and compared. This reinforces the last lesson of financial analysis: comparison. Producing a series of ratios for one company can be useful in indicating trends in its performance, but it cannot confirm whether this is good, bad or indifferent. That can only be determined by applying the three rules stated earlier.

An important lesson from the downturn in the 1990s and the financial crisis that began in 2007 is to invest in a company only when you are absolutely certain you understand the business and sector within which it operates. If you cannot see where the profits are coming from, don't invest. If you cannot understand what the company does, don't invest. In all probability it is not a failure of your analytic ability but someone practising corporate legerdemain.

The question of whether to use a rules- or principles-based system for the preparation and presentation of financial statements appears to have been answered. Financial reporting now operates under a set of mainly principles-based accounting standards kept on the straight and narrow by additional guidance and professional auditors as necessary. The key objective of the International Accounting Standards Board, "to develop, in the public interest, a single set of high quality, understandable and enforceable global accounting standards", is close to attainment. It is probable that all US listed companies will be using IFRS by 2014.

Despite the recent changes the terminology of accounting and financial reporting remains much the same, though the importance attached to some has changed. Understanding the meaning of "recognition", "fair value", "present value", "faithful representation" and others is essential to reading a set of accounts. This book is not intended to provide a detailed toolkit for financial report preparation but, rather, to give confidence in using the information contained in an annual report.

As far as possible the book is written with a light touch. It is not intended to be read from start to finish – dip in as appropriate. If you find a section hard going – move on; it will be my fault not yours.

Companies get their momentum from people, whereas financial analysis of their activities is an art. Art combined with people should be fun: if it is not, you should leave it to those who enjoy it.

1
UNDERSTANDING THE BASICS

1 The annual report – and what underlies it

ANNUAL REPORTS ARE COMPLEX and difficult to decipher – sometimes intentionally so. The increasing volume and detail of legislation, regulation, rules, accounting standards and codes of practice all contribute to this. In 1996 Deloitte Touche Tohmatsu estimated that the average company report contained some 45 pages. By 2007 this had risen to 89 pages, and today a listed company can be expected to publish more than 140 pages of corporate information. Each time there is corporate fraud or mismanagement, or a severe economic crisis, there is pressure either for a change in the role, duties and responsibilities of auditors or directors, or for the disclosure of additional or more detailed information.

The key items in an annual report are the financial statements. International Accounting Standard number 1 (IAS 1) defines a complete set of financial statements as comprising a:

- balance sheet;
- income statement;
- statement of changes in equity;
- cash flow statement; and
- notes including details of accounting policies.

These will be supported by a statement of accounting policies and other explanatory information.

A typical company annual report will contain:

- a financial summary;
- the chairman's statement;
- the CEO's review of the business;
- an operating and financial review;
- a directors' report (management discussion and analysis);
- a corporate governance report;
- a remuneration report;
- an audit committee report;
- a statement of accounting policies;

- an auditors' report;
- the financial statements;
- segmental information;
- a five-year history;
- shareholder information;
- notes to the financial statements.

There will also be, where appropriate, comparative figures for the previous year. The company can provide as much additional information, photographs, diagrams and charts as it sees fit. An environmental report is becoming increasingly common. In many cases the annual report contains 100 or more pages. Companies always face decisions as to how much detail to provide in the annual report. An annual report is expected to be timely. If information takes too long to collect the report may lose its relevance. If the cost of collecting the information is greater than the benefit of providing it, it is not worth it.

To read and use an annual report effectively, you need some understanding of the broad theory and the framework of financial accounting. The mechanics of double entry book-keeping do not need to be mastered. It is extremely unusual for a listed company to run into problems with debit and credit. The book-keeping process required to arrive at a balance sheet that balances can be taken for granted. However, some background might be useful.

Double entry book-keeping

Italy claims to have been the first country in Europe to adopt double entry book-keeping. Luca Pacioli has the accolade of being the first to publish on the subject. In 1494 he wrote *De Computis et Scripturis*. Little is known of him beyond that he was an itinerant mathematics teacher, an unsuccessful gambler and ended up in a monastery. His book included, for the first time, details of the double entry book-keeping (debits and credits) system being used in Italy.

Under this system every transaction has two entries in the books of account. Whatever amount is entered on the right-hand side (credit) of one account, the same amount is entered on the left-hand side (debit) of another account. This guarantees that at the end of the financial year it is possible to produce an income statement (profit and loss account) disclosing the profit or loss for the year and a balance sheet with assets (debit balances) equalling liabilities (credit balances). If whatever was entered on the left-hand side was also entered on the right-hand side, the total of the two sides of all the accounts must equal each other. The books must balance. In 1673 France had legislation requiring companies to prepare an annual balance sheet. It was not until the industrial revolution that book-keeping and financial reporting gained real impetus in Europe.

Who publishes accounts?

Every commercial business must prepare a set of accounts in order to agree its tax liability. Even when the organisation is a charity or otherwise tax exempt, accounts must still be prepared to allow those interested in its activities to assess the adequacy and probity of the management of its operations and assets. All public or nationalised enterprises are expected to produce and publish accounts in order to report not only to the state but also to the people.

Any company in which the public had been invited to become involved must publish an annual report containing a set of financial statements (accounts). All other companies with limited liability submit accounts to the tax authorities each year and file them, thus making them available for public scrutiny.

Limited liability

Most trading companies have limited liability. This was introduced in the 1860s to provide shareholders with some protection against a company's creditors. Shareholders (stockholders) providing a company with capital, through the purchase of stocks and shares, cannot be forced to contribute any further money to the company or its creditors. Having paid the $1 or £1 for a share or unit of stock, they need pay no more. Should the company fail they can lose no more than the $1 or £1 invested; their liability is limited to this amount.

Private and public companies

A quoted or listed company is one whose shares can be bought and sold on a stock exchange. A private company cannot offer its shares for sale to the public, so different safeguards and reporting requirements apply, compared with those for public or stock exchange listed companies.

Ownership and management

Shareholders of a private company are often directly involved in its management, often with members of the family acting as directors. Shareholders of a public company are much less likely to be directly involved in its direction. The management of a public company, its directors and managers, is normally clearly separated from the owners of the company, its shareholders. The directors act as stewards of their shareholders' investment in the company and each year are called upon to report the result of their management and the financial position of the company. At the annual general meeting (AGM) directors present the annual report and accounts to shareholders.

In the UK a public limited company (plc) must publish more information than a private company. This distinction is reflected elsewhere in Europe and the United States. The term 'public' in the plc refers to the size of the share capital of the company, so a plc does not necessarily have its shares quoted on the stock exchange. Public companies usually give a preliminary statement of the year's financial performance within a few weeks of the end of the company's financial year; formal publication of the annual report follows soon after. For private companies, there can often be considerable delay after the year end before a set of accounts is made public.

Consolidated accounts

Where one company, the parent company, has a controlling interest in other companies, its subsidiaries, it is necessary to prepare consolidated or group accounts. These incorporate all the activities of all the companies in the group to provide the consolidated financial statements, an income statement, balance sheet and cash flow statement. Since the 1900s, US and UK companies have been required to publish group accounts. The Seventh Directive on European harmonisation dealt with group accounts, and since 1970 they have been mandatory for all European Union (EU) companies. IFRS 3 and IAS 27 deal with business combinations and consolidated financial statements. The objective of consolidated accounts is to ensure that shareholders and others interested in the group of companies have adequate information upon which to assess its operations and financial position.

In addition to the consolidated balance sheet, UK companies must also provide one for the parent company, though this is often relegated to the notes accompanying the annual report. The presentation of a parent balance sheet is not required in the United States.

Minority interests

Where a subsidiary is not 100% owned, the outside or minority interest (MI) – the proportion of the subsidiary owned by those other than the parent company – is shown separately in the financial statements. Inevitably, some problems may arise in identifying ownership and control when there are pyramid structures of shareholdings.

All intra-group trading is eliminated to avoid double counting of profits, so only revenue from dealing with customers outside the group of companies is recognised in the income statement. However, minority interests must be credited with their proportion of any profits flowing from intra-group trading. What remains belongs to the parent company.

Details of subsidiaries

With a group of companies, the annual report should provide full details of all subsidiaries. The name, business, geographic location and the proportion of voting or other shares owned by the parent company should be disclosed.

If, during the year, a subsidiary has been sold or otherwise disposed of, details should be reported as part of the notes to the accounts on discontinued operations. Any gain or loss on disposal will also be disclosed separately.

The objectives of the annual report

The annual report was designed primarily to satisfy the information needs of existing and possible future shareholders. Financial reports are provided to assist and support their decision-making and to provide the basis for assessing the directors' stewardship of their investment in the company. Financial statements are not only a historic review; they also aim to assist users to predict the timing, nature and risks of future cash flows. Users should find the annual report understandable and comparable, reliable and relevant. A former chairman of the International Accounting Standards Committee (IASC) made the case for accounting standards:

> *In a rapidly globalising world, it only makes sense that the same economic transactions are accounted for in the same manner.*

The Framework

In the 1980s the Framework for the Preparation and Presentation of Financial Statements (the Framework) was developed to provide the basis for company reports. In 2001 this was adopted by the International Accounting Standards Board (IASB) as forming the basis for its work in developing accounting standards – International Financial Reporting Standards (IFRS) – that are used by companies and their auditors to guide the preparation and presentation of financial information. The Framework, for the first time, provided definitions of "asset", "liability", "income", and "expense". It provides the principles to be used in future IFRS.

The Framework is not an accounting standard but is intended to be the base reference point for all IFRS. This relieves individual accounting standards of the burden of restating definitions, principles or assumptions. The Framework defines the objective of financial statements as being not just for shareholders, but also:

> To provide information about the financial position, performance and changes in financial position of an enterprise that is useful to a wide range of users in making economic decisions.

Information on a company's financial position is mainly derived from the balance sheet and cash flow statement. An assessment of performance will focus on the income statement and the statement of changes in equity (statement of recognised income and expense).

The annual report is an important document, containing not only the statutory financial statements, tables, notes and management reports but also anything else that the company may wish to disclose. It is the formal report by directors to their shareholders of their performance during the year and the financial position of the company at the year end. It also has an important public relations role.

A listed company may have many thousands of shareholders, and even though only a few hundred are likely to turn up for the AGM, where the accounts are formally presented to shareholders, all will receive a copy. Anyone else interested in the company may also request a copy. Producing the annual report, which is often supported by audio-visual materials and internet access, is therefore a significant cost; a listed company typically spends between $500,000 and $1m on this publication.

Who uses the annual report?

Obtaining an annual report

To obtain an annual report the simplest method is to access the company's website – put the company name in a search engine. All listed companies have one, usually with a separate "investor relations" section which will include financial information. You will either be sent a copy or be able to download all of it or the sections of interest. There are also agencies offering to provide either hard copy or downloaded annual reports. In the UK the *Financial Times* (annual report service) offers a user-friendly service at www.ft.com/annualreports.

Annual reports are filed by government agencies. In the UK this is Companies House (www.companieshouse.gov.uk). In 2005 there were 1.43m accounts filed, and it mislaid only 112 of these. Securities and Exchange Commission (SEC) listed companies in the United States file their financial reports and other required information using Edgar (www.sec.gov/edgar.shtml) – the website provides free access to all such information.

All SEC listed companies file a 10-K report. This is in four parts and contains a wealth of detail and financial information. This can be accessed either through the company's own website or using the SEC website and Edgar.

Shareholders and their advisers

Shareholders range from individuals owning a few shares to institutions owning a large number, and it is a mistake to assume that the requirements of the two groups for information about the company are the same. Meeting the requirements of financial advisers, security analysts and shareholders in a single publication is even more difficult.

Shareholders own the company and use the annual report to discover how their investment has been managed by directors during the previous year. Shares are normally acquired and retained for future income and capital growth. The annual report provides the basis for assessing past trends, but shareholders will be most concerned with the level of dividends and capital growth they are likely to see in the future. In assessing this they will look at a range of measuring sticks covered in Part 2, including dividend cover, rate of return and debt/ equity ratios.

The people who advise shareholders, those who earn a living on the strength of their analyses and forecasts of company performance, will look at a wider range of measures and focus closely on indicators of the potential risk of investing in the company.

Shareholders and power

The majority of shareholders in a typical listed company may make up to 60–80% of the total number of shareholders but own less than 10% of the issued shares. The bulk of the shares – and therefore effective control of the company – is almost always in the hands of a group of institutional shareholders, usually a few hundred. These will include insurance companies, trust and pension funds, banks, private equity funds and other financial institutions. When a group of institutional shareholders get together to tackle a company they wield formidable power that cannot be ignored by even the most autocratic CEO or chairman. These are the shareholders that the directors listen to and try to satisfy. Because of this, and because they are well informed and highly competent in financial analysis, they are generally in a better position to know what is going on than small shareholders.

Lenders and creditors

Lenders – providers of long-term and short-term finance to a company – include not only banks, other institutions and wealthy individuals but also suppliers offering goods and services to a company on credit terms. They have strong incentives to assess the company's performance. They need to be assured that the company can meet the interest payments due on borrowed funds and that the loans they have advanced will be repaid when due. They are therefore likely to focus on profit and cash flow generating capability, and measures of liquidity, solvency and gearing (see Chapters 8 and 9). In assessing this a company's creditors – suppliers in particular – often rely on professional credit-rating agencies which will vet and monitor their customers.

Credit ratings for a company can run from AAA (the highest rating) through BBB (adequate) to BB (speculative) to CCC (currently vulnerable) ending with C (bankrupt). A few months before Enron's collapse, Standard and Poor gave the company's debt an AAA rating. Part of the fallout from the financial crisis that started in 2007 has been a further denting of credit agencies' reputations. In 2008 the International Organization of Securities Commissions (IOSCO) published a voluntary code of practice for credit rating agencies.

Employees and unions

Employees and their advisers or representatives turn to the annual report to help them assess a company's ability to continue to offer employment and the wages it can afford to pay.

Employees who do not turn immediately to the pages detailing what the directors have been paid usually show greatest interest in the particular part of the business – the division, factory, section or department – in which they work. Evidence suggests they have less direct interest in, or sympathy for, the company as a whole. Generally, employees are less able to read an annual report, which can create difficulties for corporate communication. Companies are therefore increasingly found to be providing employees with a separate report, briefing, or audio-visual presentation that provides a clear summary of important matters. Employees can, as well as anyone else, make use of the internet to access the company's website to see what information is available.

Government and the taxman

Annual reports and the information filed with them may be used by the government for statistical analysis. Company and personal taxation are often based on the statement of accounting profit given in annual reports. However, in most countries a company's tax liability is not fixed on the basis of the annual report but on a separate set of accounts and calculations produced for tax purposes and agreed with the tax authority. One exception to this is Germany, where a company's tax liability is fixed on the basis of the published accounts (*Massgeblichkeitsprinzip*). As a result, German companies can be expected to favour understating profits in the income statement, and understating assets and overstating liabilities in their financial statements.

Other users

Customers of a company will use its annual report to look for reassurance that it will be in business long enough to fulfil its side of any contracts it has with them. This can be particularly important in the case of, say, a large construction project or the installation of a complex management information system spanning several years, or the provision of a product or service where future continuity of delivery and quality is essential. The failure of a major supplier could have serious cost implications for the customer. The general public can also be expected to show interest in a company's annual report. They may be interested in the company's products or services, local investment and activities, or be considering taking employment with it.

The corporate persona

A company is a legal entity separate from its managers and owners. It can make contracts, sue and be sued just like an individual. Financial statements are prepared as if the company were an individual. For the purposes of law and accounting, it owns assets and incurs liabilities. Its net worth (net assets) is the amount it owes to its shareholders. The last act of a company before it ceases to exist is to repay to the shareholders the net worth (equity), if there is anything left.

Conceptual framework

Before reading an annual report, it is sensible to have some appreciation of the basis upon which it has been prepared. Financial accounting and reporting are governed by what are referred to as assumptions, concepts, principles, conventions, elements and rules. These have evolved over many years. They have been moulded by experience and linked together to provide the framework for the construction of a set of financial statements. They are applicable to every country and company.

Financial accountants, particularly auditors, are trained to be:

- Careful
- Cautious
- Conservative
- Consistent
- Correct
- Conscientious

These six Cs are evident in the preparation and presentation of the annual report. The IASB Framework identified two underlying assumptions, going concern and accrual, which together with the qualitative characteristics of financial statements provide the foundation for the corporate report.

Going concern

Financial statements are prepared at the end of the year on the assumption that they will form part of a continuing flow of such accounts into the future. It is assumed that the company will continue in business for the foreseeable future. In other words, it is a going concern. UK listed companies must provide a statement from the directors that they consider their company to be a going concern. For all companies it can be assumed that the financial statements have been prepared on the going concern basis.

Assets are shown at their "carrying value" – this is often cost less depreciation. Ideally, the balance sheet would use the fair value of all assets and liabilities. Fair value represents the market value of each item – the amount of cash for which an asset could be exchanged or a liability settled. This would offer a basis for assessing what the shareholders might receive if the company were sold or liquidated. In practice, the balance sheet contains a mixture of valuation methods – cost, replacement, present value – as well as fair values.

Normally, the value of assets on the going concern basis is greater than if the company had to be wound up and the scrap or break-up values were used. As long as it is reasonable to use the going concern assumption – the company is not going to be wound up – the carrying values shown in the balance sheet are appropriate for most purposes.

Accrual

The income statement shows the revenue generated during the year and matches it with the costs and expenses incurred in producing it. Income and expenses should be included in the income statement at the time the transaction or event took place. This is usually when it is invoiced, not when the cash relating to the transaction is received or paid. An item is recognised – brought into the accounts – when it occurs, not when cash comes in or goes out.

The accrual basis of accounting matches income and expenses for the financial year in the income statement without reference to their cash impact. The difference between the timing of the transaction and its translation into a cash movement is shown either as an accrual (money to be paid in a future time period) or a prepayment (money paid in advance for future benefit).

Recognition

Accounting standards refer to "recognition", meaning that an item has been entered in a company's financial records, the income statement or the balance sheet. Until an event or transaction has actually taken place it should not be taken into account (recognised) in arriving at the profit or loss for the year. A major customer may, at the end of a company's financial year, promise a large order. This is good news for the company. It will be recorded in the management information and control systems, and plans may be made to adjust the order book and production schedules. However, until a formal and legally binding agreement is made and executed, nothing has occurred as far as the financial accounting system is concerned. No revenue can be brought into this year's account. The transaction has not yet taken place and so is quite correctly ignored in the financial statements. Profit is made or realised only when the transaction is completed. For example, a sale is recognised only when the transaction is completed by ownership of the goods passing to the customer.

Asset values may increase as a result of inflation or market changes. This is beneficial for the company but it cannot claim that it has made a profit. Unless the asset is sold, any increase in value must be retained in the balance sheet as part of the shareholders' equity. A profit can only be recognised in the income statement when the asset is sold.

Money quantification

If it is impossible to reliably place a monetary value on a transaction or an event, it cannot be recorded in the books of account. A rule of thumb for accountants is "if you can't measure it ignore it". This is one reason accountants have such difficulties with intangibles (goodwill, brand names) or the qualitative aspects of a business. For example, the cost of a board of directors can be quantified to two decimal places and appear in the annual report each year. However, the question of what the directors are worth to the company is, at least for the accountant, impossible to answer and so they never appear in the balance sheet, as either an asset or a liability.

Accountants can be cautious in the treatment of intangibles or when quantifying "difficult" aspects of business costs and expenses. However, if it proves necessary for a measuring rod to be placed against anything, an accountant will prove well up to the task. For example, a company's employees could be quantified for inclusion in the balance sheet using human asset accounting, and there is increasing pressure to quantify and report on the environmental aspects of a business.

Qualitative characteristics

Consistency and comparability

A major dilemma for accountants is that accounting problems rarely have a single solution; usually there are several perfectly acceptable alternatives. This has given rise to the apocryphal story of a chief executive who is said to have advertised for an accountant with only one arm as he was tired of being told "on the one hand ... but then on the other hand ...".

A company could massage its profits for the year simply by changing its accounting policy; for example, by adjusting the inventory valuation or depreciation method. What may appear to be in the best interests of the company one year may not be in the next. If companies were allowed to change each year their methods of asset valuation and depreciation charging or the treatment of costs and expenses, it would be impossible to compare previous years' financial statements with the current ones. It would also be impossible to use the statements to compare the performance and financial position of a company over a number of years and with that of other companies. When comparing companies do skim the relevant section of the accounting policies statement of each one just to make sure you are comparing like with like.

Unless there is a statement to the contrary, it can be assumed that the underlying accounting policies for the preparation of this year's financial statements are the same as for the previous year. This is a requirement of IAS 1. As far as possible, from one year to the next, there should be consistency of terminology, calculation and presentation of all items included in the financial statements.

Companies can of course correctly decide to change an accounting policy in order to improve the quality of information being provided. When this occurs the notes in the annual report should clearly state the nature of the change and the reasons for it. IAS 8 provides the guidelines for changing an accounting policy.

Reliability and relevance

To be of practical use financial statements must be reliable. The IASB uses the term "representational faithfulness". The information they contain must be accurate, timely, error free, unbiased, complete and clearly reflect the substance rather than the form of transactions and events. Information is reliable if it can safely be used in the analysis of a company or in decision-making.

The information presented in the financial statements should also be relevant to users' needs. A company may show an asset in the balance sheet at a valuation based on cost. Cost is easy to find and reliable. However, the current market value of the asset – its fair value – is probably more relevant to those using the financial statements of the company. The IASB favours relevance over reliability and increasingly emphasises the application of fair value.

Substance over form

To obtain a true representation of a transaction or event it is often necessary to separate substance from form – "it's not what I say but what I mean". Merely to follow the legal form may not fully explain the commercial or business implications of what has occurred. It is more important for the basics of a transaction or event to be understood. A company's financial statements should clearly reflect the economic reality of any material transaction or event that has taken place during the year.

Neutrality

The IASB Framework makes clear that the accounting information contained in a company's financial statements should be unbiased in order to provide users with useful and, at the same time, decision-neutral information.

Materiality

Only items of sufficient importance to influence the decisions the users of financial statements might take need to be disclosed. The intention is to ensure that all appropriate information is made available to such users. Materiality is not quantified by the IASB but left to the company to decide. The 10% rule offers a rough guide to materiality in terms of size. For example, in segmental reporting, if a classification of sales revenue represents more than 10% of total revenues, it should be reported separately. IAS 1 makes clear that all material items, or classes of items (aggregation), should be shown separately in the financial statements. IAS 1 also provides limitations to the "offsetting" (netting) of revenue and expenses or assets and liabilities – this being allowed only in limited cases.

Prudence

The annual report will have a wide range of users with differing interests. It may be used as a basis for buying or selling the company's shares or even the company itself, or granting credit to, purchasing a product from, taking a job with, or lending money to the company. Because it is impossible in a single set of financial statements to meet all the requirements of all users, it is best for accountants to be cautious with the figures.

To help avoid overoptimistic definitions of profit in the income statement or asset valuation in the balance sheet, accountants developed the rule of prudence, caution, or conservatism. Profit or asset values should never knowingly be overstated. For financial accounting and reporting this can be condensed to:

- when in doubt take the lower of two available values;
- when in doubt write it off.

The Framework makes clear that prudence should never give rise to hidden reserves or excessive provisions – creative accounting. However, caution in preparing and presenting the figures appearing in financial statements is important. For example:

- value inventory at the lower of cost or fair value;
- write off potential bad debts immediately, not when all hope of collecting the money has evaporated;
- if there is any doubt about revenue, recognise it only when it is collected in cash;
- do not anticipate events – only include profits that have been realised during the year;
- take care to provide for all known liabilities and losses to date, although not to the extent of creating hidden reserves;
- recognise losses as soon as they are known, not when they happen.

When reading the financial statements in an annual report it can be assumed that all of these assumptions and qualitative characteristics have been applied. The overriding requirement for financial statements, and the objective of accounting standards, is to give a "fair presentation" or a "true and fair view" of a company's performance and position.

Accounting standards

Generally accepted accounting principles

The accounting profession developed rules and guidelines of best practice, but it was not until the 1930s that these began to be written down and codified. Every country has developed a set of generally accepted accounting principles (GAAP). These consist of a mixture of legislation, stock exchange rules, accounting standards, conventions, concepts and practice. The aim of GAAP is to ensure that the preparation and presentation of financial statements conform to the current best accounting practice.

The important words are "generally accepted" and "principles". GAAP do not comprise an unchanging set of written rules; they provide the skeleton upon which the financial statements must be fleshed out. As circumstances and theory and practice change so do GAAP. Most countries are now using IFRS and their individual GAAP are being reduced in relevance. National GAAP still exist in Europe, but the EU is gradually endorsing IFRS for listed companies – some 7,000 companies now use these.

There are some 15,000 SEC listed companies using US GAAP. In 2002 the IASB and the Financial Accounting Standards Board (FASB) – whose standards are enforced by the SEC – signed the Norwalk Agreement to work together. In 2006 they published a discussion document on their progress towards the development of a common conceptual framework (convergence) to be used as the basis for future accounting standards.

The FASB has been rules-based, producing detailed standards to be followed exactly by companies. The IASB is more principles-based, with standards indicating the way to provide financial information. The Framework provides the basic concepts that underlie the preparation of financial statements and allows standards to be principles-based rather than a set of detailed rules. There are pros and cons to both approaches. The collapse of Enron showed the shortcomings of the FASB approach, and the IASB's non-specific standards may make international comparisons difficult. Also the lack of precise guidelines can place auditors under considerable pressure. Neither approach is foolproof and combining the two is going to take some time.

European Directives

In the UK and the United States it is the accounting profession that oversees the development and implementation of accounting rules. In most of continental Europe this role is taken by government. In 1957 the Treaty of Rome set out the objectives for what has become the European Union. Directives are issued which member countries are expected to incorporate into their own legislation. The Fourth Directive (1978) dealt with accounting principles, financial statements and allied information with standard format enforced for the income statement and balance sheet. It also contained the "true and fair view" requirement in the preparation of the annual report. The Seventh Directive (1983) dealt with public quoted companies and the presentation of consolidated or group accounts, including the treatment of goodwill. This was adopted in the 1989 Companies Act in the UK.

Stock exchange listing requirements

In the United States the SEC imposes reporting and disclosure requirements on all listed (quoted) companies. In the UK the Financial Services Authority (FSA) took over this responsibility from the London Stock Exchange in 2000. The rules that companies must follow in order to be listed on the exchange are set out in the Listing Rules.

The stock exchange also reinforces the application of accounting standards by requiring companies to provide a compliance statement and an explanation of any material deviations. The overall objective is to ensure that investors have appropriate information for their buy-hold-sell decisions.

Every company listed on the stock exchange must comply with its listing requirements. This may call for revision of the presentation and content of the financial statements. Foreign companies listed on the SEC often have to disclose additional information to that required in their home country. In 1993 Daimler-Benz complied with US GAAP when it became the first German company to be listed in New York.

International accounting standards

Since 2005 all EU listed companies have had to use IFRS, and many other countries are opting for IFRS compliance. In 1990 the Financial Reporting Council (FRC) was set up in the UK to promote good financial reporting. In 2001 the Accounting Standards Board (ASB) replaced the Accounting Standards Committee (ASC), which had overseen the introduction of some 22 Statements of Standard Accounting Practice (SSAP). The first international accounting standards came from the International Accounting Standards Committee (IASC), set up in 1973 just after the United States set up the Financial Accounting Standards Board (FASB).

The IASC was reorganised in 2001 – by which time it had published 41 standards – after the International Organisation of Securities Commissions (IOSCO) agreed to endorse IFRS. The IASC Foundation now oversees the International Accounting Standards Board (IASB) with a Standards Advisory Council (SAC) and the International Financial Reporting Interpretations Committee (IFRIC).

The objective of the IASC is to bring about international convergence and harmonisation of corporate reporting through the adoption of IFRS. In 2006 the chairman of the IASB stated:

> A common financial language, applied consistently, will enable investors to compare the financial results of companies operating in different jurisdictions more easily and provide more opportunity for investment and diversification. The removal of a major investment risk – the concern that the nuances of different national accounting regimes have not been fully understood – should reduce the cost of capital and open new opportunities for diversification and improved investment returns.

From November 2007 foreign SEC listed companies have been exempt from reconciling their accounts with US GAAP as long as they have complied with IFRS. This has considerably eased the complexity and cost of an SEC listing for these companies.

Normally, the IASB publishes an Exposure Draft (ED) to allow comment and discussion on a proposed standard before it is formally issued as an IFRS. The IASB website (www.iasb.org) contains useful information on IFRS. Deloitte also offers a useful website (www.iasplus.com). It is worth having a look at any of the large accounting firms' websites to see what is available.

Sir David Tweedie has been chairman of the IASB since 2001. Described by the *Scotsman* newspaper as "the most hated accountant in Britain" – a title that does not seem to bother him – his latest clash with companies was over defined benefit pension schemes. He says: "I did not put the final nail in the coffin – I just measured it." He is the driving force behind the adoption of fair value accounting. His term of office ends in 2011.

International Acccounting Standards

IAS 1 Presentation of Financial Statements (revised 2007)
IAS 2 Inventories (revised 2003)
IAS 7 Cash Flow Statements
IAS 8 Accounting Policies (revised 2003)
IAS 10 Events After the Balance Sheet Date (revised 2003)
IAS 11 Construction Contracts
IAS 12 Income Taxes
IAS 16 Property, Plant and Equipment (revised 2003)
IAS 17 Accounting for Leases (revised 2003)
IAS 18 Revenue
IAS 19 Employee Benefits (revised 2004)
IAS 20 Accounting for Government Grants
IAS 21 The Effects of Changes in Foreign Exchange Rates
IAS 23 Borrowing Costs (revised 2007)
IAS 24 Related-Party Disclosures (revised 2003)
IAS 26 Accounting and Reporting by Retirement Benefit Plans
IAS 27 Consolidated and Separate Financial Statements (revised 2003)
IAS 28 Accounting for Investment in Associates (revised 2003)
IAS 29 Financial Reporting in Hyperinflationary Economies
IAS 31 Financial Reporting of Interests in Joint Ventures (revised 2003)
IAS 32 Financial Instruments (revised 2003)
IAS 33 Earnings Per Share (revised 2003)
IAS 34 Interim Financial Reporting
IAS 36 Impairment of Assets (revised 2004)
IAS 37 Provisions, Contingent Liabilities, and Contingent Assets
IAS 38 Intangible Assets (revised 2004)
IAS 39 Financial Instruments: Recognition and Measurement
IAS 40 Investment Property (revised 2003)
IAS 41 Agriculture

International Financial Reporting Standards

IFRS 1 First-Time Adoption of IFRS
IFRS 2 Share-Based Payment (revised 2008)
IFRS 3 Business Combinations
IFRS 4 Insurance Contracts
IFRS 5 Non-current Assets Held for Sale and Discontinued Operations
IFRS 6 Exploration for and Evaluation of Mineral Resources
IFRS 7 Financial Instruments: Disclosures
IFRS 8 Operating Segments

Statement of accounting policies

IAS 1 requires that the annual report contains a statement of accounting policies that the company has applied in preparing its financial statements. This will normally be found in the notes "Significant Accounting Policies". IAS 8 defines accounting policies as:

The specific principles, bases, conventions, rules and practices applied in preparing and presenting financial statements.

The objective of a set of accounting policies is to provide the basis for the faithful presentation of a company's performance and financial position. For each major item companies are expected to comply with all applicable accounting standards, and the statement of compliance is normally found within the accounting policies statement. Where there is no standard, management is expected to use appropriate judgment in the selection of the accounting policy to apply in its presentation and to disclose this. Substance over form is most important in such management decisions.

A statement of accounting policies will normally include:

- the basis of preparation of consolidated financial statements;
- conformity with IFRS;
- foreign currency translation;
- the treatment of intangible assets;
- the valuation of non-current assets;
- employee benefit calculations;
- income tax calculation;
- financial instruments.

It can be assumed that a company's accounting policies will be applied consistently from year to year (IAS 8). A company can change an accounting policy if this is required by a new standard, or the change will improve the relevance or reliability of the information being presented. Any changes in accounting policies will be set out in the annual report. When a company makes any such change, you should read the auditors' report to see if it gives the company a clean bill of health. If the auditors believe that some aspect of the financial statements does not comply with legislation, accounting standards or GAAP, they have a duty to make this clear in their report to shareholders.

Auditors

Every listed company must employ an auditor. Auditing developed in the 19th century to protect shareholders' interests. Auditors are professional accountants who check the accounting records and all other relevant sources of data and information, and report that the financial statements give a true and fair view (faithful presentation), and have been properly prepared in accordance with all relevant legislation and GAAP.

Auditors are independent of management. They are employed by the shareholders, not the directors of the company. They report directly to shareholders at the AGM. In the UK, the main professional body is the Institute of Chartered Accountants in England and Wales (ICAEW), and in the United States it is the American Institute of Certified Public Accountants (AICPA).

All countries have many firms of auditors dealing with small and medium-sized companies, but for listed companies, particularly if they are multinational, there are only a few suitable auditing firms. These are capable of offering full professional services anywhere in the world. They are as multinational as any company they may deal with and their names are well known. The largest (with total fee income for 2007) are:

- PricewaterhouseCoopers ($25.1 billion);
- Deloitte Touche Tohmatsu ($23.1 billion);
- Ernst & Young ($21.1 billion);
- KPMG ($19.8 billion);
- BDO International ($4.7 billion);
- Grant Thornton ($3.5 billion).

Size is important. A small firm of auditors, threatened with losing the business of a major company, might find the prospect made it more amenable to management's wishes. A large firm might not like losing the account any more than the small one, but it would not miss the income to the same degree. Bernard Madoff's $50 billion hedge fund was apparently audited by a three-person firm: a 78-year-old retiree and two assistants. This fact alone should have set alarm bells ringing well before the fraud was discovered at the end of 2008.

However, experience of corporate misadventure through the 1990s and the financial crisis that started in 2007 cast some doubt on the effectiveness of large auditing firms as a safeguard to shareholders. One particular problem in the 1990s was that, as a general rule, for every $1 charged for audit fees, professional firms seemed to generate more than $1 of non-audit related income. Can complete independence be guaranteed if the auditing firm is reliant on consultancy or other fees from the same company? In one year, Arthur Andersen, then one of the largest international audit firms, as auditors of Enron, received $25m; in the same year it received $27m for consultancy work. In June 1999 Rite Aid, a US drugstore chain, where the SEC found "widespread accounting fraud schemes" resulting in an overstatement of profits between 1997 and 1999 of some $1 billion, gave its auditors $1.5m in consultancy contracts.

With the increasing complexity of business and the penchant for litigation, the auditors' role has become difficult, risky and unrewarding. Auditing firms, in agreement with a company's directors and shareholders, often limit their liability. In the UK auditors are allowed to apply to shareholders for a liability limitation agreement (LLA). Previously, as with Arthur Andersen and Enron, auditors had unlimited liability. An LLA sets a limit to their liability in the law courts. Most EU countries have some form of limit to auditors' liability.

Auditing standards

Most countries have a set of auditing standards. These are the basis of the work of auditors and are mandatory for members of the profession. The International Auditing and Standards Board (IAASB), the standard setting committee of the International Federation of Accountants (IFA), has responsibility for International Auditing Standards (IAS), and International Auditing Practice Statements (IAPS).

Auditors' report

The purpose of an audit is to provide an expert and independent view of a company's financial statements. The auditors' report normally describes the respective responsibilities of management and the auditors for the preparation and presentation of the financial statements, the basis upon which the audit was conducted, and finally a formal opinion. The audit report states that the financial statements have been prepared properly in accordance with an appropriate financial reporting framework – IFRS, GAAP – and appropriate legislation. In the United States the audit report is likely to include the following:

In our opinion, the financial statements present fairly, in all material respects, the financial position of the company and the results of its operations and its cash flows for the year in conformity with US GAAP.

The auditor has the responsibility to:

Obtain sufficient appropriate audit evidence about the appropriateness of management's use of the going concern assumption in the preparation and presentation of the financial statements and to conclude whether there is a material uncertainty about the entity's ability to continue as a going concern.

For a UK listed company the audit can be expected to take, on average, some 60 days to complete. The annual report will include details of the auditors' fees for the statutory audit and any non-audit fees. The statutory audit fees for a large multinational company can range from $5m to $50m – in 2007 British Airways paid £2m and Barclays paid £25m.

True and fair presentation

In the UK reference may be made to the "true and fair view" requirement of financial reporting. This term is not used in the United States, where companies must prepare their financial statements in accordance with GAAP. The requirement for a true and fair view first appeared in the 1947 UK Companies Act and was adopted in the EU's Fourth Directive, where it is seen to be the prime objective of annual reporting. There is no definition of true and fair in the UK legislation or the Fourth Directive, but most people know what it means. The IASB uses the term "fair presentation":

The faithful presentation of the effects of transactions, other events and conditions in accordance with ... the Framework. The application of IFRS, with additional disclosure when necessary, is presumed to result in financial statements that achieve a fair presentation.

Some audit reports now use "present fairly, in all material aspects", rather than "true and fair view".

Qualified report

Always read the auditors' report. It is extremely important. When auditors feel it necessary to make any concerns they have public this should influence any view taken of the company and its management. If auditors are not satisfied with any aspect or the information provided to them or in the preparation and presentation of the financial statements, they have a duty to draw this to shareholders' attention. They qualify their report.

The auditors will detail the area of concern and indicate how this may influence the standing of the company. A qualified report over the application of an accounting standard or a change in accounting policy may reflect nothing more than a basic disagreement on principle between auditor and management and is not necessarily a serious problem. However, an auditor might state, for example:

> *This indicates the existence of a material uncertainty which may cast significant doubt about the company's ability to continue as a going concern.*

This is about as bad as it can get, and makes the auditors' report the most important page in the annual report. In effect, the auditor is saying, there is a likelihood that this company will fail.

The final resort of an auditor is to resign. In 2008 the third largest travel operator in the UK, XL Leisure Group, failed, leaving tens of thousands of people stranded abroad, and many thousands more lost their pre-booked and paid for holidays. In 2006 KPMG had resigned from the audit of one of the main XL subsidiaries after deciding there were "material errors" in the financial statements and warned that as a result these did not "give a true and fair view of the profit and state of affairs of the company".

Auditors and fraud

It is a common misapprehension that the auditors' main role is to search for fraud. An 1896 legal case in the UK provided a useful definition of the auditor as "a watchdog not a bloodhound". That a company has a clean audit report does not guarantee that there has been no fraud or, indeed, that the company will not fail the day after the annual report is published. In 2006 the Association of Certified Fraud Examiners (ACFE) published research suggesting that only 10% of fraud was initially detected by auditors, whereas 40% was disclosed by whistle-blowers.

Traditionally, auditors were employed only to ensure the presentation of a set of financial statements that provided a true and fair view.

Auditors must satisfy themselves that the company's internal control systems are adequate. It was a combination of less than effective auditing and sloppy internal management control that led to the demise of Barings Bank in 1995. In the United States auditors have responsibility for designing and completing an audit that gives:

> Reasonable assurance that the financial statements are free
> from material misstatement either by fraud or error.

Directors are required to make clear that they have complete confidence in their internal control systems, and that they consider the financial statements free from fraud and material misstatement. The auditor also ensures that the information contained in the directors' report is consistent with the financial statements.

Bannerman and Sarbanes-Oxley

Bannerman Johnstone Maclay were auditors of a company which failed in 1998 owing some £13m to Royal Bank of Scotland (RBS). In 2002 RBS sued the auditors, claiming that the financial accounts had misstated the true position of the company. This proved to be an important case (referred to as Bannerman) defining the duties and liabilities of auditors. The auditors claimed there was no duty of care to third parties, but lost the case. The judge ruled that as the auditors had not made it clear they were denying any duty of care to third parties using the audit report it could be assumed that this duty was accepted. The absence of any disclaimer was the key. An appeal in 2005 was dismissed. Following the Bannerman ruling PricewaterhouseCoopers was the first major firm to change its audit opinion statement to include:

> We do not, in giving this opinion, accept or assume
> responsibility for any other purpose or to any other person to
> whom this report is shown or in whose hands it may come
> save where expressly agreed by our prior consent in writing.

Most audit reports now contain a "Bannerman Disclaimer" – the auditors do not accept any responsibility to third parties using the annual report.

The new millennium saw a number of financial reporting frauds, the most infamous being Enron and WorldCom. In 2002, 186 large US companies filed for bankruptcy – WorldCom owing over $100 billion. In 2002 the Public Company Accounting Reform and Investor Protection Act – referred to as the Sarbanes-Oxley Act (SOX) – was passed. Directors are now expected to take responsibility for the effectiveness of the internal control system, and each year to review and report on it in the annual report.

The SOX created the Public Company Accounting Oversight Board (PCAOB) to protect investors and to ensure full transparent corporate reporting and the application of the highest auditing standards. The PCAOB sets the standards for auditing and auditors; there is no comparable body in the UK or European Union. Firms are banned from undertaking non-audit work for companies they audit.

Corporate governance

In the 1990s, after a series of examples of blatant mismanagement (if not fraud) in public companies, corporate governance became a major issue in both the UK and the United States. Additional disclosure was demanded so that shareholders and others interested in a company might gain confidence in its management and likely future viability.

In the UK in 1998 the Hampel Committee concluded that a board of directors should always act in the best interests of their shareholders and in doing so adopt the highest principles of corporate governance – "the system by which companies are directed and controlled". Hampel reinforced and expanded on the recommendations of the Committee on the Financial Aspects of Corporate Governance (Cadbury Code, 1992), and the Greenbury Code (1996) and resulted in the publication of the Combined Code. This was followed in 1999 by the Turnbull Committee dealing with the internal control of companies, the Higgs Committee (2003) looking at the effectiveness of non-executive directors and the Smith Committee (2003) dealing with audit committees. Companies are expected to follow the Combined Code on Corporate Governance and state this in their annual report.

In the United States in 1999 the New York Stock Exchange (NYSE) and the National Association of Securities Dealers Automated Quotations (NASDAQ) made independent audit committees a requirement for all listed companies. In 2003 the SEC laid down that the majority of any board of directors should be independent.

An annual report will contain a detailed corporate governance report as well as additional reports from the chairman and directors.

The chairman's report

Each year the chairman is expected to publish a report. This is not mandatory, there are no accounting standards or legislation requiring it, but it is generally accepted practice. A chairman can say whatever he or she wants, and this is not subject to strict audit. It is a personal statement in which anything goes – attack the government or spread a little home-spun philosophy. There is normally an overview of performance, often with only the bright spots highlighted, and a comment on the general business outlook. It is rarely found to be downbeat and is almost certain to be biased – to be read with caution and healthy scepticism.

The directors' report

The annual report contains a list of all members of the board of direct-ors with brief personal details. New appointment and retirements are noted. At the AGM directors will be put forward in rotation for re-elec-tion with a formal vote by shareholders taking place at the meeting.

Directors are accountable to shareholders. They have overall respon-sibility for the management of all a company's assets and equity. Part of their responsibility involves providing shareholders with not only finan-cial statements but also adequate information on the principal aspects of the business. At the AGM shareholders have the opportunity to raise any questions they wish. Such questions are not limited to the content of the annual report but may be on any topic. One of the key tasks of a company's chairman is to manage the AGM.

Each year directors provide shareholders with a written report. This identifies the main business activities of the company, and makes com-ment on the performance and financial position. If the directors con-sider that likely future developments may affect the company, they should draw this to shareholders' attention.

Operating and financial review

In the UK the annual report should include an operating and financial review (OFR), similar to the management discussion and analysis (MD&A) statement required of listed companies in the United States. The OFR or MD&A is a good starting point for studying a company. It is intended to be read and understood by anybody and therefore is rela-tively free of specialist terminology and jargon. If figures are included, such as those concerned with gearing or earnings per share, they should be clearly linked with those appearing in the financial statements. There should be reference to accounting policies with full discussion of any changes in the way in which the financial statements have been prepared or presented.

It should not focus just on good news and victories, as is so often the case with statements by the chairman or CEO. It would be unreasonable to expect a company to publish its corporate plan, but it should discuss business trends. Each year the OFR sets out the historic performance and activity of the company together with some indication of management's view of likely future developments. Any major deviation from these should be explained the following year. It is intended to:

> Assist the user's assessment of the future performance of the reporting entity by setting out the directors' analysis of the business.

Ideally, there are three sections offering a description of the business, its objectives and overall strategy, and its actual performance and financial position.

Pro forma figures

When faced with uncertainty, poor performance, or the need to hide incompetence or fraud, directors may be attracted to presenting "pro forma" figures in their reports to investors. They develop their own measures of performance that do not necessarily correlate with the published financial statements or support objective analysis.

If you find the terms "adjusted", "normalised" or "underlying" being used in the review of a company's performance, be on your guard. Examples of such measures may be found in the use of earnings before interest, taxation, depreciation and amortisation (EBITDA – see Chapter 6). A company showing a loss in its published income statement could produce a positive EBITDA figure. If in their discussion of performance directors choose to use a measure other than one firmly based on the reported financial figures and GAAP, a clear explanation must be provided.

The hindsight factor

There is only one attribute needed to ensure perfect financial analysis and investment: hindsight. A few days after a major event anyone can articulate precisely what occurred and the impact it had on a company and its share price.

It is easy to criticise the annual report as an ineffectual document. There are numerous examples of companies failing shortly after publishing apparently healthy figures. With hindsight there may have been clear evidence of directors' incompetence, if not misrepresentation and fraud. It is often the poor auditors who bear the brunt of criticism over their apparent inability to discover and draw attention to the real situation before shareholders lost their investment. However, the annual report is all we have and so we have to make the best use we can of it.

2 The balance sheet

THE BASIS OF FINANCIAL ANALYSIS is the ability to read the accounts. This is a necessary skill for any manager and essential for those with ambitions for a seat on the board. The balance sheet is one of the key financial statements provided by a company in its annual report. It is sometimes called a statement of assets and liabilities or a statement of financial position (the IASB is keen on this title), but most usually a balance sheet. Those with little or no financial knowledge often view it as a puzzle, and one best left alone. Others see it as the pinnacle of the accountant's necromantic art, with some spectacular effects but no real substance.

The balance sheet provides much of the data and information necessary to support the analysis of a company's performance and position. It is the starting point for an assessment of a company's liquidity and solvency (Chapter 8), gearing (Chapter 9) and the calculation of rates of return on assets, capital or investment (Chapter 6).

Balance sheet presentation

Proof of the book-keeping

Originally, a balance sheet was prepared at the end of the financial year to provide proof of the accuracy of the double entry book-keeping system. It listed all the balances in the books of account at the end of the year – hence the name. If the two sides of the account balanced with assets (debit balances on the left-hand side) equalling liabilities (credit balances on the right-hand side), it could be assumed that proper records had been maintained throughout the year.

The balance sheet can be viewed as a set of old-fashioned kitchen scales. On one side is a bowl containing the assets (items of value the company owns or has a right to receive in the future), and on the other side is a bowl containing the liabilities (amounts the company owes to its shareholders or others providing finance and credit). For any business, one side of the scales represents what it has got and the other where it got the money from. The two sides must balance. It is not possible for a business to have more assets than sources of finance, to use more money than is available, or to have more finance available than is used.

The balance sheet originated as the final statement in the book-keeping process and was never intended to show the value of a business. It was one of a continuing chain of year-end accounts. The balance sheet continues to fulfil its role as the final proof of the books of account, but in recent years it has gained a more central role in financial reporting. The IASB Framework favours a balance-sheet-first approach to income and expenses. Income may be recognised when there is an increase in future economic benefits arising from an increase in an asset or a decrease in a liability. Any such changes are taken either to the income statement or to shareholders' equity.

The balance sheet can be seen as presenting the fair value of assets and liabilities at the end of the year; the income statement contains the changes in them over the year. Changes in shareholders' equity are dealt with separately. The income statement shows the change in the wealth of the company from year to year; the balance sheet, taking into account all income and value changes, shows its financial position at each year end.

The year-end position

The balance sheet provides a snapshot of the financial state of a company at the year end, setting out is financial position on the last day of the financial year. The basic equation of the balance sheet is:

$$\text{Assets} = \text{liabilities}$$

Under the rules of double entry book-keeping, assets appear on the left side of the balance sheet and liabilities on the right. The UK was an exception to this rule, with companies displaying assets on the right-hand side of the balance sheet. This idiosyncratic behaviour dated back to the 1860s, when a civil servant made an error in the example of balance sheet presentation incorporated in a Companies Act. Assets were shown on the right instead of the left, and UK accountants followed the letter of the law for more than 100 years.

Where to now?

Traditionally, attention focused on the income statement as disclosing the profit or loss for the year. Income and expenses were matched for the year and any "leftovers" taken to the balance sheet. It was the calculation of the profit or loss for the year that was seen as most important. The balance sheet took second place as a less important statement. The emphasis on

fair value reporting has meant that the balance sheet has gained importance in a move to show the current value of assets and liabilities
employed. There has been some criticism of accountants forcing banks
and other financial institutions to apply fair value accounting during the
financial crisis that started in 2007. Rather than, as previously, showing
their assets – including sub-prime loans – at historic cost, companies were
pressured to show them at market value. The result was a substantial
write-down of asset values which, it was argued, added momentum to
the financial crisis and loss of confidence in the banking sector.

What to show

It is not necessary to prepare an income statement to discover the
change in shareholders' interest (profit or loss) for the year. If, at the end
of the year, all the assets of the company are set down on one side of the
page and all the liabilities on the other, the two sides will not balance.
The difference represents the profit or loss for the year. If net assets
(shareholders' funds, equity) have increased, a profit has been achieved;
if they have decreased, there has been a loss. When the income statement is prepared the final figure (profit for the year or net income) will
provide the necessary "proving" balancing figure for the balance sheet.
The IASB appears keen to focus on seeing the change in balance sheet
net assets as representing total company performance for the year.

Fair value

An important issue is what value to place on the assets and liabilities in
the balance sheet: their cost, or fair (market) value. The cost of an asset
can be defined with some accuracy; its true value is uncertain until it is
actually sold. Whatever method of valuation is adopted, any changes in
the value of assets and liabilities occurring during the year will have an
impact on the shareholders' stake in the business. The figures appearing
in any balance sheet are a mixture of cost and some estimate of market
value.

In recent years there has been a positive move towards using fair
value as the basis for balance sheet presentation. Fair value represents
the current exchange price for an asset or liability. The FSAB (FAS 157)
defined fair value as:

> The price that would be received to sell an asset or paid to
> transfer a liability in an orderly transaction between market
> participants at the measurable date.

The intention is that the balance sheet should, as far as possible, reflect the current market values of a company's assets and liabilities. This can only improve the appreciation of a company's financial position and performance.

Balance sheet building blocks

A balance sheet normally consists of five basic building blocks. These appear in the balance sheet of any company, irrespective of the nature of the business or the country or countries within which it operates. The way in which the five building blocks are set out depends partly on what is common practice or legally required within a particular business sector or country.

For most companies and countries the balance sheet displays total assets and total liabilities. IAS 1 requires that these are classified as either "current" or "non-current" depending on their expected life span. Current assets and liabilities are short-term and circulate as part of the operating cycle of the business. It is assumed they are received or paid in cash within a year. Any other assets or liabilities are defined as non-current. The long-term assets and liabilities employed in the business are defined as non-current – they are not expected to be paid or received within one year.

On one side of the balance sheet, non-current assets added to current assets gives the total assets employed at the end of the year.

Non-current assets	90
Current assets	60
Total liabilities	**150**

There are only three possible sources of funds that can be applied to finance total assets. Shareholders provide funds by purchasing shares or stock and allow the company to retain profit (equity). The company may undertake long-term borrowing (non-current liabilities) or use short-term borrowing and creditors (current liabilities) to finance the business. These sources of finance are set out on the other side of the balance sheet.

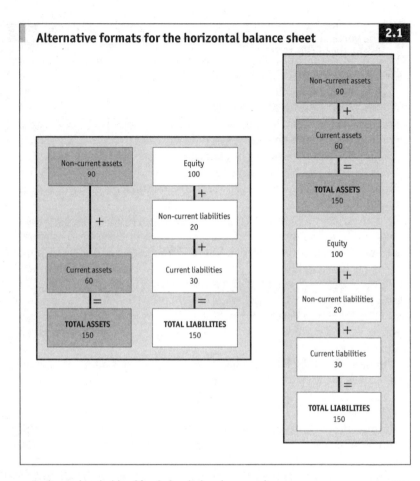

2.1 Alternative formats for the horizontal balance sheet

Equity or shareholders' funds (capital and reserves)		100
Non-current liabilities (long-term creditors and borrowing)		20
Current liabilities (short-term creditors and borrowings)		30
Total liabilities		**150**

Non-current assets + current assets = equity +
non-current liabilities +current liabilities

Total assets = total liabilities

2.2

The vertical balance sheet presentation adopted in the UK in the 1970s

How these three sources are combined to finance the total assets employed is central to understanding the financial structure – the gearing or leverage – of a company. In assessing the adequacy or safety of a company's balance sheet, the proportion of finance provided by the shareholders is compared with that derived from other sources: outside borrowings, loan or debt, and short-term creditors.

UK presentation 1970s-style

Having proved their obstinacy on the question of which side of the balance sheet to place assets, UK accountants remained out of step with those in other countries. The traditional horizontal presentation of the balance sheet was replaced by a vertical one that linked current assets and current liabilities to highlight net current assets. Net current assets are defined as current assets less current liabilities (see Figure 2.2). The fact that a company had more short-term assets than short-term

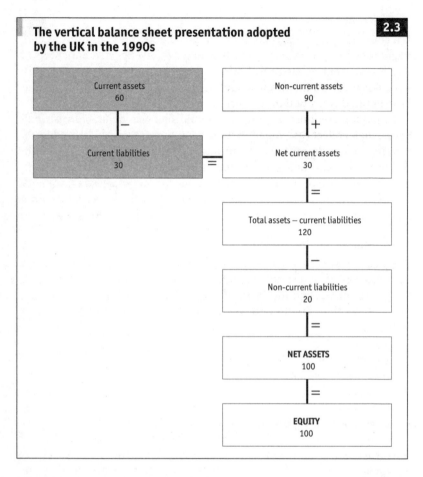

The vertical balance sheet presentation adopted by the UK in the 1990s 2.3

liabilities was taken as a simple indicator of financial health and solvency – the ability to pay creditors

Highlighting net current assets was seen as providing useful information on the extent to which a company could, if necessary, quickly pay its short-term creditors by using its short-term assets. Current assets, if not already in the form of cash balances, are assumed to be capable of being turned into cash within the company's normal operating cycle (12 months). Current liabilities are creditors due for payment within 12 months.

Net current assets

If a company is to pay its creditors within the next few months, where might it find the necessary cash? It would not be expected either to sell any non-current assets or to borrow long-term to pay short-term creditors. For most companies it would be reasonable to expect this cash to be generated from within the current asset building block.

In paying creditors, a company would first use available cash balances, then collect cash owed to it by customers (receivables), and lastly turn its inventory into cash. A surplus of current assets over current liabilities – net current assets – in the balance sheet indicates that a company has more short-term assets that can be turned into cash reasonably quickly than short-term liabilities that require cash for payment in the near future.

IAS 1 balance sheet format

The balance sheet format is guided by IAS 1, which provides for the classification of assets and liabilities as either current or non-current. IAS 1 does not define the form of presentation, but it does set out the list of items that should appear as individual lines in a balance sheet including:

Non-current assets
Property, plant and equipment
Investment property
Intangibles assets
Investments valued using the equity method

Current assets
Inventories
Trade and other receivables
Cash and cash equivalents

TOTAL ASSETS

Current liabilities
Trade and other payables
Short-term borrowings
Taxes payable

Non-current liabilities
Long-term liabilities
Deferred tax

TOTAL LIABILITIES

Equity
Share capital
Retained earnings
Other reserves
Minority interest

TOTAL EQUITY AND LIABILITIES

This is the most usual format for a balance sheet. Total assets match total liabilities and shareholders' equity. In the UK, some companies show net assets balanced against shareholders' equity.

Net assets = (total assets – total liabilities) = **Shareholders' equity**

Liabilities

The IASB Framework defines a liability as:

> A present obligation of the enterprise arising from past events, the settlement of which is expected to result in an outflow from the enterprise of resources embodying future benefits.

Equity

One building block in the balance sheet indicates the amount of finance shareholders (stockholders) have provided for the company. This can have a variety of titles – capital and reserves, shareholders' funds, stockholders' interest, net worth – but equity is the most likely. Equity is what is left when liabilities are deducted from assets.

Equity = total assets – total liabilities = net assets or net worth

The term net worth is a good basis for understanding what this building block represents. If the company with the example balance sheet used previously in this chapter were to close down and turn its assets into cash (a process known as liquidation), there would be $150 cash available. It would repay its borrowings and long-term creditors (non-current liabilities) $20, and short-term creditors (current liabilities) $30, leaving $100 in the bank. This $100 is the net worth or equity of the company. After all borrowings and creditors (liabilities) have been paid, what is left belongs to the shareholders. The final step, before the company ceases to exist, would be to repay to the shareholders the $100, representing their investment or stake.

IAS 1 suggests three subdivisions of equity (stockholders' interest): issued share capital, reserves and accumulated earnings or losses. The section of a company's balance sheet giving details of equity normally contains four main headings:

- Called-up share capital
- Share premium account
- Other reserves
- Retained earnings

Shareholders have acquired the issued shares or stock of the company and are its owners. The shareholders' stake represents a long-term source of finance (capital) to the company. The two principal items are share capital, the shares issued to shareholders, and the retained earnings, representing the profit retained (ploughed back) over the life of the company.

Retained profit

Under normal trading conditions a company retains some of the profit each year to assist growth and investment for its future development and success. In allowing the company to retain a part of the earnings made in the year rather than taking all the profit as dividends, shareholders are, in effect, lending this money to their company. Thus retained profit is a liability to the company and is shown as such in the balance sheet.

Share capital

Only shares or stock that have been issued and paid for by shareholders are shown in the balance sheet. These are referred to as the called-up or issued capital of the company. A company may have the ability to issue more shares from its authorised share capital. The number of authorised shares is the maximum that a company can issue. Most US companies disclose this information on the face of the balance sheet. In other countries, the authorised and issued share capital is usually set out in the notes to the accounts. The par, nominal or face value of the shares will also be disclosed.

A company may issue shares that are only partly paid for with the balance due at some future date. Details will be provided in the notes.

Share price and the balance sheet
Shares are always shown in the balance sheet at their nominal or par value, for example, 25p, 10¢, €10. The market price at which these shares change hands is irrelevant; there is no attempt in the balance sheet to reflect the stock exchange value of shares.

If a company is wound up or liquidated, it sells its assets, turning them into cash. This is used to repay short-term and long-term creditors (the liabilities of the company), and what is left (net worth or equity) is returned to the shareholders, who may receive more or less than the nominal value of their shares.

Ordinary shares
Ordinary shareholders are a company's risk-takers. They may lose their investment completely if the company fails and there is insufficient money available to pay the creditors. They are the last group to receive any money from a company in liquidation. However, ordinary shareholders can lose only the nominal value of the shares they own, although they will normally have paid more than the nominal or par value of the shares on the stock exchange. They cannot be called upon to contribute any more funds to a company. Ordinary shareholders thus have a limited liability.

The bulk of most companies' share capital is provided by ordinary shares (called common stock in the United States). In acquiring shares a shareholder obtains a stake or a share of the equity of the company. IAS 32 defines equity shares. Legally, the owner of ordinary shares has a right to share the profits and assets of the company as well as certain rights and obligations connected with its management. Ordinary shareholders have no rights to dividends. Each year the directors decide whether or not to declare a dividend and the amount to be paid.

IAS 1 requires full details of share capital to be disclosed and divides shareholders' interest into three sections: issued capital, reserves and accumulated profit or loss. A company may have several different types or classes of ordinary shares. Shares may carry different voting rights, with some shares having more or less than one vote per share. There may be differences in their rights to participate in profits being preferred or deferred.

Treasury stock

It is possible for a company to purchase ("buy back") and cancel or hold its own shares. These are referred to as Treasury shares or stock and form part of the company's equity. The result of share repurchase is to reduce the number of shares outstanding and increases the value of those remaining. IAS 32 calls for the purchase of shares to be shown in the statement of changes in equity. To protect creditors there are legal limitations to the proportion of shares a company may repurchase. A company cannot "trade" in its own shares, and if the shares are later sold at a profit this remains in equity and cannot be taken to the income statement. IAS 1 requires Treasury stock to be deducted from equity. No gain or loss on the sale, purchase, issue or cancellation of a company's own shares is taken to the income statement.

Preference shares

Preference shares were introduced in the 19th century to allow investors to participate with less risk in companies. Preference shareholders normally receive their dividend payment before the ordinary shareholders receive anything, and if the company is wound up they get their capital back before the ordinary shareholders. In other words, they rank preferentially for dividend and capital repayment. In return for these benefits preference shares usually have a fixed rate of dividend and few, if any, rights regarding the management of the company. Issuing preference shares allows a company to raise long-term capital with a known cost: the dividend paid. However, the preference share dividends are not tax allowable as would be interest paid on a long-term loan.

A company may issue cumulative preference shares. If in one year there is insufficient profit to pay the preference share dividend, the obligation will be carried forward to the following year when the arrears will be paid before the ordinary shareholders receive anything. Preference shares may be offered with the right to share (participate) in profits beyond their fixed dividend. These are called participating preference shares.

Normally, preference shares are irredeemable. They form part of the permanent capital of the company and are not expected to be repaid.

Sometimes a company issues redeemable preference shares. These may have a fixed date upon which they will be repurchased (redeemed), or the company may have the right to redeem then at any time. In rare circumstances, a company may issue participating redeemable preference shares.

Convertible shares

The term convertible can attach to either shares or loans. Convertible shares may be issued providing the owner with the right, at some time in the future, to convert them into ordinary shares.

A bank may be approached by a company for a loan. The company wants to pay as little interest as possible, and the bank wants the best security for both interest and capital. The bank may be persuaded to charge a lower than normal rate of interest in return for the right to convert the loan into ordinary shares at an agreed future date and price formula. The bank has security, as the money provided is not part of the company's equity but a loan. Also, if the company flourishes and its share price improves, the bank can make a profit by converting the loan into shares. Convertible redeemable preference shares may be issued, although they rarely are.

Reserves

A reserve is the setting aside of earnings in the balance sheet and is shown as part of equity. There are two types of reserves: revenue and capital. The retained earnings accumulated over the life of the company will normally be the largest revenue reserve. Revenue reserves are considered free for distribution to shareholders as dividends. Capital reserves (legal or non-distributable reserves) are not considered distributable and so cannot normally be used for dividend payments. Examples of these are share premium account and revaluation reserves. When foreign operations are translated into the parent company's currency for inclusion in the balance there will be differences in opening and closing carrying values. These differences are not taken to the income statement – they have not been realised – and so are shown within equity as a reserve.

Share premium account

If a company issues shares to new or existing shareholders, it offers them shares of the normal nominal value. It will take full advantage of the fact that its shares are being traded on the stock exchange at a price above their nominal value. So a company with $1 nominal value shares, taking account of the current quoted share price, decides to offer new shares at a price of $4 and the issue is taken up. As each share is issued and paid for the company's balance sheet is adjusted.

$$Cash + \$4 = equity + \$4$$

For each share issued the company increases its share capital by $1. The remaining $3 is the extra amount above the nominal value, or the premium, that shareholders are willing to pay for a share. The share premium must be shown in a separate account as part of equity and is deemed a capital reserve.

$$Cash + \$4 = share\ capital + \$1\ and\ share\ premium + \$3$$

A capital reserve can be used only for legally determined purposes; for example, it cannot be used to pay dividends to shareholders, but it can be used to cover the expenses of share issues.

Retained earnings

As a company generates and retains profit, the shareholders' stake increases proportionately. The balance sheet figure for retained earnings shows the total amount of profit retained by the company over its life. Retained profit is a revenue reserve. It can be used to pay dividends to shareholders and for almost any other purpose a company wishes.

Revaluation reserve

A company may be allowed to revalue non-current assets. Where the fair value of non-current assets increases this may be reflected in an adjustment to the value of the assets shown in the balance sheet. IAS 16 requires fair value – "the amount for which the asset could be exchanged between knowledgeable, willing parties, in an arm's-length transaction" – to be used in revaluing assets.

As far as possible the balance sheet should reflect the fair value of assets and liabilities. However, the increase in value of a non-current asset does not necessarily represent an immediate profit for the company. A profit is made or realised only when the asset is sold and the resulting profit is taken through the income statement. Until this event occurs the prudence rule requires that the increase in asset value is retained in the balance sheet. Shareholders have the right to any profit on the sale of company assets, so the shareholders' stake (equity) is increased by the same amount as the increase in asset valuation. A revaluation reserve is created and the balance sheet still balances.

Changes in equity

Equity is the amount left if all assets achieved their carrying values and all liabilities were paid. What is left – the net worth or net assets of the company – is the amount available to shareholders after all assets and liabilities are liquidated. This is usually called shareholders' or stockholders' equity. Share capital and retained earnings can be expected to make the largest contribution to the figure for equity. If the company has repurchased any shares (Treasury stock), these will be shown at their cost as a deduction from shareholders' equity. IAS 32 requires this information to be included in the statement of changes in equity.

The income statement provides details of all operating income and expenditure for the year with the after-tax profit (net income). A number of accounting standards require that certain gains or losses do not pass through the income statement but are taken directly to equity. There are also transactions made directly with shareholders such as dividend payments or share issues. IAS 1 requires a statement of changes in equity to be presented in a company's annual report. A Statement of Recognised Income and Expense (SORIE) takes the net income (after-tax profit) for the year and adjusts it for all items not recognised in its calculation for the income statement. This will include all changes in equity except share issues or dividends (these will appear in the notes accompanying the statement). The final step is to highlight the total recognised income for the year and show its division between equity and minority interest.

A typical SORIE will include:

Gains on revaluation of asset	XX
Foreign currency translation differences	XX
Actuarial valuation changes	XX
Cash flow and net investment hedges	<u>XX</u>
Net income recognised directly in equity	**XX**
Profit for the year	<u>XX</u>
Total recognised income for the year	**<u>XX</u>**
Attributable to equity shareholders	XX
Minority interest	<u>XX</u>

IAS 8 requires that any adjustments made because of a change in accounting policy or previous accounting errors are shown and described.

Companies may present a Statement of Changes in Equity (SOCE) – statement of stockholders' equity – which will include all transactions with owners including share issues and dividends. This should make clear what has brought about the change in net assets during the year. The statement begins with the opening balance of equity, then makes all necessary adjustments including net income for the year to arrive at the year-end figure for equity appearing in the balance sheet.

A typical SOCE will include:

Shareholders' equity January 1st	**XX**
Net income for the year	XX
Foreign currency translation	XX
Actuarial gains or losses	XX
Dividends	XX
Share issue	XX
Shareholders' equity December 31st	**XX**

Reference may be made to "comprehensive income". This is defined as the change in net assets during the year, except those relating to transactions with owners (share issue and dividends). The IASB and the FASB are looking towards replacing the income statement and changes in equity statement with a single comprehensive income statement.

Non-current liabilities

Equity is a permanent source and current liabilities (creditors due for payment within one year) are a short-term source of finance to a company. Between these two extremes is the third building block on the liabilities side of the balance sheet: non-current liabilities (long-term creditors and borrowing). These are sources of finance that do not have to be repaid within the coming year and are often termed "debt". In most companies debt consists of a mixture of long-term creditors and medium-term and long-term borrowings.

The notes supporting the balance sheet should provide details of repayment dates of all loans and the rate of interest applying to them. Often a debenture appears as part of the long-term financing of a company. A debenture is a loan secured on the company's assets, normally with an agreed rate of interest and a fixed repayment date. It is possible for a company to issue a convertible debenture offering similar rights to those outlined for preference shares.

The time when major loans fall due for repayment is an important factor in assessing the future viability of a company, because on the date of repayment the necessary cash must be available.

Another type of borrowing is through loan stock. Loan stock does not form part of equity (the ordinary shareholders' stake) and may or may not have the right of conversion into ordinary shares. It is often issued with warrants. The loan stock is not convertible, but the warrants allow the holder to purchase a fixed number of ordinary shares at an agreed future price and date. The advantage for the company is that the loan stock is repayable only on the set redemption date but new capital can be raised through the warrants.

Current liabilities

To an accountant, the term current means short-term, with short-term being taken as less than one year. A current liability – a creditor due for payment – is therefore an obligation that the company can be expected to fulfil within the 12 months following the date of the balance sheet.

The current liabilities building block in the balance sheet normally contains four main headings:

- Trade and other payables
- Short-term borrowings
- Taxes payable
- Provisions

The figure for trade payables comprises the money the company owes to its suppliers for goods and services delivered during the year. In most types of businesses suppliers are paid within 30–60 days, with the company taking 1–2 months from the delivery of the goods or services before making payment. Any creditors not due for payment within the 12 months necessary for them to be included as a current liability will be shown as a non-current liability in the balance sheet.

Until a company pays its creditors it has the used of the cash owed to them. Thus creditors act as a source of finance. Companies exceeding acceptable levels of use of short-term creditors to finance their business may be viewed as employing an aggressive financing strategy or they may be overtrading (see page 78).

All borrowings due for repayment within 12 months of the balance sheet date appear within current liabilities. In the UK, an overdraft, a form of short-term flexible borrowing, is technically repayable on demand so it is shown as a current liability. This will be the case even if there is an agreement with the bank to have the overdraft as a permanent source of finance.

The figure for tax shown in current liabilities can be taken as the amount owed by the company due for repayment within the next financial year. Remember that there is no guaranteed match between the reported earnings for the year and the amount of tax actually paid. A heading of "deferred taxation" may be found. This represents the difference between the amount of tax owed and that recognised in the income statement (see Chapter 3).

One explanation for the taxation differences is that the company may depreciate its non-current assets using the straight line method of depreciation but, in calculating its taxable profit, use a different depreciation method – normally an accelerated rate method. As an incentive to investment a company may be allowed to charge 125% of the asset cost as tax allowable depreciation, or it may be allowed to charge the total cost against taxable income in the first year of operation. A difference arises in the amount charged in the income statement to arrive at the profit for the year and that used in the tax calculation. Some tax is "deferred" to future years.

Provisions

The term "provision" may appear within either non-current or current liabilities in a balance sheet. When a company has an obligation that is likely to require payment in the future, but the amount is uncertain, it is prudent to earmark resources for this event, that is, make a provision. A provision is "a liability of uncertain timing or amount" and is made when:

- a company has a present legal or constructive obligation as a result of past events;
- it is probable that an outflow of resources embodying economic benefits will be required to settle the obligation; and
- a reliable estimate can be made of the amount of the obligation.

IAS 37 recommends the use of present value calculations where this improves the quality of the information provided. An example is when a company sells a product to customers with a replacement warranty.

Some products will have to be replaced, and the company should be ready to meet this obligation. However, the exact number of products that will have to be replaced cannot be precisely defined. The company considers that, based on previous experience, only 1% of products will require replacement within one year of sale. If it sells 10,000 units of the product and the replacement cost is $50 per unit, a provision of $5,000 could be created.

First year replacement $50 × (10,000 × 0.01) = $ 5,000

The expected value of warranty costs of $5,000 will be shown as part of the year-end current liabilities. Where the liability extends for more than one year ahead, IAS 37 requires discounting techniques to be used to provide a present value (see below) and the provision would appear in non-current liabilities.

Provisions were originally developed to allow companies to show that they had prudently set aside resources to meet future expenses that were "either likely to be incurred, or certain to be incurred but uncertain as to amount or date". Companies soon realised that they could take advantage of provisions to massage their earnings. A company would make a provision for the anticipated losses on closing down a business or the costs of major restructuring following an acquisition. Significant amounts of one year's profit would be set aside. Then the company would discover it had overprovided for the event and would bring the provision back to boost a future year's profit. These were called "big bath" or "kitchen sink" provisions. They proved a simple but effective tactic for an executive brought in to turn a company round. Investors expected to suffer in the first year and were delighted when "profit" returned in the second.

Big bath provisions have effectively been outlawed by IAS 37, which sets out clear rules for the creation of a provision. Management's intentions alone are not a sufficient reason to create a provision. There must be an unavoidable obligation on the company to incur the expense being provided for. A simple check is to apply the "year-end test": if a company ceased to trade at the balance sheet date, would it still have to pay the amount involved? If not, there can be no provision made as it relates to future, not past, business activity.

Contingent liability

Sometimes a company faces a possible future event that is uncertain and difficult to measure – a contingent liability or asset. It may be involved in a law action where the outcome is still unknown. IAS 37 defines a contingent liability as:

> A possible obligation that arises from past events whose existence will only be confirmed by the occurrence or non-occurrence of one or more uncertain future events not wholly within the control of the entity.

There is a problem of accurate measurement and so it cannot be recognised in the financial statements. However, users of the annual report should be made aware of its existence as it may well influence their view of the company. The information will be provided in the annual report notes. It is possible, but unusual, to find a contingent asset listed in the notes.

Assets

The IASB Framework defines an asset as:

> A resource controlled by the enterprise as a result of past events and from which future economic benefits are expected to flow to the enterprise.

Two building blocks appear on the assets side of the balance sheet: non-current or long-lived assets (these used to be called "fixed assets") and current or short-term assets. Non-current assets are mainly tangible, such as the physical assets used to undertake the business of the company. They include land and buildings, plant and equipment, vehicles, and fixtures and fittings.

Non-current assets

Non-current assets are divided into two classes: tangible and intangible. Tangible assets have a finite useful working life. Investment in them ties up the company's available financial resources for a number of years. Tangible assets are depreciated, amortised or written off over their useful life. They are shown in the balance sheet at their carrying value – normally cost less accumulated depreciation.

IAS 16 provides the basis for the provision of information on tangible assets. There is usually a single figure in the balance sheet for property, plant and equipment (PP&E). These are assets used on a continuing basis in the company's business activities. The figure shown is their balance sheet value, net book value (NBV) or written down value (WDV), which represents their cost, or fair value, less the accumulated depreciation charged over their life.

To be recognised – included in the accounts – an asset must have a clearly defined cost or value that can be reliably measured. There are a number of ways to value an asset: historic cost, current replacement cost, net realisable value, present value (discounted expected future cash flows) or fair value (market value). Purchase price or cost of is commonly the basis for asset valuation. Where the asset was acquired not by cash payment but other means – issue of shares or exchange of assets – then, if possible, fair value is used as the basis of valuation.

The initial cost of an asset may include all expenses necessary to get it into a working state – labour, materials and other costs are capitalised – as long as this does not result in the carrying value exceeding its fair value.

As with almost every figure appearing in the balance sheet, it is to the notes in the accounts that you must turn to find useful details. At a minimum there should be, for each major component of tangible assets, details of:

- cost or fair value at the beginning of the year;
- accumulated depreciation charged at the beginning of the year;
- amount of depreciation charged during the year;
- any additions or disposals made during the year;
- net carrying amount (balance sheet) value at the end of the year;
- freehold and leasehold property.

Government grants

Government grants or incentives are often available to encourage investment in PP&E. IAS 20 allows the grant either to be deducted from the value of the asset or to be shown as "deferred income" in the balance sheet and written off over the life of the asset. Whichever method is adopted the reported earnings of the company are identical. For example, a company purchases an asset for $10,000 and receives a government grant of $2,000. The asset has an expected useful working life of four years. The asset may be shown in the balance sheet at $8,000 and depreciated at $2,000 per year. The alternative is for the balance sheet to show the asset valued at $10,000 and deferred income of $2,000. The asset is depreciated at $2,500 per year with deferred income of $500 per year set against this, providing a $2,000 per year net charge in the income statement.

Capitalisation of expenses

Companies used to have considerable flexibility in deciding whether or not to capitalise expenses. Rather than charging an expense in the income statement, it was taken to the balance as an asset and profit was increased by reducing the amount of expenses being charged against income. Currently, only the borrowing costs associated with a non-current asset, where it takes a considerable time to get it operational, may be capitalised. This treatment is governed by IAS 23, with the cost added to the carrying value of the asset and expensed (taken to the income statement) over its life as part of the depreciation charge.

Depreciation

IAS 16 defines depreciation as "the systematic allocation of the depreciable amount of an asset over its useful life". Depreciation is not an attempt to measure the change in value of an asset but a means, over its useful working life, of charging its cost to the income statement. Depreciation, or amortisation, can be viewed as representing the setting aside of income to provide for the future replacement of physical assets. It is to be expected that all assets, except land, are depreciated over their useful working life. As assets are used their value reduces. They become worn out, run-down, or obsolete and need replacing in order to maintain or improve the productive efficiency of the business.

Depreciation is a provision, a setting aside of current income to meet future eventualities, so it could be shown in the balance sheet as part of equity in the same way as retained earnings.

Equity	$	Non-current assets	$
Depreciation provision	100	Tangible assets at cost	200

However, it has been traditional policy to deduct depreciation from the asset value in the balance sheet.

Non-current assets	$	$
Tangible assets at cost	200	
Less depreciation	100	100

Depreciation is charged as an expense in the income statement; this reduces reported profit. It is also deducted from the value of non-current assets set out in the balance sheet, thus reducing the value of the company's assets. The income statement is charged with the use of the assets and the balance sheet is adjusted to compensate. See Chapter 3 for details of the depreciation charge.

Inflation and non-current assets

Inflation can complicate the valuation of assets because $1 at the beginning of the year will purchase more than $1 at the end of the year. When inflation is low, it is reasonable to use historic cost – what the asset cost when acquired – as the basis for the valuation of a company's assets and depreciation.

A company that had not revalued property purchased in 1980 would face two problems in relation to its balance sheet. First, the property would be undervalued because to replace it would cost significantly more than the 1980 figure. Undervaluing assets may improve the reported profit of the company, as a result of a lower than realistic depreciation charge, but it may prove dangerous by making the company an attractive target for takeover. If the published balance sheet value was used to set the acquisition price, it would be far below fair value (current market value). Second, if the property needs replacing or major investment to maintain it, the company may not have been setting aside sufficient profits, through depreciation, for this to be possible.

For example, an entrepreneur starts a company in 2003 with an investment of $10,000, which is used to purchase a non-current asset. The balance sheet at this point is as follows:

	$		$
Non-current assets	10,000		
Cash	0	Share capital	10,000

The asset has a useful working life of five years and, following IAS 16, is depreciated or written off in the income statement at the rate of $2,000 per year. Each year the company makes a profit of $2,000 (after depreciation). In 2008 the company's balance sheet would appear as follows.

	$		$
Non-current asset cost	10,000	Share capital	10,000
Less depreciation	10,000	0 Retained earnings	10,000
Cash		20,000	20,000

The $20,000 cash balance is the result of five years' retained profit ($2,000) and five years' depreciation ($2,000). The business has doubled in size between 2003 and 2008.

The entrepreneur decides to replace the asset and continue the business. However, at the end of 2008 an identical asset to that purchased in 2003 costs $20,000; the price has doubled because of inflation. The investment is completed and the balance sheet shows the following:

	$		
Non-current asset	20,000		
Cash	0	20,000 Equity	20,000

The company is now in exactly the same position it was five years before; it has a new asset and no cash. Has the company really made the $10,000 profit shown in the balance sheet? Indeed, if it had been paying tax at 50% it would be necessary to borrow money to replace the asset at the end of 2008. This example illustrates the problems of financial reporting under conditions of inflation and the benefits of fair value accounting – using the current market value of assets and liabilities.

The overriding rule of faithful presentation (incorporating prudence), supported by that of capital maintenance (see Chapter 6), requires that a company take account of the impact of inflation in the reporting process. There are many ways of countering or reflecting this in corporate reports. One approach is to take an appropriate index of inflation, such as the retail price index, and apply this to the assets and liabilities of a company to bring these to current values – current purchasing power (CPP) accounting. The simplest method is to use fair value – the current market value – as the basis for valuing assets and charging appropriate depreciation rates. IAS 29 deals with the issues of hyperinflation.

Asset revaluation and sale

The historic cost or a revaluation provides the basis for accounting for tangible non-current assets. Under conditions of inflation, using historic cost as the basis for depreciation will overstate real earnings. Revaluing assets will overcome this problem. IAS 16 requires that fair value –

current value – be the basis of any asset revaluation. When an asset is revalued all other similar assets must also be revalued. This avoids the potential problem of having varying valuation methods within an asset class. The amount of any revaluation is taken to a revaluation reserve in equity.

Once a revaluation reserve is created it remains within equity. The increase in asset value cannot be taken into the income statement. If at some time after revaluation the fair value of the asset falls, the resulting loss of value is deducted from the revaluation reserve; it is not taken into the income statement.

If a company purchases an asset for $100,000 with an expected ten-year life, it will have a carrying value of $50,000 at the end of five years. If the asset is then revalued to $70,000 a revaluation reserve of $20,000 is created, and the balance sheet still balances. For the remaining five years the depreciation charge will be $14,000 per year ($70,000 ÷ 5). This is produced by charging the income statement with $10,000 (as in previous years) and reducing the revaluation reserve by $4,000.

Two years later the carrying value is $42,000, and the asset is sold for $50,000. IAS 16 requires the profit on the sale of $8,000 to be taken to the income statement, and the revaluation reserve of $12,000 ($20,000 less $8,000 depreciation) to be transferred to retained profit.

Foreign exchange

If a company trades or makes investments or acquisitions in another country, it usually has to deal in a foreign currency. A foreign subsidiary will keep its records in its own currency. For consolidation purposes these will have to be translated into the currency of the parent company. IAS 21 provides the guidelines for foreign currency transactions. You may find reference to three different definitions for currencies involved in foreign operations:

- Local currency – in which a subsidiary keeps its records.
- Functional currency – in which the parent company trades.
- Presentation currency – used in the group's financial statements.

Reference may also be made to the following:

- Spot rate – the exchange rate at the date of the transaction.
- Closing rate – the spot rate at the balance sheet date.
- Average rate – the average exchange rate for the year.

If exchange rates remained constant, accountants would have few problems. Unfortunately, for both accountants and companies, exchange rates fluctuate, not only from year to year but also from minute to minute.

As an example, if a company purchased a machine in France for $100,000 when the exchange rate was $1 = €1.25, it would appear in the balance sheet at $80,000 (100,000 ÷ 1.25). If the machine was purchased on credit and at the end of the year the amount was still owing and the exchange rate had moved to $1 = €1.10, the account payable (a monetary item) would be re-translated to $90,909 (100,000 ÷ 1.1) and the currency translation difference of $10,909 (loss) would be taken to the income statement.

If the $100,000 (at $1 = €1.25) represented the acquisition of a foreign subsidiary at the beginning or the year and at the end of the year the rate had moved to $1 = €1.10, the $10,909 currency difference would be taken not to the income statement but directly to equity (IAS 21).

If a UK company sells a machine for $10,000 to a US customer when the exchange rate is $1 = £0.63, the transaction is recorded as sale and receivable of £6,300. If, by the time payment is made, the pound has strengthened against the dollar to $1 = £0.57, only £5,700 will be received and an exchange rate loss of £600 will need to be recognised in the income statement.

If rather than normal trading and investment activity a company makes an acquisition in a foreign country, consolidated accounts will have to be prepared. To consolidate a subsidiary, some basic rules of procedure are required. There are several options available in choosing the exchange rate that best reflects trading during the year (for the income statement) and the year-end position (for the balance sheet). The options are:

- average exchange rate for the year;
- exchange rate at the time of the transaction (spot rate);
- exchange rate at the end of the financial year (closing rate).

It is reasonable and practical to use the exchange rate applicable at the year end (the balance sheet date) for the consolidation of overseas assets and liabilities. It is most common for the net worth of a foreign subsidiary to be brought into the accounts at the exchange rate applicable at the balance sheet date. Any gain or loss does not reach the income statement but is retained in the parent company's equity. For trading transactions, either the exchange rate at the date of the transaction or an average rate is used with the profit or loss taken to the income statement.

Hedging

It is normally accepted that a prudent company would endeavour to reduce or minimise its exposure to risk through exchange rate fluctuations by covering the potential risks. For example, a company might borrow in the foreign currency a sum equivalent to the amount of the investment it is going to make in the foreign subsidiary. Or the company might take a "put" option to sell one of its long-term investments for an agreed sum in the future. This approach, which is called hedging, means that any change in exchange rates is automatically adjusted on both the asset and liability side of the balance sheet. IAS 7 requires each type of hedge to be disclosed and fully described.

Do not mix up hedging with hedge funds. A hedge fund – the name comes from "hedging your bets" – is a private investment company that oversees the investment of its clients' money, not just in financial instruments, but in more or less anything, anywhere, as long as there is a profit to be made.

Hedging is used not only for foreign exchange and foreign operations but also to protect companies against changes in interest rates, cash flow exposure, or specific asset values. IAS 39 deals with fair value and cash flow hedge accounting.

Most hedging is accomplished through the use of derivatives. This is a difficult subject and all you really need to know when you see references to hedge accounting is that the company considers it has taken the necessary steps to counter the potential risks involved in the acquisition or holding of the assets concerned.

Hedge accounting adjusts the timing of the recognition of any gains or losses on either the hedged item or the hedging instrument so they appear in the same accounting period.

Financial instruments

Reporting on financial instruments is a complex issue requiring three accounting standards. IAS 32, mainly concerned with definitions of debt and equity, defines a financial instrument as:

> *Any contract that gives rise to a financial asset of one entity*
> *and a financial liability or equity instrument in another entity.*

The most common equity instrument is an ordinary share. A bank loan is a financial instrument as are accounts payable and receivable.

During the 1980s there was widespread misuse of complex financial packages (compound financial instruments) or derivatives, mixing debt and equity, in order to disguise the true level of a company's borrowings. The result has been weighty accounting standards attempting to contain the problem. Some examples are as follows.

- Convertible debt – carries the right to exchange for equity shares at some future date until which time interest is paid.
- Subordinated debt – in the event of liquidation it is repaid before the shareholders, but only after all other liabilities have been settled.
- Limited recourse debt – secured only on a particular asset.
- Deep discount bond – a loan with low interest issued at a substantial discount to its repayment value. A zero-coupon bond receives no interest.

IAS 39 deals with the recognition and measurement of financial instruments. IFRS 7, applicable from 2007, sets the disclosure requirements.

All financial instruments are recognised at their fair value when the contract is made and shown in the balance sheet. There are four classes of financial instrument that may appear in a balance sheet.

- Financial assets at fair value through profit or loss – held for short-term profit.
- Held to maturity investments – held with no intention to sell.
- Loans and receivables – not for short-term sale.
- Available-for-sale financial assets – any other financial asset.

Once an instrument has been classified it cannot be moved to another category. The notes should provide information on the company's financial risk management objectives and policies with specific details of hedge transactions. IFRS 7 requires a company to provide sufficient information for the users of its financial statements to be able to assess the importance of financial instruments to its financial position and performance and to appreciate the nature and extent of the risks involved. Qualitative and quantitative information must also be provided on the nature and extent of risks from financial instruments.

As yet there is no single measurement, valuation method, or accounting treatment applied to all financial instruments. If you are lucky the company you are studying will make things clear in its statement of accounting policies, but, unfortunately, there is no guarantee that the next company you look at will follow the same methods.

In 2008 the IASB published a discussion document, *Reducing Complexity in Reporting Financial Instruments*, and the FASB released a similar document. Hopefully the reporting requirements of this most difficult area will be improved through simplification.

Derivatives and risk

The term derivative is applied to many financial instruments. These can be difficult to understand, but all "derive" their value from an underlying item such as a share price or an interest rate. A derivative has little or no initial cost and so the traditional historic cost value fails to reflect the true financial importance or potential impact of the contract.

For example, a company using a commodity such as coffee beans, copper, or oil to generate revenue might insure against future price rises by agreeing to fix the future price paid for its raw materials with a forward contract. The raw material becomes the underlying item of a commodity futures derivative. The company is hedging the risk and uncertainties of the future market price and has certainty as to its future costs. The company offering the derivative is, in effect, betting that the future commodity price will be lower than the agreed contract price.

Derivatives are traded, allowing anyone to enter the "casino" and place a bet on prices rising or falling. The demise of Barings Bank in 1995 was brought about by Nick Leeson's gambling in Japanese futures markets.

Option contracts

A common derivative is an option contract. For example, X buys from Z the option to purchase 1,000 shares in company A for $3 per share at any time in the next six months. X is the holder of the option and has a financial asset. Z has a contractual obligation (financial liability) to sell the shares at $3. If the shares rise above $3, X will exercise the option and make a profit. If the shares rise to $3.20, X makes a $200 profit and Z makes a $200 loss.

A premium is normally paid for an option. The shares in company A are the underlying financial instruments from which the option derives its value. $3 is the exercise price of the option. If the option is not exercised and lapses, it has no value for X ("out-of-the-money"); if the price rises above $3, it becomes "in-the-money".

Intangible assets

It is to be expected that the majority of assets shown as non-current assets in the balance sheet are tangible, but there are often other long-term assets that are described as intangible. These comprise the second classification of non-current assets to be found in the balance sheet. As a general rule accountants and auditors do not like intangible assets, which are fraught with potential danger. As their name implies, they are not physical items capable of normal identification and verification as are property, plant and equipment.

Intangibles are dealt with in IAS 38, which describes them as "an identifiable non-monetary asset without physical substance". They are assets that the company owns. They are expected be used to generate future income and are capable of separate identification and measurement. Examples of intangibles likely to be found within the non-current asset building block are as follows:

■ **Marketing-related**
- trade names or trade marks
- internet domain names and newspaper titles

■ **Customer-related**
- customer lists and relationships

■ **Artistic-related**
- plays, operas, ballets, musical works and song lyrics
- books, magazines, newspapers
- audiovisual materials

■ **Contract-based**
- licences, royalties
- advertising contracts
- lease agreements
- construction permits
- employment contracts

■ **Technology-based**
- technology and trade secrets (processes, formulas)
- computer software
- databases

Brand names and know-how

Until recently it was not considered prudent for companies to include intangibles such as trade or brand names or knowledge-based assets such as intellectual property rights (IPRs) in the balance sheet. Reference is sometimes made to "intellectual capital" as an intangible asset. This has been defined as:

> The possession of knowledge and experience, professional knowledge and skill, good relationships, and technological capacities, which when applied will give organisations competitive advantage.

In the late 1980s in the UK, some companies, mainly in the food and drinks sector, began to include brand names they acquired – and in some cases developed – as an asset in their balance sheets. Their argument was that brands were a valuable commercial asset and that excluding their value from the balance sheet resulted in a potentially dangerous undervaluation of the company. It is reasonable to consider such assets as important for many companies. Brands such as Coca-Cola, St Michael, McDonald's and KFC are worth something in their own right.

IAS 38, introduced in 1998, was the first standard to tackle the treatment of intangible assets in financial reports. Brands, software programs, copyrights and similar intangibles create many problems for accountants. They have no real physical substance and are developed over a number of years with the cost being charged as an expense in the income statement. This development cost may bear no relationship to their market value. They have a useful life of more than one year, bring positive economic benefits to the company and can be sold. The only time their true value can be determined is when they are bought or sold. Therefore, IAS 38 does not allow companies to capitalise internally developed brands or similar intangibles. Marks and Spencer does not include St Michael in its balance sheet.

When a company purchases a brand name there is a clearly defined value or price, and this can be used to put the asset in the balance sheet. In a recent balance sheet Christian Dior showed only its acquired brands – for example, Veuve Cliquot (€244m) and Parfums Christian Dior (€610m) – in its balance sheet. Clearly, in attempting to place a value on some companies it is unwise to ignore intangibles such as brands or software programs.

Treatment of intangibles

It is important to study the notes in a company's annual report on intangible assets, particularly if they are appearing for the first time. The balance sheet notes should provide details of the basis of their valuation.

Tangible assets are depreciated; intangible assets are amortised. The amortisation charge for intangibles will depend on whether they are seen as having a finite or an indefinite useful life. Normally the straight line method of amortisation will be used to write off the asset over its useful life. In 2007 Diageo indicated that its major brands were responsible for some 60% of sales revenue. Brands were valued at £4,085, representing almost 30% of the total assets of the company, including Johnnie Walker (£625m), Captain Morgan (£598m) and Smirnoff (£411m). These brands are assumed to have an infinite life and so are not amortised, but their value is reviewed each year.

In valuing a company or assessing its financial position, the treatment of intangibles can be crucial. It can be argued that intangibles are by their nature of debatable value and should be ignored in placing a value on assets employed in a company. Their inclusion can make it difficult to get an appreciation of the assets that might act as valid security to creditors and providers of funds to the company. Alternatively, if a company is being valued as a going concern on a continuing business basis, more often than not intangibles form an integral part and should not be ignored. Although difficult to value, they are essential to placing a realistic valuation on a company. Prudence and caution may say remove intangibles, but commercial reality may say the opposite.

Goodwill

One intangible that has presented many difficulties for accountants is goodwill. Goodwill arises from business combinations: takeovers and mergers. IFRS 3 and IAS 27 deal with business combinations and consolidated financial statements. Goodwill is defined as the amount paid by one company for another over and above the fair value of the net assets appearing in its balance sheet – purchased goodwill. Brands and other intangibles therefore often form part of goodwill.

Goodwill is an important intangible and can arise only when dealing with a group of companies. It is produced when one company acquires another. On acquisition all the assets and liabilities of the subsidiary that can be separately identified are valued at their fair value. IFRS 3 defines goodwill as:

> *Future economic benefits arising from assets that are not capable of being individually identified and separately recognised.*

IAS 38 states:

> *Goodwill acquired in a business combination represents payment made by the acquirer in anticipation of future economic benefits from assets that are not capable of being individually identified and separately recognised.*

The calculation of goodwill is straightforward – the fair value of the identifiable net assets acquired less the purchase price. It is its treatment in the balance sheet that is complex and has been the subject of considerable difference of opinion.

For example, company A offers to purchase company B for $2,000 cash. Their balance sheets are as follows.

($)	A	B			A	B
Assets	5,000	2,000	Equity	4,000	1,500
			Payables	1,000	500
	5,000	2,000		5,000	2,000

Company B has net assets of $1,500. Why might company A be prepared to pay $500 more than the balance sheet value of B? There could be many reasons. Company B may have intangible assets such as brands, patents, or valuable research and development, which, though of value, do not appear in the balance sheet. Company A may wish to gain the benefit of B's management team with its flair, experience and expertise (management does not appear in either company's balance sheet). Or A may be attracted by the potential future profit streams that it considers can be generated from B.

Goodwill can arise only as the result of a business combination: one company acquires another. It is not recalculated each year but will be covered in the impairment of asset values undertaken each year (see page 74). Goodwill will be particularly significant where service or people-oriented businesses are concerned. If an advertising agency or an insurance broker is acquired, it is reasonable to assume that the principal assets will be the employees of the company and their client contacts, rather than the tangible assets. The net assets, or balance sheet value, of such companies might be minimal and the resultant goodwill high.

Company A decides that $2,000 represents the fair value of the net assets of B and so is an acceptable price to pay. Company B's shareholders agree and it becomes a subsidiary of A, and consolidated accounts are prepared. Everyone is happy, except the accountant of company A. There is a basic mismatch in the transaction. Company A has paid $2,000 for assets in B which are valued at $1,500. The books do not balance.

Cash paid out	$2,000	Assets acquired	$1,500

There is $2,000 cash going out and only $1,500 assets coming in. To solve this dilemma the accountant simply adds goodwill valued at $500 to the assets acquired in company B. The books now balance.

Cash paid out	$2,000	Assets acquired	$1,500 + goodwill $500

However large or complex the balance sheet of the company being acquired or however fierce and acrimonious the takeover battle, the calculation of goodwill is the same.

Goodwill = total acquisition price – fair value of net assets acquired

Accounting for goodwill
The considerable conflict and debate generated by goodwill arise not so much from its calculation but from its treatment in the accounts of the acquiring company. The $500 of goodwill could be treated as an asset in company A's balance sheet and written off (amortised) over a reasonable number of years in the income statement or deducted from shareholders' funds in equity.

Until 1998 UK companies did not write off goodwill in the income statement but charged it directly against reserves in the balance sheet. Thus it was possible for the elimination of goodwill to have no impact on the reported profit appearing in the income statement. When FRS 10 was issued the UK fell into line with the practice adopted by most other countries. Goodwill was shown as an asset in the balance sheet and written off over its estimated useful economic life – normally not more than 20 years – using the straight line method of amortisation. In 2004 IFRS 3 was issued, which made goodwill arising on acquisition an intangible asset with an indefinite life and so not subject to amortisation.

Negative goodwill

It is possible for an acquisition to be made for less than the balance sheet value of net assets. The acquirer has made a good purchase or the acquisition is loss-making and seen as having poor future prospects. For example, BMW sold the Rover car division for £1. Rover did not last long under the new management. IFRS 3 requires that negative goodwill be recognised immediately and taken to the income statement as a gain.

Acquisitions and mergers

When one company acquires another, the acquiring company must bring the acquisition into its accounts as part of non-current assets – "investment in subsidiaries". IAS 27 requires consolidated or group accounts to be prepared by the parent company.

A special purpose entity (SPE) or variable interest entity (VIE) may have been created for off-balance sheet leasing or other activities. Even though the parent company does not have legal control over such companies they should be treated as a normal subsidiary and consolidated following the "substance over form" rule. The precise relationship between the parent company and the subsidiary should be made clear in the accompanying notes.

Continuing with the example used earlier, company A's balance sheet reflects the transaction with cash being reduced by $2,000 and replaced by an investment in company B's shares valued at $2,000. When an acquisition is made all the assets and liabilities of the subsidiary must be recognised by the parent company at their fair value. The fair value of A's assets is $1,500, and goodwill is $500. This is the "acquisition accounting" or "purchase method" of dealing with business combinations.

($)	A	B			A	B
Assets	3,000	2,000		Equity	4,000	1,500
Investment in B	2,000	____		Payables	1,000	500
	5,000	2,000			5,000	2,000

IAS 27 requires the aggregation method of consolidation to be used where "the financial statement of the parent and its subsidiaries [are combined] line-by-line by adding together like items of assets, liabilities, equity, income and expenses". Following the acquisition a consolidated balance sheet is prepared.

Group AB ($)

Assets	5,000	Equity	4,000
Goodwill	500	Payables	1,500
	5,500		5,500

Minority interests

In practice, often less than 100% of a company's shares are acquired. As a rule, when more than 50% of the shares of one company are acquired by another it is necessary to bring the subsidiary into the parent company's consolidated accounts. If 80% of the shares are acquired the remaining 20% constitute a minority interest (MI). IAS 27 defines a minority interest as:

> That proportion of the profit or loss and net assets attributable
> to equity interests that are not owned directly or indirectly ...
> by the parent.

If company A purchases only 80% of company B's shares for $2,000, A still controls B. It owns the majority of B's shares and has so gained a subsidiary company which it will consolidate into its accounts. Goodwill is $800 as it has paid $2,000 for $1,200 of B's net assets (80% of $1,500). The 20% ($300), a minority, of B's shares are owned by outside, non-company A shareholders. Company B is not a wholly owned subsidiary. IAS 27 requires that the "minority interests shall be presented in the consolidated balance sheet within equity, separately from the parent shareholders' equity". It is assumed that the minority interest is an equity contributor to the group rather than a creditor. This is referred to as the "equity concept of consolidation" with the minority interest seen as having a share in the total equity of the group. The company's equity ($4,000) will be shown as part of the $4,300 (including the MI) total equity appearing in the balance sheet.

Group AB ($)

Assets	5,000	Equity	4,000
Goodwill	800	Minority interest	300
		Liabilities	1,500
Total assets	5,800	Total liabilities and equity	5,800

The minority interest ($300) is also entitled to 20% of the earnings of company B and this will be shown as a separate line in the consolidated income statement as an allocation of the group's net profit or loss for the year. Details of minority interests will also be shown in the consolidated statement of changes in equity.

Shares rather than cash

Company A might consider issuing shares to acquire company B rather than using cash. If A's $1 nominal value shares are quoted at $2 on the stock exchange, it could issue 1,000 shares ($2,000) in exchange for company B. If B's shareholders agree, the acquisition can take place without any cash being involved. Company B is now a wholly owned subsidiary and the group balance sheet is as follows.

Group AB ($)

Assets	7,000	Share capital	3,000
Goodwill	500	Share premium	1,000
		Reserves	2,000
		Liabilities	1,500
Total assets	7,500	Total liabilities and equity	5,500

The share premium arises from the issue of 1,000 $1 shares at $2 each.

Pooling of interests

Until the adoption of IFRS 3 in 2004 it was possible for acquisitions to be treated under the "merger accounting" or "pooling of interest method". In 1998 the DaimlerChrylser combination used this method, then allowable under US GAAP. It was assumed that two companies came together to run a joint business rather than one taking over another. Both companies shared equally in the management and earnings of the group. There is no goodwill created as the assets are taken into the consolidated balance sheet at their carrying value – not necessarily their fair value. IFRS 3 banned the pooling of interest treatment of mergers and acquisitions. It is now possible to write off goodwill only if there is impairment (see page 74).

Reverse takeover

It is sometimes the case that the acquirer becomes the subsidiary of the acquired company. This occurs when a small company takes over a larger one. The acquirer issues enough shares to exchange for shares in the acquiree for control to pass. For business combination accounting all that matters is which company has the controlling interest – the acquirer.

Associates, joint ventures and significant interest

There are several accounting standards that deal with the various issues of the investment by one company in another: IFRS 3 (replacing IAS 22 in 2004 and revised in 2007) covers business combinations; IAS 27 consolidated financial statements; IAS 28 investment in associates; and IAS 31 interests in joint ventures.

A joint venture is where two or more companies share the control of another. A partnership is formed with co-operation on decision-making and control of the business. IAS 31 defines a joint venture as:

> A contractual arrangement whereby two or more parties
> undertake an economic activity that is subject to joint control.

The joint venture maintains its own accounting records and presents financial statements. There is normally a profit sharing agreement between the parties involved.

An associate is a business where the investor has a financial interest or investment and some degree of control. IAS 28 defines an associate as:

> An entity ... over which the investor has significant influence
> and that is neither a subsidiary nor an interest in a joint
> venture.

Associates and joint-ventures appear in the balance sheet as non-current assets.

When one company owns or controls more than 50% of the shares of another that company is treated as a subsidiary, and it is consolidated into accounts of the parent company. If company A owns less than 50% of the shares of company B and is thus a minority shareholder, it will show the investment as part of non-current assets in its balance sheet, and the share of B's annual profit will be taken into A's income statement – "share of profits of associates".

A simple guideline has developed where 20% share ownership is taken as the defining level of "control" – the level used under US GAAP. If a company owns less than 20% of the shares of another, it is treated as an investment in an associate in the balance sheet and any income received is taken to the income statement.

It is often difficult to judge the degree of control one company has over another. This was a grey area well exploited in the 1990s when the use of associates and joint ventures was a popular means of creating SPES or special purpose vehicles (SPVs) allowing companies to disguise the true nature of their involvement in an activity. It was possible for a company to disguise its true debt position and create fictitious revenue and profits. Enron claimed profits and hid enormous debt from investors through the creative use of a complex web of SPVs – some 3,000 at the time of its collapse. Remember the golden rule: beware if you cannot understand what a company is doing or where its profits are coming from.

Where between 20% and 50% of the shares are owned it is assumed there is some degree of control. IAS 28 provides a detailed list of factors that may define a significant interest or influence such as controlling the board or active participation in management decision-making. Even where an investor has no legal control over another company but can control that company, it must be consolidated in the investor's accounts – substance over form.

Equity and proportionate consolidation methods
For both associates and joint ventures "substance over form" is the ruling factor in presentation. The equity method of accounting is used to bring them into the financial statements. IAS 28 provides the guide for this approach, which is similar to that for accounting for subsidiaries. The broad aim is to show the investment in the associate as equal to the investor's share of the associate's equity, adjusting year by year for dividends and movements in reserves. The investor's balance sheet, within non-current assets, initially shows the investment at its cost and adjusts each year for the investor's share of the profit or loss – which is taken to the income statement. No goodwill can arise with an associate – it is not a subsidiary – but an annual impairment review must be completed and, if necessary, the carrying value of the investment reduced. Full details of associates should be found in the notes to the financial statements.

The equity method is a simple means of providing information on an investment but does not necessarily provide full disclosure of the financial implications involved. For example, the associate may have heavy borrowings which are not fully disclosed as only the investor's share of the net assets is shown in the balance sheet. The exact level and quality of the associate's profit is also not visible. Make sure you read all the information provided on associates and joint ventures carefully.

IAS 31 endeavours to make sure that economic substance takes precedence to form in proposing the proportionate consolidation method for the treatment of joint ventures. Using this method the investor's balance sheet will show its proportionate share of the assets and liabilities jointly controlled and the income statement the proportion of income and expenses. The share of each asset and liability, income and expense is added to those appearing in the investor's own financial statements. Normally full details of the joint venture will be provided in the notes to the accounts.

Current assets

A current asset is held for trading purposes. The three main headings found in this section of the balance sheet are inventory, receivables (debtors) and cash. Any item appearing within the current asset heading can be taken as either being cash or capable of being turned into cash within the company's normal business operating cycle – typically 12 months.

Inventory

Year-end inventory normally consists of a mixture of raw materials, work in progress and finished goods. In the UK it is sometimes referred to as stock. For retail companies, the year-end inventory consists almost entirely of finished goods in the shops or in the warehouse. IAS 2 defines inventory as:

> Assets held for sale in the ordinary course of business; in the process of production for sale; or in the form of materials or supplies to be consumed in the production process or in the rendering of services.

The basic rule for inventory valuation is that it should be shown in the balance sheet at the lower of cost or net realisable value – cost or fair value. The balance sheet figure is the lower of what it cost to make or acquire and what someone might reasonably be expected to pay for it.

Receivables

Receivables (debtors, accounts receivable) represent the amount owed to a company by customers for goods or services that have been provided but at the end of the year have not yet been paid for. The amount due at the year end is shown as trade receivables.

If a company has experienced bad debts during the year, these should have been accounted for in the income statement. It is standard practice for a company to make a regular provision each year for bad or doubtful debts; a percentage of sales revenue is assumed to be non-recoverable. The figure for receivables appearing in the balance sheet can be taken as good debts that the company realistically expects to collect in the next few weeks under normal terms and conditions of trade.

Most sales are paid for by customers within two or three months. Be cautious when the terms "long-term receivables" or "deferred" receivables or revenue appear. This indicates that the company has made sales but is shifting some or all of the income into future years, possibly as a means of smoothing volatile or uncertain earnings. Alternatively, the company may be suffering sales resistance and offering customers extremely generous and extended credit terms.

Present value accounting

The use of present value accounting in the preparation of financial statements has become increasingly common. In the United States, Concepts Statement 7 (CON 7) provides guidance for calculating fair values.

If a company sells a product to a customer for $10,000 with 12 months' interest-free credit, what figures should appear for revenue in the income statement and receivables in the balance sheet? It is the present value (PV) of $10,000 that should be shown – the value of $10,000 to be received in one year's time. If the appropriate interest rate is 10%, this is $9,091 ($10,000 × 0.9091). $9,091 represents the amount you would have to invest now at 10% interest to obtain $10,000 in one year's time – it is simple arithmetic to prove this for yourself. In the following year $909 "interest" will be recognised in the income statement.

To make the calculations discount tables are used – or, ideally, the inbuilt features of a spreadsheet such as Excel. If $10,000 is to be received in five years' time with an interest rate of 10%, the present value is $6,209 (discount factor 0.6209). This is the sum that would need to be invested now at 10% compound interest to accumulate to $10,000 after five years. Discounting is compounding in reverse. There are also annuity tables available to allow ease of calculation for regular streams of income or expense. The annuity present value for a five-year income stream at 10% interest is 3.7908. The present value of $1,000 per year for five years with 10% interest is therefore $3,791.

The risks and uncertainties of future cash flows should, where possible, be taken into account. Probabilities can be applied to arrive at an expected value.

Possible cash flow	$10,000	$40,000	$60,000	
Probability	20%	60%	20%	
Expected value	$2,000	$24,000	$12,000	**$38,000**

The expected value of the likely cash flows is $38,000. If an asset is being valued fair value will be used – the present value of the expected cash flow using an appropriate discount rate. Using a 10% discount rate for $38,000 receivable in one year would give a fair value of $34,546 ($38,000 × 0.9091) for the balance sheet.

Debt factoring and securitisation

Companies sometimes enter factoring arrangements, whereby they "sell" their receivables or other debts to another company and have immediate cash available for use in the business. The receivables are sold at a discount to a factor who then collects the full amount due. Receivables are usually factored "with recourse", allowing the factor to claim reimbursement from the company if the customer fails to pay. The alternative is "without recourse", where an appropriately higher discount to the factor will be required. Details of any significant factoring arrangements should be given in the notes to the annual report.

The term "securitisation" may be linked to trade receivables or other assets. It refers to the packaging of assets for sale to generate immediate cash flow, and was first developed by American banks in the 1970s to raise finance from the sale of mortgage loans.

The 2007 credit crisis was probably triggered by somewhat excessive and casual trading in securitised mortgage loans. In 2000 Credit Suisse issued a collateralised debt obligation (CDO) of some $340m, of which 5% was sub-prime debt (US mortgages). By the end of 2006 it had lost $125m in value.

A simple definition of a sub-prime mortgage is where the property value was lower than the amount of the mortgage at the time of the loan – surely not a sensible business activity to be involved in. Packages of highly suspect (sub-prime) mortgages were put together and traded by financial institutions in a reckless "pass-the-parcel" game. For several major companies and their CEOs it proved fatal to be left holding the parcel when the music stopped.

Cash and investments

Cash is defined as being the cash held by a company at the balance sheet date, including all deposits repayable on demand and net of any overdrafts. These are sometimes referred to as cash equivalents or liquid resources. Investments are included in current assets only if they are short-term. Any investments shown in this section of the balance sheet can be taken as being liquid, that is, capable of being turned into cash within a reasonably short time.

Impairment of asset values

To assess a company's performance or financial position, it is essential to have a realistic figure for the value of assets employed – ideally their fair value. If the value of a company's assets falls and is unlikely to recover – a permanent diminution – the balance sheet should reflect this and the income statement should take the loss.

Assets should never knowingly be overvalued: an asset should not be shown in a balance sheet for an amount greater than can be realised from it. IAS 36, as amended in 2004, requires that companies undertake a regular impairment test of both current and non-current assets to make sure that their carrying value does not exceed their fair value less selling costs (the recoverable amount).

All intangibles, including goodwill, must have an impairment test each year, because these assets are considered to have more uncertain value than others appearing in the balance sheet. At the end of the first year following an acquisition, companies must review the associated goodwill for impairment. For all other assets a test should be completed if the company has any indication that the asset is impaired. The value of an asset may fall because of many adverse events or conditions, such as obsolescence or damage, or significant or permanent changes in the marketplace.

An impairment review consists of comparing the carrying values of the assets against their recoverable amount. The recoverable amount is the higher of the asset's fair value less any disposal costs likely to be incurred or its value in use. Value in use is the net present value of the future cash flows the asset is expected to generate. To arrive at the value in use of an asset, the future cash flows are estimated and then discounted using discount tables to produce a net present value.

For example, a company owns an asset with a carrying value of $100,000. The asset could be sold for $70,000. It is expected to generate $15,000 per year for the next three years when it will have a disposal value of $50,000.

	Cash flow	PV factor	PV	
Year 1	15,000	0.9091	13,636	
Year 2	15,000	0.8264	12,396	
Year 3	15,000	0.7513	11,269	
End value	50,000	0.7513	37,565	**$74,866**

The carrying value is $100,000, the fair value is $70,000 and the value in use is $74,866. The value in use figure is therefore used in the balance sheet. An impairment of $25,134 ($100,000 – $74,866) is recorded in the income statement. In future, the value in use will provide the basis for the annual depreciation charge.

An impairment review may reduce the carrying value of an asset that has previously been revalued, with the reduction in value being charged against the revaluation reserve, not the income statement.

The financial crisis that started in 2007 was not helped by companies being coerced into using fair value accounting. If the balance sheet is required to reflect the current market value of an asset – a mortgage loan – this may be close to zero at the time the financial statements are prepared. There is no market for the asset – it is a toxic loan. The company reduces the carrying value of the asset resulting in an even more gloomy and fragile picture being presented.

The impairment of asset values reduces shareholders' equity and can affect rates of return and gearing measures (see Chapter 6). Although impairment testing may appear to overcome many of the problems previously met in company valuation, it must be remembered that the only "facts" being offered are based on estimates and forecasts made by the reporting company.

This form of accounting treatment can cause volatility in earnings solely because of non-current asset valuation changes. Today it is accepted that it is better to live with this possibility and have balance sheets that attempt to show a realistic value of the current worth of a company. At least goodwill can never be revalued upwards.

3 The income statement

THE INCOME STATEMENT (previously called the profit and loss account in the UK) deals with the operating activities of a company and is intended to provide a report on its performance during the year. The statement gives details of a company's income and expenditure for the year. Where sales revenue is greater than expenses a profit is produced; the reverse results in a loss – hence profit and loss account.

Profit considerations

Different profits for different purposes
A considerable amount of time could be spent discussing various definitions of profit. A starting point for an accountant might be that "a profit is produced when income is greater than costs"; for an economist it might be "what you can spend during the week and still be as well off at the end of the week as at the beginning". The accountant's definition necessitates the practical application of the principles of recognition, realisation and accrual. The economist's definition would probably include capital maintenance as one of financial reporting's basic principles or rules.

Profit can be defined as the difference between a company's equity or net assets at the start and end of a period. Profit can arise only when equity has increased. For example, a company starts business with equity of $1,000 and uses this to purchase an asset that is later sold for $1,500. Inflation is 10% per annum, and the replacement cost of the asset at the end of the period is $1,300. What profit has the company made?

The simple answer, of course, is $500. Traditional historic cost accounting shows an opening equity of $1,000, closing equity of $1,500 and, ignoring inflation, a profit for the period of $500.

Profit =	sales revenue	–	cost of sales
$500 =	$1,500	–	$1,000

If the purchasing power of the company is to be maintained, the impact of inflation must be taken into account. Financial capital maintenance calls for $100 (10% of the opening equity) to be set aside, resulting in a profit of $400.

If the intention is to maintain the physical operating capability of the company, sufficient funds must be available to replace the asset and continue the business. Operating capital maintenance requires $300 to be earmarked for the replacement of the asset and profit becomes $200.

What happens if an investment held by a company increases in value during the year? If the investment has not been sold (realised), should the increase in value be included in income for the year? Economists would argue yes. Accountants weighed down with prudence and realisation issues generally say no. There does seem to be evidence that IFRS are moving towards acceptance of the recognition of events or transactions that have not yet been realised.

One of the difficulties in reading an income statement is to decide what should be taken as "the" profit for the year. This depends on what is being looked for and why. There are different profits for different purposes. It is impossible to have a single profit figure for a company, let alone a single profit for all companies. That is why you will find several different profits appearing in the income statement. After following accounting standards and satisfying the auditor, companies must still be allowed some flexibility as to which figures they highlight in the financial report.

Matching and accrual

The income statement covers a company's financial year, which normally, but not always, consists of 12 months or 52 weeks. If the income statement's main purpose is to show the profit for the year, it is important that income and expenditure be matched to relate to the year in question. There is often a difference between when a transaction occurs (cash is paid or received) and when it should appear, or be recognised, in the income statement. For example, what happens when materials are used to produce products that are sold this year but the customer is not going to pay until the next financial year? Or when materials have been received and paid for this year but not yet used in production? In the income statement, the income produced during a financial year is set against the expenses associated with that income: income and expenditure are matched.

Profit is not cash

It must not be assumed that the profit displayed in the income statement is represented by cash at the end of the year. A company can show a profit for the year, but this does not mean it has cash available. Even if a company makes no investment in assets to sustain the business for the future, a profit in the income statement is no guarantee that adequate cash or liquid assets appear in the balance sheet at the end of the year.

When preparing an income statement, an accountant includes the total sales revenue produced during the year. This figure includes both cash and credit sales. A company offering customers credit terms is, in effect, lending them its money until payment is made. A sale is made, and therefore included in the income for the year, but no cash may have been received.

Money owed by customers is referred to as either trade receivables or debtors. Credit sales are included in the figure for sales revenue in the income statement and appear in the balance sheet as a heading within current assets. When customers pay the amount due, the figure for receivables is reduced and the cash balance increased by the same amount in the balance sheet.

A company taking advantage of credit terms offered by its suppliers for materials and services for use during the year may not pay for them by the end of the year. Until the suppliers are paid, the money owed (trade payables or creditors) is shown in the balance sheet within current liabilities. When the suppliers are paid, the figure for payables reduces and the cash balance is reduced by the same amount.

The timing difference between the recognition of a transaction or event and the associated cash movement can have important implications for a company.

Overtrading

What happens when credit given exceeds credit taken? A company may be achieving a healthy profit margin on sales but, at the same time, offering its customers much better, longer, credit terms than it can obtain from its suppliers. The terms of credit given and taken have no impact on the profit disclosed in the income statement, but they can significantly affect the cash position or liquidity of a company.

For example, a company starts the year with $2,000 cash. With no credit given or taken, sales revenue is $10,000 and the cost of sales is $8,000. A profit of $2,000 is shown in the income statement and a cash balance of $4,000 in the year-end balance sheet.

$2,000 cash + ($10,000 sales revenue − $8,000 cost of sales) = $4,000 cash

If credit is given and taken, at the end of the year the company is owed $5,000 of the $10,000 sales revenue and owes its suppliers $1,000. The cash position then changes.

$2,000 cash + ($5,000 sales revenue − $7,000 cost of sales) = $0 cash

In both examples, the net current assets have moved from $2,000 at the start of the year to $4,000 at the end. However, with the credit policy adopted in the second example, the cash position has deteriorated from $2,000 at the beginning of the year to zero at the end. Although the company may be trading profitably, it is running down its liquid resources to possibly dangerous levels. This is often referred to as overtrading: profit being generated at the expense of liquidity.

If a company extended further credit or a major customer became a bad debt, it would be forced to borrow money to keep trading. Before such an event occurred, the company might be well advised to look for alternative forms of finance for its future operations and growth.

Since the dangers of overtrading are so clear, why do companies get into such positions? Overtrading is most commonly associated with growth. A traditional means of increasing sales revenue is to offer good credit terms to customers. If the financial implications of the sales policy are not taken into account, a company may show rapid growth in revenue and profit but run out of cash and be unable to continue trading.

Another reason for adopting a generous credit policy is because everyone else does. If a business has traditional terms of trade with customers or if the majority of companies in a sector decide to change their credit terms, it is difficult for one company, particularly a small one keen to gain market share, to act differently.

How long is a year?

The standard reporting period for all companies and all countries is 12 months and accounts are presented each year. Although this is logical and useful, the calendar year is not necessarily the best timescale for company reports. Annual reports may be suitable as a basis for assessing the performance and position of retail companies but not for companies involved in gold, oil or gas prospecting or planting oak trees.

In connection with a company's income statement, it is important to be aware that occasionally the year may consist of more or less than 52 weeks or 12 months. It is common for companies to have a trading year end for the last Friday of one month of the year or to be operating on internal reports covering 13 periods of 4 weeks in the year. As a result, some years may have 53 rather than 52 weeks. If this is the case, it must be taken into account before using the figures for analysis or drawing any conclusions from comparing one company with another. Though, in practice, this does not have much impact on the analysis of the company concerned.

More significant is where there is a major change in the financial year end. A company may wish to move its year-end reporting into line with other similar companies, or it may have become part of a group of companies having a different year end. This can cause problems for financial analysis, particularly if seasonality is involved, such as a retail company moving from an end-December to an end-March year end.

Continuing and discontinued businesses

The income statement will normally show revenue and profit divided into that produced from continuing operations, discontinued operations and acquisitions made during the year. This makes it easier to analyse the company, with details of continuing operations providing the basis upon which to forecast likely future performance.

Any material events or items that will assist a user of the annual report should be disclosed. If a company acquires another during the year and the resulting revenue or profit is more than 10% of the total of the group, it would be reasonable to assume that this information will be disclosed separately, either on the face of the income statement or in the notes.

If a company disposes of or otherwise divests itself of a business this is called a discontinued operation (IFRS 5). When this occurs, the comparative figures are restated to highlight the revenue and profit or loss of that business. The division of operating profit between continuing and discontinued operations is shown in the same way. This makes it easier to assess revenue and profit trends and therefore what the company is likely to achieve in the forthcoming year from its continuing businesses.

Associates and joint ventures

IAS 28 requires that the fair value and percentage of ownership in associates be disclosed and the equity method be applied to the investment (see Chapter 2). Summarised information should also be supplied for each associate's assets, liabilities, revenue and profit. The company's share of the profit or loss of associates will be shown separately in the income statement.

IAS 31 deals with joint ventures with the objective of ensuring the reporting of economic substance over form. Details of joint ventures should be provided, including the ownership percentage. The company may adopt either the equity or the proportionate consolidation method (see Chapter 2) in accounting for joint ventures. Whichever method is adopted, full details should be provided on the assets, liabilities, revenues and expenses. The company's share of the profit or loss of a joint venture will be shown separately in the income statement.

Segmental reporting

It is interesting to know a company's total sales revenue for the year, but it is much more useful to be able to see in which businesses and where in the world that revenue was generated. Foreign operations may be seen as being more risky than home-based businesses, and it is useful to know where a company is making sales and profit.

One of the most useful notes in a company's annual report to help you understand what it does, where and how well is that provided by what is called segmental information or reporting, or disaggregated information. The segmental report analyses a company's turnover, profit and assets employed by major sector of activity and location. From this it is possible to study individual businesses within a group or conglomerate and to use the data to compare them with other, perhaps single business, companies.

Generally, the three main areas of interest are revenue, profit and assets employed. For segmental reporting the most common definition of profit is operating profit and of assets is net operating assets. Revenue will be divided into that from external customers – as shown in the income statement – and that from other segments (internal customers). The total assets and liabilities will be shown together with depreciation and capital expenditure for each segment. Comparative figures will be provided in every case. Companies may opt to provide more than the minimum required disclosure. Some provide segmental cash flow information and employee numbers and location.

A segment can be defined using the materiality rule of 10%. If a business represents more than 10% of turnover, profit or net assets of a company, it can be expected to be reported separately in the segmental analysis report. UK companies have been providing segmental details since 1967 and US companies since 1970. IAS 14 provides the guidance for segmental reporting, leaving the choice of whether to use business or geographical segments as the basis for reporting to the company. These are normally referred to as operating segments.

IFRS 8 (issued 2006 and effective in 2009) requires the primary segment to be identified as the basis for the report:

> *The dominant source and nature of an entity's risks and*
> *returns shall govern whether its primary segment reporting*
> *format will be business segments or geographical segments.*

It is assumed that the company will refer to its internal management and control systems to define segments for disclosure purposes. This allows the review to be completed from a management viewpoint. The result should be to provide users with relevant and useful information. The EU adopted IFRS 8 in November 2007.

A business segment can be defined by reference to:

- the nature of the products or services;
- the nature and technology of production;
- the types of markets in which the company trades;
- major classes of customers;
- distribution channels.

A geographical segment can be defined by reference to:

- proximity of operations;
- similarity of economic and political conditions;
- relationship with operations in other geographical areas;
- special risks associated with a particular country.

There are often practical problems of allocating costs and expenses. For example, how can the total cost of a group's directors be allocated, by product or by market? Such costs are defined as common costs, and when they are not spread among the segments they appear as a single line in the segmental report. Intersegment trading may create some technical problems for accountants and directors and will be shown separately in the report.

Presentation format

IAS 1 does not enforce a single form of presentation but offers a list of items that should appear on the face of the income statement. It also requires the disclosure of all material items of income and expense. Fair value is the basis for measuring revenue. Companies may show expenses either by their nature (for example, employee costs, depreciation) or by their type (for example, cost of sales, marketing, administration). The company may provide additional information to improve the usefulness of the statement.

A typical income statement format and presentation showing expenses by function is as follows.

	$
Revenue	1,000
Cost of sales	(550)
Gross profit	**450**
Other income	10
Selling expenses	(60)
Administrative expenses	(50)
Other expenses	(40)
Operating profit	**310**
Finance costs	(30)
Share of profit of associates	20
Profit before income tax	**300**
Income tax expense	(110)
Profit from continuing operations	190
Profit from discontinued operations	10
Profit for the year	**200**

If the costs and expenses are shown by their nature the profit for the year will not change, but the headings used to arrive at it will.

	$
Revenue	1,000
Other income	10
Changes in inventories	(200)
Materials consumed	(210)
Employee benefit expenses	(160)
Depreciation and amortisation	(90)
Other expenses	(40)
Finance costs	(30)
Share of associates	20
Profit before tax	**300**

Once the after-tax profit is reached its division between the shareholders (equity holders) of the parent company and any other share-holders (minority interest) will be shown.

Profit attributable to:

Equity holders of the parent (90%)	180	
Minority interest (10%)	20	**200**

This is followed by the statement of total recognised income and expense for the year or statement of changes in equity (see Chapter 2).

Total recognised income and expense for the year

The income statement then details all other recognised income and expense for the year. These are added or deducted from the profit for the year to arrive at the total recognised income and expense for the year.

	$
Profit for the year	**200**
Currency translation differences	5
Gains in property revaluation	20
Actuarial gains on defined benefit plans	30
Share of other recognised income of associates	15
Other recognised income and expense	(20)
Total recognised income and expense for the year	**250**

The total recognised income and expense for the year will be shown divided between parent and minority shareholders as previously.

Total recognised income and expense attributable to:

Equity holders of the parent (90%)	225	
Minority interest (10%)	25	**250**

The final key figure shown in the income statement – normally at the end – is that of earnings per share (EPS). This is calculated by dividing the after-tax profit by the number of equity shares in issue. If the company has 1,000 shares, the EPS is 25.

Earnings per share	**$0.25**

Earnings per share will be shown from continuing and discontinued operations and as basic and diluted (see Chapter 6).

Nuts and bolts

Sales revenue and recognition

The first figure appearing in an income statement is normally that of sales revenue, turnover or income for the year. IAS 18 deals with sales revenue. In most cases it is shown net of any sales taxes. However, some companies quote gross revenue. Watch out for this when comparing companies within a sector for size, growth, or profitability; many of the ratios discussed in this book will be distorted if gross rather than net revenues are used as their base.

The income statement should provide a single figure for sales revenue. Be warned, it should not be assumed that there can be only one correct figure. A sale is not always easy to define. Is sales revenue to be recognised when the order is placed, when the customer's cash is received, or when the order is shipped? How should revenues flowing from a five-year service and rental contract or a three-year construction project be treated?

Deciding which figure to use for sales revenue is not as simple as it might seem. In 2001, the ASB published a discussion paper, *Revenue Recognition*, of over 150 pages. Businesses face a variety of problems in deciding at what point a sale should be recognised in the income statement. It may be assumed that when the right to or ownership of the goods or services has passed to the customer that is the point at which a sale is included in the income statement.

Internet and software companies have caused problems for accountants as they try to devise rules for sales revenue recognition. There are B2C (business to end consumer) and B2B (business to intermediate consumer) transactions as well as barter deals to sort out. Is there revenue to recognise when two websites "swap" advertising space? The rule here is that if the value involved cannot be quantified, no revenue should be recognised – if you can't measure it, don't use it. Another potentially fraught area is the treatment of customers' rights of return.

Revenue is used as the basis for assessing the past, current and likely future performance of a company. It is a key factor in profitability – normally, the higher the sales revenue the greater the profit. Revenue recognition is a problematic area; more company restatements of financial statements result from this than from any other factor. Issues of consistency, comparability, prudence, accrual, realisation, recognition and substance over form have to be faced. A simple test is whether, following the transaction, a quantifiable asset – the right to receive income in the future – and a liability – the obligation to deliver – have been created. If this is the case, the revenue should be recognised in the income statement. IAS 1 states that income should be recognised when "an increase in future economic benefits related to an increase in an asset or a decrease in a liability has arisen and can be measured reliably".

IFRS 1 ensures that the income statement includes comparative and consistent figures for the previous year. The US Securities and Exchange Commission (SEC) requires public companies to provide comparative figures for the current and previous two years. Figures for earlier years will be included in the company's five-year or ten-year historic performance table to be found elsewhere in the annual report.

Creating sales
In the 1990s there were numerous examples of creativity enabling companies to show substantial and consistent revenue growth, at that time mistakenly seen as a key indicator of performance and success. These included:

- goods on sale or return to customers treated as sales;
- secret "side agreements" giving customers the right to cancel a sale, but including it in the sales revenue for the year;
- all potential income from long-term contracts taken immediately rather than spread over the life of the agreement;
- taking a sale into income before the customer signs the contract;
- failing to make adequate provision for bad debts;
- sending invoices to customers for fictitious deliveries in the hope, owing to their poor internal control systems, that they will pay;
- taking 100% of a sale as income even though the customer has paid only a 10% deposit;
- shipping goods early before the customer expected and including them as sales revenue for the current year – an extreme example was, when the customer refused delivery, to hire a warehouse, ship the goods to it and record the sales revenue immediately;
- grossing up sales, as when a travel agent sells a $1,000 ticket on which 10% commission is earned, but takes the full $1,000 as sales revenue;
- treating investment income and interest as operating sales revenue;
- lending money to customers to finance their purchases – the loan goes to the balance sheet and the "sale" to the income statement;

- showing income from the sale of non-current assets as operating revenue.

The early 2000s added to the list with the SEC bringing to light:

- "channel-stuffing" – McAfee persuaded distributors of its software to hold excessive levels of inventory, using a SPE to repurchase unwanted inventory;
- making sure advertisers have funds to place adverts – Time Warner induced companies to place online adverts, which also enabled it to inflate its internet customer numbers to increase confidence in performance.

Such creativity is not, at any time, easy to spot. Moves by accounting bodies and stock exchanges have considerably reduced the scope for creativity in financial reports. Some of the analysis discussed later can help to highlight inconsistencies or blips in financial statements and at least trigger a caution signal.

Cost of sales

Cost of sales can be considered the cost of materials and employees and other direct and indirect costs incurred in generating sales revenue including:

- direct materials;
- direct labour;
- all direct production overheads including depreciation;
- inventory change;
- hire of property, plant and equipment;
- product development expenditure.

Companies do not normally provide any further analysis of the cost of sales, although additional information may be found in the notes on the income statement.

Often details of employee numbers, non-current asset depreciation, leasing, and research and development will be found in the notes.

Change in inventory

Cost of sales includes the change in inventory between the beginning and end of the financial year. This is part of the matching process. Sales revenue for the year should be charged only with the cost of goods used in producing that revenue. Any items remaining unsold at the end of the year should not be charged against the year's revenue.

Companies adopt either the perpetual method of inventory control where the records are updated each time a transaction occurs, or the periodic method where inventory is taken every now and again – including the year end. The balance sheet value of a retail company's inventory is often calculated by taking the selling price of the goods on shelves at the end of the year and deducting the normal profit margin – the retail method.

The value placed on inventory can be an important factor influencing the reported profit of a company. The basic accounting routine applied to arrive at the cost of sales charge in the income statement is as follows.

Opening inventory + purchases for the year =
goods available for sale – closing inventory = cost of sales

Inventory is often attractive not only to employees (shrinkage and wastage are euphemisms for theft) but also to those preparing a company's accounts for the opportunities it may allow for creativity. For example, if a company, for whatever reason, were to increase the value of inventory at the end of the year by $1,000, there would be an automatic improvement of reported profit of $1,000. Cost of sales is reduced by $1,000 to bring about the profit increase. A simple form of creative accounting is where a company keeps old and obsolete items valued at their cost in year-end inventory.

($)	Low inventory value		High inventory value	
Sales revenue		10,000		10,000
Opening inventory	1,000		1,000	
Purchases	8,500		8,500	
	9,500		9,500	
Closing inventory	3,500	6,000	4,500	5,000
Profit		**4,000**		**5,000**

Profit is improved and the balance sheet value for inventory increased. Nothing physical has occurred to the inventory; only its value has been changed. For every $1 added to the value of closing inventory there is an extra $1 at the bottom line of the income statement. Inventory and its valuation is an area attracting close scrutiny from a company's auditor.

Valuing inventory

Although companies may be reluctant to admit that inventory is worth less than it cost to produce, the prudence requirement in financial reporting ensures that the simple rule of showing inventory at the lower of cost or net realisable value (fair value) is followed. The lower inventory figure shows caution in both the balance sheet valuation and in defining the profit for the year.

IAS 2, originally issued in 1975 and revised as part of the proposed improvements to international accounting standards in 2003, deals with inventories. The most common method of valuing inventory is called first in first out (FIFO). This assumes that the oldest inventory items are used first. As inventory is used or sold, it is charged to production or sales at the earliest cost price. Until it was banned in 2003 a method called last in first out (LIFO) – the reverse of FIFO – was commonly used by American companies.

The second means of inventory valuation is the weighted average cost method. The two methods are illustrated below using an example where 2,000 units of materials are purchased, 1,600 used in production, leaving 400 in the closing inventory.

Purchases	$	FIFO	$
1,000 units × $5	5,000	1,000 × $5	5,000
1,000 units × $7	7,000	600 × $7	4,200
2,000	12,000	1,600	9,200

The cost of sales charge in the income statement is $9,200 and the closing inventory (400 units) is valued at $2,800 (400 units × $7). If prices are rising, FIFO may be assumed to value inventory close to its replacement cost in the balance sheet ($4,200) but the charge for cost of sales in the income statement ($9,200) will be comparatively low.

Purchases	$	Weighted average
1,000 units × $5	5,000	
1,000 units × $7	7,000	
2,000	12,000	$12,000 ÷ 2,000 units = **$6 per unit**

The cost of sales is $9,600 (1,600 units × $6) and the closing inventory is valued at $2,400 (400 units × $6).

Always read the notes relating to inventory valuation. They should show that the company has taken the lower of cost or net realisable value to produce the balance sheet value of closing inventory.

When cost is the basis for valuing inventory this normally includes the costs of raw materials and supplies, wages and appropriate over-heads (indirect expenses). Read the notes supplied in the annual report to see if there has been any change in the calculation of the cost of inventory. This may be done to adjust the reported profit for the year. Companies should be consistent in their valuation methods; if this is not the case there should be a good reason for the change.

If only a single figure for inventory is provided in the balance sheet, read the notes supplied to see the split between the three headings: raw materials, work in progress and finished goods. A substantial or continuing increase in the level of finished goods may point to trading problems.

Sometimes reference may be made to a "product financing arrange-ment" where the company has "sold" inventory to a finance institution, agreeing to repurchase this at a set price (including financing costs) and date in the future. The company gains immediate access to cash with the inventory acting as security for the loan. On the agreed date the com-pany repurchases the inventory for delivery to customers. Details of any such arrangements should be included in the notes to the accounts.

Gross profit

Gross profit is the first profit shown in the income statement using the by nature classification of expenses. This is produced by deducting the cost of sales from sales revenue. Other operating costs and expenses are deducted from gross profit to provide the operating profit and profit before income tax for the year.

Auditors' fees

The fees paid to the company's auditors will be shown under the administrative expenses heading in the income statement. This figure should clearly distinguish between fees for audit and fees paid to the same firm for other work such as consultancy assignments – unlikely nowadays – or special investigations.

Employee details

As part of the annual reporting process, companies disclose details of full-time and part-time staff, either the number at the end of the finan-cial year or, more commonly, the average during the year. The total pay-ment to employees is also shown. The employee or staff cost heading covers all wages and salaries, social security costs, pensions and other employment-related payments.

Anyone legally contracted to work for the company is an employee, including part-time workers and directors. Where a company has a contract with a self-employed person, who by definition is not an employee of the company, the money is normally included under the other costs and charges heading. Directors who have a service contract with the company are classed as employees. Thus the total cost of directors is included in the figure for staff or employee expenses. There will be separate notes that deal in some detail with directors' remuneration and rewards.

Pensions

The reward for long service with a company is normally a pension. In 1991 it was discovered that Robert Maxwell had misappropriated some £450m from his company's pension fund. This illustrated the importance of keeping the pension fund separate from the control of the company. In 1992 the Cadbury Committee made recommendations on accountability and corporate governance. Pension funds now have assets that are legally separate from the company and cannot be touched even in the event of the company's bankruptcy. There are two types of pension scheme:

- Defined contribution scheme. The employer pays a regular amount (normally a proportion of the wage or salary of the employee) into the pension fund. On retirement the employee receives a pension dependent on the size of the pension fund and its returns from investment. The company has no obligation to pay beyond its agreed contribution to the pension fund.
- Defined benefit scheme. The pension is linked to the employee's salary level or years of service. The company has an obligation to pay the pension whether or not the pension fund has sufficient assets or income. The company takes actuarial advice as to how much to put into the fund to allow future payment to retired employees. This will include the calculation of the average life expectancy of employees and the revaluation each year of the pension fund to produce a surplus or deficit.

The aim of accounting for pensions is to match the pension cost against income when it is paid. To defer any expense recognition until a pension is actually paid does not adequately match income and expense. In the early years there will be a low level of expense which rises rapidly in later years. Matching the expected future cost against current income is crucial.

IAS 19 deals with employee benefits, but not the financing of pension schemes. To avoid fluctuations in a company's earnings due solely to changes in the actuarial valuations of a pension fund, a "corridor approach" is adopted. An estimated band (corridor) is set for the higher of 10% of the fair value of the assets at the start of the year or 10% of the present value of the obligations at the end of the year. Only if this corridor is exceeded are any actuarial differences taken to the income statement. The IASB and the FASB are working together on a project to review IAS 19. It is expected that the outcome will be for a pension fund surplus or deficit to be recognised in the accounts as a separate item.

The notes to the financial statements should offer full details of the company's post-employment benefits including a reconciliation of the movements during the year and the net asset or liability reported in the balance sheet.

Directors' remuneration

The actions and activities of a company's directors form an important part of corporate reporting. In most countries there has been a flow of legislation, regulation or stock exchange requirements covering disclosure of details of a company's financial dealings with its directors.

The Cadbury Report stated:

> The overriding principle in respect of board remuneration is that of openness. Shareholders are entitled to a full and clear statement of directors' present and future benefits, and of how they have been determined.

The Combined Code requires that three or more non-executive directors form a remuneration committee. This committee is to develop and oversee the company's remuneration policy and the individual rewards of each executive director and the chairman. The committee will consider benefits in kind, share-based payments and any long-term incentive schemes. In the UK the Directors' Remuneration Report Regulations (published in 2002), the Combined Code on Corporate Governance, updated by the Financial Reporting Council in 2006, and stock exchange listing rules govern the directors' report, which includes the remuneration committee report. This provides full details of the scope, membership and workings of the committee. Details of the individual directors' remuneration packages are normally shown here. There may also be details of the number of board meetings attended during the year by each director.

Included in the remuneration committee report will be details of directors':

- salary and benefits (including increases during the year);
- bonuses and long-term incentives (cash and shares);
- key performance targets used in bonus schemes;
- service contracts;
- pension schemes.

Share options

Rather than being paid in cash employees may be given shares in their company. If employees are given shares the cost of this can be set as the current market price of the shares (fair value). A popular means of providing executives with the incentive to manage a successful company is to offer them shares or share options. If management performs well the share price will rise and they will benefit. It can be argued that share options offer management rewards but no penalties, and that they focus attention on short-term gains that may not be in the long-term best interests of the company. Management does not have the same "downside" as shareholders if things go wrong.

Many companies operate share (stock) incentive plans (SIPS). These give all employees the opportunity of owning shares in their company. Other companies offer selected employees, as a reward for past or as an incentive for future performance, the right to purchase shares at a favourable price. Share options can be a more effective means of providing employees with net income than straightforward taxable remuneration. In the 1990s many e-companies offered share options. The cost to the company was negligible, and no cash was involved. The potential reward for the individual could be significant, and this was expected to ensure loyalty and top performance. In 2000, when many of these companies joined the "99% Club" – their share price dropped to 1% of its previous level – the true value of the share options was revealed.

IFRS 2 (130 pages in length) deals with share-based payment schemes. A key issue is the timing: when does the benefit from the share option occur? When should it be recognised in the income statement? Is it on the granting of the option or when the option is exercised? Whether it is even appropriate to charge the income statement with the fair value of share options has been the subject of fierce debate between business-men (anti) and accountants (pro). The accountants appear to have won.

Share options act to reduce shareholders' investment: when shares are issued their holding is worth less. There is a transfer from share-holders to management. IFRS 2 requires that the cost of the option be set at the time it is granted not when it is exercised. Share options are not revalued each year. The value of the option is set with reference to the fair value of the shares when granted. If a comparable market price is not available an option pricing model – such as the Black-Scholes-Merton (BSM) formula, or the Cox, Ross and Rubinstein binomial model – may be used. The pricing model must take into account the:

- exercise price of the option;
- expected term of the option;
- current market price of the share;
- expected volatility of the share price;
- dividends expected to be paid; and
- risk-free interest rate.

If a share option, expected to be taken up in five years' time, is offered when the current share price is $10, with a risk-free interest rate of 4%, the option value is $1.78 per share.

PV of $10 at 4% in 5 years $= \$ 8.22$ $\$10 - \$8.22 = \mathbf{\$1.78}$

The time value of money (present value) is used to calculate the value of $10 received at the end of five years with an interest rate of 4% as $8.22. If $8.22 is invested for five years at 4% interest, in the first year it would earn $0.33 interest, in the second year $0.34 and so on until the capital value at the end of the fifth year is $10. This calculation is com-pleted using present value factor (in this case 0.8219) tables found in any spreadsheet application.

The risk-free interest rate is normally taken to be that of government Treasury notes with a similar lifespan to that of the option. Any divi-dends that would have been received on the shares are similarly dis-counted and the total deducted from the option – they have been forgone – to produce the net value. The fair value of an option is charged to the income statement over its expected life – this is the period it is earned by the employees. A compensating adjustment is made to equity which will show the share options granted as a separate item.

The remuneration committee report and notes should provide full details of each director's options awarded or exercised during the year and the number of shares involved at end of the year. There are some weighty notes in the annual report. Do not be put off as their study may well repay the effort of analysis.

Make a loss, take a profit

There have been many examples of directors receiving substantial sums in return for giving up their tenure of incompetence in managing loss making companies. Charles Prince of Citigroup appears to have left the company in some disarray – in 2007 there was a $43 billion asset write-off relating mainly to sub-prime mortgages – but he had pension and stock options of some $29m, a final-year bonus of $10m and the use of an office and chauffeur for five years. He is, not least, to be remembered for his statement:

> When the music stops ... things will get complicated. But as
> long as the music is playing, you've got to get up and dance.

Other financial institutions have found themselves forced to make more than generous final payments to executives – for example, Stanley O'Neal of Merrill Lynch walked away with some $160m in stock, options and benefits – who had taken their company to the brink, and sometimes over the edge, of the precipice. Any payment in compensation for loss of office and any significant payments made to directors, including former directors, should be fully disclosed in the annual report.

Best practice requires directors' rewards to be firmly based on appropriate objective performance-related measures. Directors may be rewarded above their basic salary in relation to internal performance targets, such as sales revenue or profit, or with reference to the relative share price of the company. An increase in a company's market capitalisation might prove effective as a basis for executive reward schemes. Whatever approach a company adopts, it should be clearly set out for shareholders in the annual report.

Greenbury and Hampel (see Chapter 1) recommended that directors be given service contracts of no more than one year's duration. The Combined Code on Corporate Governance (2003) ensures that shareholders are provided with sufficient information on each director to decide on their re-election at least every three years. In the United States the SEC plays a leading role in corporate governance.

The annual report gives details of the directors' aggregate remuneration or emoluments and identifies the total amount paid to directors for services in connection with the management of either the holding company or any subsidiary. Pensions paid to past directors will also be shown. The disclosure should make it possible to identify all the payments made. For example, if a retired director is allowed to continue using a company car, the estimated value of this benefit should be shown separately within the disclosure on post-employment benefits.

Operating profit

An important measure and indicator of performance of a company is the profit made from running the business; that is, the profit generated from its operations. If gross profit is not shown, this is normally the first profit disclosed in the income statement. Operating profit is calculated by deducting the cost of sales plus other operating expenses from sales revenue. IAS 1 does not require that the operating profit be shown on the face of the income statement but most companies do so. It is reasonable to assume that the operating profits of different companies can be compared on a common basis.

Depreciation and profit

Capital maintenance is an important factor in corporate reporting. To continue in business, a company is expected at least to maintain the current level of investment in operating assets and to replace these assets as they wear out or become obsolete. Capital employed is on one side of the balance sheet and assets on the other. If assets are maintained, so must capital be maintained. One way of achieving this is through depreciation, the setting aside of current revenue for future reinvestment in the business. The cost of the asset is charged against income over its useful working life. IAS 16 requires all tangible assets, except land, to be depreciated, and defines depreciation as "the systematic allocation of the depreciable amount of an asset over its useful life".

It is possible to consider depreciation in at least three ways:

1 In the balance sheet a company is expected to provide a reasonable

representation of the fair value of its assets. In normal circumstances a new car is worth more than an old car. As an asset gets older and its value decreases, it is to be expected that this change in value is reflected in the balance sheet.

2 As a company carries on its business, it uses resources. It incurs costs and expenses, uses labour and materials (direct costs), and uses up some of the value of the non-current assets, property, plant and equipment employed in the business. To produce a profit or loss in the income statement, all costs and expenses are deducted from revenue. The direct costs are charged and some allowance made for the cost of using the non-current assets during the year. Part of the value of property, plant and equipment has been used up during the year (indirect costs). To reflect this an amount is charged in the income statement. Thus depreciation may be considered to be the cost of the various non-current assets being used during the year.

3 If a company is to continue in business, at some stage it will have to replace its non-current assets as they wear out or become obsolete. To provide for this eventuality the company prudently sets aside funds. Depreciation is charged in the income statement but is not actually paid out to any third parties; it is retained in the company.

A company that fails to charge depreciation breaches not only the requirement of prudence in financial reporting but also the fundamental requirement of capital maintenance.

Calculating depreciation

There are many ways of calculating depreciation. For example, a company purchases an asset with an expected working life of four years for $10,000. The company makes a profit of $3,000 per year, 50% of which is distributed as a dividend to shareholders. At the end of the fourth year the replacement cost of the assets is $10,000.

If no depreciation were charged, the company would retain $6,000 profit (50% of $3,000 for four years). At the end of the asset's life there would not be sufficient funds available in the balance sheet for replacement. Had the company charged $2,500 per year for depreciation (writing off the asset over the four-year working life), the net profit would have been only $500 each year. If 50% of this had been paid to shareholders as dividend, there would have been only $1,000 of retained profit at the end of the fourth year.

Straight line depreciation

The simplest and most commonly used method of calculating depreciation is the straight line method. The cost or value of the asset is divided by its anticipated useful working life to produce the annual depreciation charge.

Cost of asset	$1,000
Estimated useful working life	4 years
Depreciation charged in the income statement per year	$250

Diminishing balance depreciation

A second method, often required by tax authorities, is the diminishing balance method. This is sometimes referred to as accelerated depreciation as the higher charges occur in the first few years of the asset's life.

Cost of asset	$1,000
Depreciation rate per year	50%

In the first year $5,000 depreciation is charged in the income statement. This reduces the carrying value of the asset to $5,000, and so in the second year the depreciation charge is $2,500. Under this method the asset is never written down to a zero value.

Sum of the digits method

A third approach is the sum of the digits method. The expected useful working life of the asset is four years. All the digits – 1,2,3,4 – are added together, producing a total of 10. If the asset life was ten years the sum would be 55. In the first year the depreciation charge is 4/10ths of the asset value ($4,000), in the second 3/10ths, and so on until in the final year 1/10th is charged to fully depreciate the asset.

The three methods would depreciate the asset at different rates.

Year	Straight line $	Diminishing balance $	Sum of digits $
1	2,500	5,000	4,000
2	2,500	2,500	3,000
3	2,500	1,250	2,000
4	2,500	625	1,000
Total	10,000	9,375	10,000

The three methods of calculating depreciation will, each year, result in a different charge for the asset being made in the income statement and in its carrying value in the balance sheet. Depreciation is important when assessing the performance and position of a company.

Depreciation policy

Always read the notes on non-current assets and their depreciation carefully. A company's asset valuation and depreciation policies should be reasonable, prudent and consistent. If this is not the case, you need to satisfy yourself that income is not being manipulated. It is possible to boost reported profit if all expenses relating to an asset, including the interest charges for its finance, are capitalised rather than charged to the income statement. Compare the company's policy with that of others in the same sector to make sure there is conformity.

It is not difficult to imagine a situation in which a company would prefer not to operate a prudent depreciation policy. Low profitability might be bolstered by not charging any depreciation in the first year of a new asset being brought into operation. The company might argue that as the new investment – particularly if it is property – was operational for only part of the year, it is reasonable that it should not be subject to depreciation. Thus the new investment would generate revenue but not be burdened with the depreciation. Once such an approach is accepted, the consistency rule will ensure its application in future years.

Taxing matters

The pre-tax profit reported in a company's accounts is unlikely to be the profit used to calculate the eventual tax liability. A simple means of assessing this is to estimate the actual tax rate being paid on a company's reported profit. This can be done by using the pre-tax profit and income tax expense appearing in the income statement. The resulting figure can then be compared with the rate of company taxation for the country involved. Generally, the actual company tax rate will be found to be lower than the standard rate imposed by government. The rate of tax being paid should be disclosed, and the amount due at the end of the year shown in the balance sheet as part of current liabilities.

IAS 12 deals with accounting for income taxes. The intention is for the balance sheet to show the amount of tax due by the company at the end of the year and the income statement to make the necessary adjustment from the previous balance sheet to achieve this aim.

Tax allowable depreciation

If companies were allowed to set their own rates of depreciation in arriving at taxable profit without any external controls or guidance, no company would need to end up with a tax liability. The standard practice in most countries is to have two rates of depreciation, one that is allowed and accepted for tax purposes and a second that is applied by companies in their financial reports. Inevitably, there is a difference between the profit a company declares to its shareholders and the profit it declares to the tax authorities. Accounting profit is defined under generally accepted accounting principles (GAAP); taxable profit is defined by IAS 12 as:

> *The profit for a period, determined in accordance with the rules established by the taxation authorities, upon which income taxes are payable.*

Deferred taxation

Depreciation is often the cause of a significant difference between a company's reported and taxable profit. A company has little option but to accept the tax rules prescribed by the country or countries in which it operates. If tax incentives are offered to encourage investment, any company can be expected to take full advantage of them. However, this can affect the reported after-tax profits of a company. This is the result of what is called timing or temporary differences.

A company may have interest income during the year of $5,000 which will be included in pre-tax profit. If tax is paid only when the interest is received in cash and at the end of the year $1,000 is still due, the company's taxable profit will not be the same as its accounting profit. The impacts of investment and the associated tax implications may not occur in the same time period. This can distort the reported after-tax profits and is overcome by use of a deferred taxation account, sometimes referred to as a tax equalisation account.

IAS 12 requires a company to show the amount of tax that relates to the pre-tax profit being reported. This is not the same as showing the actual amount of tax paid in the financial year. The income statement should show the amount of tax due to be paid in the current year (current tax expense). The balance sheet should show the future tax liability (deferred tax liability). Deferred tax will be calculated using the expected future tax rates that will apply to the transaction involved. There may be both deferred tax liabilities and deferred tax assets. A deferred tax asset is where tax will be recoverable in future years including unused tax losses and credits.

Reconciling the books

Companies keep at least three sets of books. One is for management to enable them to run the company; the second is for the tax authorities to calculate the annual tax liability; and the third is presented to the shareholders in the annual report. The three sets should, under normal sound accounting practices, be capable of reconciliation.

Capital or revenue

The decision on whether an item should be treated as capital (balance sheet) or revenue (income statement) in the year reinforces the links between the balance sheet and the income statement in connection with the treatment of non-current assets. Revenue expense is related to the normal business activity of the company or is concerned with maintaining the non-current assets. Capital transactions are normally intended to provide a long-lasting asset to the company.

The treatment of research and development (R&D) costs is a good example of the potential importance of the expense or capitalise decision. The result of this decision can have a significant impact on both the income statement and the balance sheet.

For example, a company invests £100,000 in R&D each year. It is expected that the new products and services delivered by the R&D will come on stream over the next ten years. The company's policy is to provide shareholders with a regular $25,000 dividend as shown in year 1:

($)	Year 1	Year 2a	Year 2b
Profit for the year	150,000	75,000	75,000
R&D expense	100,000	100,000	10,000
Profit	50,000	(25,000)	65,000
Dividend	25,000	0	25,000
Retained profit	25,000	(25,000)	40,000

The company experiences a downturn in business, profit is halved in year 2 and there is insufficient profit available to pay the dividend (year 2a). There is little the company can do in operational terms (generating additional revenue or reducing costs), but it might be tempted to consider a change in its policy for the treatment of R&D.

It could be argued that a better form of presentation and a more accurate reflection of the events would result from spreading the investment in R&D. That is, it would be better to spread the amount spent on R&D over the years when the new products and services result. It could be argued that it is unfair accounting treatment to burden one year's sales revenue with what is really ten years' investment in R&D.

The company opts to charge only one-tenth of the R&D spend against year 2 sales revenue, and to continue writing it off over the next nine years. The charge in the income statement is $10,000 (year 2b) and the balance, $90,000, is capitalised as a non-current asset in the balance sheet.

The impact of this change in accounting presentation is that the company in year 2b shows a profit of $65,000, and so may pay the dividend to its shareholders. It also exhibits a new asset, R&D valued at $90,000, in the balance sheet. Although it is not possible to fault the book-keeping involved in this exercise, it might be possible to raise questions about the validity of displaying R&D as an asset in the balance sheet.

There were many examples of companies capitalising R&D and then discovering that under pressure it was impossible for it to be translated quickly into positive cash flow. In response to this, and to avoid the potential misrepresentation or error in companies' financial reports, R&D became subject to an accounting standard which enforced the prudence rule and required companies to write it off as incurred.

IAS 38 defines research as:

> Original and planned investigation undertaken with the
> prospect of gaining new scientific or technical knowledge and
> understanding.

Development is defined as:

> The application of research findings or other knowledge to a
> plan or design for the production of new or substantially
> improved ... products ... or services before the start of
> commercial production or use.

The future economic benefit likely to flow from research is uncertain. It is an intangible internally developed asset and, as with internally generated goodwill, it cannot be capitalised. IAS 38 provides a list of criteria which must be met for development expenses to be capitalised.

The example of R&D may now be only of historic interest, but many of the same issues face companies today regarding such intangibles as brand names (see Chapter 2). When a company is so desperate to show a profit that it throws the rule book away it is not unusual to see expenses capitalised. The 1990s provides examples of companies:

- adding maintenance and repairs to non-current asset values;
- capitalising software that had dubious real value;
- capitalising internal software costs;
- capitalising marketing and advertising expenses.

Once this is done the cost is written off over a number of years or treated as a one-off non-recurring or special charge not affecting the current year's reported profit. With the CEO insisting "we have to hit our numbers", reducing real capital expenditure and capitalising operating expenses were crucial to WorldCom's creative accounting, contributing some $3.8 billion to the overall $11 billion fraud.

Interest

Interest paid by a company on borrowings and interest received on investments is shown either on the face of the income statement or in the notes. Often the income statement figure is for net interest payable, that is the interest payable less the interest received and any interest capitalised.

The total interest payable during the year should be divided into interest relating to short-term borrowings, such as bank loans, repayable on demand or within 12 months, and interest on loans falling due within five years.

Capitalising interest payments

If a company borrows money to complete a major project, such as building a new factory or hypermarket, it is possible, under IAS 23, to capitalise the interest payments and write them off following the company's normal depreciation policy. Although this is acceptable as the interest expense has been incurred to allow the asset to be built, it does increase the reported profit. The notes in the accounts should clearly indicate how much interest has been capitalised during the year.

When looking at the interest paid by a company, perhaps for use in an interest cover measure, it is best to use the total interest payable figure. That a company has capitalised a proportion of its interest payments does not affect how much interest it has to pay.

Effective interest method

When a company invests or borrows money for a number of years in return for interest payments, there are some issues of recognition and valuation to be tackled. A company sells a product for $50,000 with a down payment from the customer of £10,000 and five annual instalments of $10,000. If the current cash price for the product is $40,000, and the ruling interest rate is 5%, what should be shown in the accounts? It would not be correct to record a sale of $60,000 immediately in the income statement. IAS 18 requires the transaction to be shown as part sales revenue and part interest income spread over the life of the contract.

The effective interest rate must be calculated. This is the rate that discounts the expected future income or expense stream to equal the current carrying amount of the asset or liability. This is undertaken using discounting techniques.

Using the present value of an annuity table (regular amounts paid for a defined number of years) it can be seen that the 5% factor for five years is 4.3295. If $10,000 is to be received for the next five years its present value is $43,295. If $43,295 were invested today at 5% interest, in five years' time it would be worth $50,000. Alternatively, if a loan was taken out for $43,295, it would be repaid (plus interest) with five annual payments of $10,000 according to the example below. The second column gives the 5% interest charge on the reducing balance and the third column the amount of the principal which is being repaid.

Year	Payment	5%	Principal	Balance
				43,295
1	10,000	2,165	7,835	35,460
2	10,000	1,773	8,227	27,233
3	10,000	1,362	8,638	18,594
4	10,000	930	9,070	9,524
5	10,000	476	9,524	0

The present value can be used to calculate the amount to be brought into the income statement as recognised revenue. The company should recognise $53,295 ($10,000 down payment + PV $43,295) income in the first year. Each year the company would bring into the income statement the interest shown in column 3 of the example ($2,165 and so on).

Operating and finance leases

A further example of the distinction between capital and revenue items is found in the treatment of leases. IAS 17 provides the guidelines for the treatment of lease agreements and defines a lease as:

> An agreement whereby the lessor conveys to the lessee in return for a payment or series of payments the right to use an asset for an agreed period of time.

Should lease payments be treated as an operating expense (income statement) or as the acquisition of a non-current asset (balance sheet)? The decision will affect reported profit for the year. The reporting of lease arrangements was manipulated by companies in the 1990s to bolster profits and disguise asset ownership.

The main criterion is whether the rights and associated risks and rewards of ownership of the asset pass to the lessee. If they do, the lease is capitalised and taken into the balance sheet (a finance lease). If they do not, it is assumed that the asset is being rented and the lease payments are included as an operating expense in the income statement (an operating lease).

A finance lease is:

> [One] that transfers substantially all the risks and rewards incidental to ownership of an asset. Title may or may not be eventually transferred.

Substance over form requires that if the lease in effect transfers ownership to the lessee it is treated as the acquisition of an asset. Any other type of lease agreement is an operating lease. An operating lease shows the lease payments as an expense in the income statement and there are no entries in the balance sheet.

A company may enter a sale and leaseback agreement where an asset is sold and immediately leased. This is often undertaken with an office block. The lessee receives cash but still has complete use of the asset. The lease will be treated as a finance or an operating lease depending upon the terms involved.

A finance lease is recognised in the balance sheet at the fair value of the leased asset or the present value of the minimum lease payments (MLP). If a lease is agreed for an asset with an immediate payment of $10,000 and three annual payments of $10,000, and an implicit interest rate of 10%, it has a discounted present value of $34,869 (down payment + $10,000 × PV factor 2.4869). The present value of minimum lease payments is $34.869. An asset and a lease liability are recognised and depreciated over the lease period.

IAS 17 requires that leases be classified according to their life – within one year, 2–5 years and longer than five years – with the present values and MLPs shown for each class of lease.

Dividends

The profit attributable to shareholders forms the potential source of dividend payments. A dividend can only be paid from profit. If a dividend were paid from capital, the capital maintenance rule would be breached. The dividends the company has paid (interim dividends) and the amount the directors have proposed for the year (final dividend) are normally shown as a single figure in statement of changes in equity.

When a dividend is declared as 10% this relates to the nominal value of the shares involved, not their market value. A company with $1 or £1 shares paying a 10% dividend is offering shareholders 10¢ or 10p per share.

It is common for companies to offer shareholders a scrip or stock dividend – the alternative of taking additional shares rather than a cash dividend. This has the advantage of not reducing the company's cash balances and of offering shareholders the possibility of increased capital gains and future dividends.

No profit, no dividend

Basic good housekeeping would suggest that a company with little or no profit should not be expected to pay a dividend. Technically, it is possible for a company with a loss for the year to pay a dividend. As long as it has sufficient distributable reserves in the balance sheet, and of course enough cash, a dividend can be declared.

Retained profit

After all costs and expenses, interest and dividend payments have been covered, the retained profit (net income or surplus) is what is left. This is taken to the balance sheet to add to the accumulating shareholders' interest (equity).

Pro forma profits

Always make sure the profit figures you are using are taken from the published income statement. A recent trend is for companies to offer "pro forma" financial information to investors. In 2002 the International Organisation of Securities Commissions (IOSCO) recommended care when using non-GAAP figures:

> Investors should be aware that non-GAAP pro forma earnings measures are not prepared in accordance with the accounting standards applied to financial statements and may omit or reclassify significant expenses.

In the United States the Sarbanes-Oxley Act of 2003 was supported by the SEC with firm rules covering all pro forma financial information released by listed companies

Interim reports

The annual report is not the only financial statement available to assist in the analysis of a company's performance and position. Listed companies are required to publish interim reports. These normally cover a period of three or six months. The objective is to keep investors aware of company performance. IAS 34 details the minimum content for an interim report. The report should assist in identifying any changes in the organisation, trends or volatility of company income, liquidity and cash flow generation. It should also bring investors up to date with new activities or circumstances arising since the last annual report. Comparative figures are provided.

There are two views of an interim report. American companies see it as part of the annual reporting process (integral view) and expenses are spread over the appropriate period. UK companies see it as a separate report (discrete view) to be prepared in exactly the same manner as the annual report, and expenses are recognised as incurred with no spreading. A company can opt to present a complete set of financial statements rather than the "condensed format" which includes a condensed:

- balance sheet;
- income statement;
- changes in equity statement;
- cash flow statement.

Also disclosed are:

- ◪ earnings per share;
- ◪ dividends paid;
- ◪ segmental analysis;
- ◪ statement of accounting policies and methods;
- ◪ management discussion of events.

It is quite likely that a company will publish its interim statements only online. Shareholders will not be mailed copies.

Preliminary announcements

Companies are expected to make a preliminary announcement of annual results and dividend within 120 days of the financial year end, with most companies complying within 90 days. The preliminary announcement contains information similar to that of an interim report, and, ideally, provides some linkage to the final quarter or second half of the year. It acts as a quick overview of the annual report and normally forms the basis for press releases by the company and media comment on its performance.

Receipt of a preliminary announcement was a major advantage for analysts as it was not mailed to shareholders. The internet now makes it possible for anyone using the company's website to have almost as speedy access to this information as the professionals.

4 The cash flow statement

A COMPANY'S INCOME STATEMENT can show a healthy profit for the year, but this does not guarantee that it has the cash necessary to survive. Profit is not cash. Profit is an accounting measure; cash is a physical item. In the 1970s and 1980s many apparently profitable companies failed because of a lack of cash. This increased pressure for financial reports to give more emphasis to a company's cash flows, liquidity and borrowings. Thus the cash flow statement became the third significant financial statement to be presented by companies in their annual reports. Cash flow statements were introduced in the United States in the late 1970s and the UK in the early 1990s.

No cash, no business

Profit is part fact, part opinion and occasionally part hope. Different assumptions, views and accounting treatment will produce different profits. Low profitability or loss-making operations may be distressing or embarrassing for management but not necessarily terminal for a company. Companies can survive without profit as long as they have cash available. Even a profitable company cannot survive without cash.

Every activity of a company is translated into cash at some time. Companies use it to pay employees and suppliers and customers use it to purchase products and services. It is necessary to allow investment in assets to support growth and to pay interest and dividends to providers of financial resources, and to pay taxes. At any time there is a single indisputable figure for cash, which can be physically counted and checked.

What is cash?

Cash is normally understood to be the notes and coins used in the day-to-day transactions of companies and individuals. For the purposes of accounting and financial analysis the definition of cash is slightly broader, including not only coins and notes but also money held in bank accounts. These cash or near-cash assets form part of a company's liquid assets. A starting point for assessing the strength of a company's cash position is to look at the changes in the amounts of cash held at the beginning and end of the year. All that is required is two consecutive balance sheets. An increase in cash held could be taken to be a good sign representing an improvement in liquidity. However, in making an assessment of a company's liquidity, any short-term borrowings, such as overdrafts in the UK, should be deducted from cash and bank balances to identify the net position.

Cash balances

For most purposes cash can be taken to include all cash and bank balances net of overdraft or other borrowings repayable on demand; in other words the cash a company has readily available for immediate use. Although cash is essential in the running of any business, it is, except for any interest it may earn, a non-productive asset that can be used to increase productive resources or to repay debt, thus reducing interest charges and improving profitability. A company with a shortage of cash may be in trouble. A company with a lot of cash may not be operating as profitably as it could be. But you have to be careful about reading too much into the cash balance given in the annual report. A large figure may simply reflect the setting aside of money to pay for machines in the following financial year.

What matters

Working capital

To consider only the movement in cash and liquid assets over a period of time does not provide a sufficient basis for understanding the financial changes a business is experiencing. A better view of a company's financial position can be obtained if the scope of analysis is expanded to cover all current assets and current liabilities. Current assets are likely to be turned into cash, if they are not already in this form, within a fairly short period. Similarly, current liabilities will have to be paid in cash within 12 months of the balance sheet date, if not much sooner. By deducting current liabilities from current assets to produce net current assets or liabilities, you get what is commonly called the working capital of a company. Changes seen to be occurring within the working capital of a business can be important indicators of its performance and position.

As a business is managed there is a continual movement of financial resources or funds including cash, as Figure 4.1 shows. In a typical business, inventory is produced or purchased, suppliers deliver raw materials, operating costs and expenses are incurred and customers buy the products. All these transactions are completed either in cash or on credit

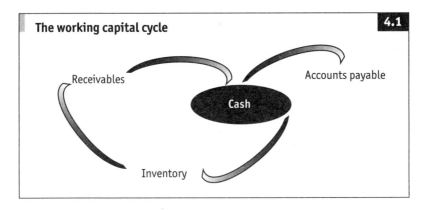

The working capital cycle   4.1

terms. Current assets and liabilities change to reflect the impact of transactions made to enable the business to operate.

There are problems, however, in using working capital as the basis for analysing the financial changes of a business. Concentrating on working capital movements alone ignores other sections of the balance sheet, such as changes in non-current assets, shareholders' funds and long-term borrowings. Also it is possible for a company to control the level of current assets and liabilities at the time the balance sheet is drafted. Immediately before the end of the financial year customers can be chased for payment so that the balance sheet shows an unrepresentative low level of receivables; payment for plant and equipment can be delayed to allow a higher level of cash balances; and suppliers can be paid earlier or later than normal to adjust the level of credit.

Funds flow

For all businesses there are movements of cash resulting from transactions and events outside the area of working capital. There is more to a business than just the working capital cycle. Non-current assets may be bought or sold, dividends, interest and tax paid, loans raised or repaid and shares issued or repurchased. When these items are included, a better foundation is provided for the analysis of movements in a company's financial resources. If all the changes between two consecutive balance sheets are analysed, every financial movement will be covered. This is called funds flow analysis.

Funds can be defined as being any source of finance allowing a company to acquire assets. Cash raised from shareholders is a source of funds (finance) that can be used in the business. Additional credit taken from suppliers, although not cash, acts as a source of funds, enabling the level of inventory held to increase. Any liability increasing during the year acts as a source of funds available for use on the other side of the balance sheet to increase assets.

Sources and uses

The balance sheet is the starting point for discovering what funds have been generated during the year and how these have been used in the business. The balance sheet equation, assets = liabilities, ensures that in any year a company cannot use more funds than it generates or generate more than it uses; in other words, sources = uses. If more funds are generated than can be immediately used for operational purposes, paying interest and dividends or repaying borrowings, the surplus will appear in the year-end cash balances. Holding more cash is a use of funds.

Sources of funds

A company considering making an investment can fund it by:

- using existing cash balances;
- generating cash from operations;
- raising capital from shareholders;
- borrowing money;
- changing credit terms;
- selling assets.

Sources of funds fall into two categories: internal and external. Internal sources are largely under the control of the company. A proportion of internal funds can be expected to be generated through the income statement. Shareholders can be an internal source of funds, but they also make demands on cash for payment of dividends. External sources comprise suppliers giving credit payment terms to the company and banks and other institutions providing short-, medium- or long-term finance.

In looking at the changes that have taken place between two balance sheets, a decrease in the value of an asset or an increase in a liability can be assumed to act as a source of funds to the business. However, common sense indicates that the revaluation of property during the year will show an increase in assets matched by an increase in liabilities (equity); since this does not indicate any actual movement in financial resources it should be ignored.

Sources = increases in liabilities and/or decreases in assets

Uses of funds

The funds available to a company during the year can be used for:

- increasing current assets;
- decreasing current liabilities;
- purchasing non-current assets;
- repaying borrowings;
- repurchasing shares;
- covering operating losses.

A change in customer credit policy resulting in an increase in receivables at the end of the year is a use of funds. Customers are, in effect, being allowed to borrow more of the company's money. Until they pay for the goods or services received they are tying up valuable financial resources that could be used elsewhere in the business. An increase in the value of an asset or a decrease in a liability, such as the purchase of a new machine, payments to suppliers or the repayment of a loan, can be assumed to have consumed funds.

Uses = increases in assets and/or decreases in liabilities

Funds flow statement

A statement displaying the changes in a company's financial position can be called a:

- funds flow statement;
- statement of changes in financial position;
- source and application statement;
- cash flow statement.

A funds flow statement is produced by comparing two consecutive balance sheets and identifying the changes that have occurred. This can be done by deducting, line by line, one balance sheet from the other. The differences represent an increase or decrease in an asset or liability. All the changes that have occurred during the year are thus identified as representing either a source or a use of funds.

($)	Year 1		Year 2		+/-
Non-current assets					
Plant and equipment	210		250		+40
Depreciation	110	100	120	130	+10
Current assets					
Inventory	60		75		+15
Debtors	30		40		+10
Investment	0		10		+10
Cash	10	100	15	140	+5
Total assets		200		270	
Equity					
Share capital	100		110		+10
Retained earnings	60	160	80	190	+20
Loan				20	+20
Current liabilities					
Accounts payable	30		40		+10
Taxation	10	40	20	60	+10
Total liabilities		200		270	

If the year 1 balance sheet is deducted from that of year 2, the changes represent either a source or a use of funds during the year.

Sources	$	Uses	$
Retained earnings	20	Plant and equipment	40
Depreciation	10	Inventory	15
Share issue	10	Accounts receivable	10
Loan	20	Investment	10
Accounts payable	10	Cash	5 __80__
Tax	10		
	80 __80__		

The treatment of depreciation

In the example above, depreciation (amortisation) of $10 has been included as a source of funds. Although depreciation is charged in the income statement as an expense for the year, there is no cash movement. If the assets on which the depreciation charge is based were paid for in cash at the time of their acquisition, there will be no further cash movements associated with them until their disposal. Depreciation is a non-cash expense.

It would be possible to show only the $30 net change in non-current assets after depreciation ($40 – $10) instead of showing the $40 investment in plant and machinery and the $10 depreciation charge separately. However, this could conceal the true financial movements associated with non-current assets. The depreciation charge of $10 has been generated by the company from its operations and is available for reinvestment in assets during the year. The company has not only maintained its productive resources but also increased them. It is better to view the changes that have taken place during the year as the company having spent $40 on additional plant and machinery.

It is important to understand that although it is common practice to refer to depreciation as a source of funds, this is technically incorrect. A change in depreciation policy has no impact on cash. A company cannot generate funds by changing its depreciation rates. If it decided to increase the depreciation charge from $10 to $20, this would reduce the reported profit by $10. The combined retained earnings ($10) and depreciation ($20) remain at $30, and there is no impact on the end of year 2 cash balance of $15.

From funds flow to cash flow

Until 1991 all UK companies had to provide a Statement of Source and Application of Funds in their annual report. The accounting standard (SSAP 10) offered considerable flexibility on content presentation. With companies adopting slightly different reporting formats it proved hard to compare funds flow. Also the statement merely showed the changes taking place in the interval between two balance sheets. It did not provide the additional information necessary to assess a company's ability to meet its obligations, including payments to suppliers, shareholders and others as they fell due.

Pressure for change grew as users of financial statements made clear their dissatisfaction with the level of disclosure. They wanted to see clearly where financial resources were being generated, how they were being applied in the business, and the resultant changes in liquidity and borrowings. By 1990 most major UK companies were providing a cash flow statement which covered only the actual cash movements experienced during the year, rather than a funds flow statement.

Cash balance changes

It is sometimes helpful to adjust the presentation format of the funds flow statement to highlight the changes that have occurred in cash balances.

($)		
Opening cash balance		**10**
Sources		
Share issue	10	
Loan	20	
Retained earnings	20	
Depreciation	10	
Increase in payables	10	
Increase in tax payable	<u>10</u>	<u>80</u>
		90
Uses		
Increase in inventory	15	
Increase in receivables	10	
Investment	10	
Plant and equipment	<u>40</u>	<u>75</u>
Closing cash balance		**15**

Cash flow

The cash flow from sales revenue is not the same as the sales revenue figure appearing in the income statement. It is the actual cash received and does not, as under accrual accounting, include credit transactions with customers. Cash inflows from customers and cash outflows to suppliers are produced by adjusting the total amounts of these by the credit element involved.

If sales revenue for the year is $150 then the cash inflow can be calculated as:

$$\text{Cash inflow} = \text{sales revenue} + (\text{opening} - \text{closing receivables})$$
$$140 = 150 + (30 - 40)$$

The $30 owed by customers at the start of the year has been collected, and from the year's sales of $150 only $110 cash has been received ($150 less closing receivables of $40). The actual cash inflow from sales is $140 ($30 + $110).

Cash outflow to suppliers can be calculated in the same manner:

Cash outflow = purchases + (opening – closing accounts payables)

Cash flow and profit

The management of profit and cash is the key to any successful business. There is little point in a company having profit but no cash – its long-term survival is likely to be difficult to manage. Equally, there is no advantage, apart from short-term survival, in having cash but no profit.

An appreciation of cash flow is essential to fully understanding the financial position of a company. There have been many examples of major companies disclosing a profit in their annual report, only to go into liquidation or receivership soon after because of a lack of liquid resources. A company could report an increase in working capital with inventory and receivables increasing during the year disguising the fact that cash was depleted to a dangerous level. The following example shows net current assets increasing from $25 to $30 but cash balances are run down to zero.

($)	Year 1	Year 2
Inventory	20	30
Receivables	10	20
Cash	5	0
	35	50
Accounts payable	10	20
Working capital	**25**	**30**

A company may be creative in arriving at its reported profit for the year, but it is much more difficult, if not impossible without fraud, for it to create cash. Sales revenue may be increased by offering attractive credit terms to customers, but if the resulting receivables cannot be collected, cash balances will be run down and there may be difficulty in acquiring new inventory to service future business. Non-current assets may be revalued to produce an apparently healthier balance sheet, but there is no change in cash balances. In recent years there has been a shift in emphasis, with the cash flow statement being seen as an integral and important part of the annual report.

The profit produced from operations (running the business) should be an important element of cash flow. If a loss is incurred, there is a positive internally generated cash flow only if the depreciation charge for the year exceeds the loss. Depreciation, a non-cash item, is added back to the profit for the year in the same way as in the funds flow statement.

A company may show a profit from making a credit sale to a customer but experience a reduction in cash balances. For example, a $150 sale to a customer and the associated materials and labour costs of $110 are recorded when the transaction is completed and included in the income statement for the year. However, there may be no increase in cash balances. If the suppliers have been paid $60 of the $110 cost of sales, but the customer has not paid the $150 owed, the income statement will show a gross profit of $40 and the balance sheet cash balances will be reduced by $60.

	$		$
Sales revenue	150	Cash inflow	0
Cost of sales	110	Cash outflow	60
Profit	40	Cash flow	(60)

Capitalising expenses and cash flow

By deciding to capitalise some of its expenses, interest payments or product development costs, a company can move the charge from the income statement into the balance sheet, thereby improving the reported profit. However, the cash movements associated with the year's expenses remain unchanged. Following the capitalisation of an expense it would be possible for the income statement to show a profit and the cash flow statement to show a negative cash flow from operations.

Cash flow and dividends and tax

Operating cash flow is what remains after paying the direct costs and expenses of the business. Ideally, it is sufficient to cover interest on borrowing and income taxes, and then provide the source of dividends to shareholders. Where a company incurs a loss, it is still possible to declare a dividend as long as there are sufficient revenue reserves in the balance sheet and cash available to make the payment. But a company that continues to deplete reserves and cash resources in order to pay dividends will eventually run into trouble.

A simple rule of good housekeeping is that companies should pay shareholders dividends only from sound and positive cash flows. They should not have to rely on selling non-current assets or borrowings. A company making a dividend payment from declining operating cash flow may satisfy the short-term needs of shareholders but not have sufficient funds to reinvest in the business to provide for future growth and continuing profitability.

The cash flow statement will show the cash outflows for dividends, interest and income tax during the year. The tax paid in one year is normally based on the previous year's profit – there is a delay between generating the profit and paying the tax. The income tax expense in the income statement will not match that appearing in the cash flow statement. For reasons of clarity and simplicity, timing differences for payment of interest, dividends and non-current asset investment are ignored in the examples used in this chapter.

Working capital and cash flow

Any change in the amount of inventory held and the credit given to customers or taken from suppliers has an impact on both reported profit and cash flow. Increasing the amount of credit taken from suppliers acts as a source and an increase in credit offered to customers is a use of available financial resources.

The relationship between current assets and current liabilities can be explored by looking at the movements that have taken place within working capital. Continuing with the example used earlier in this chapter it can be seen that financial resources ($60) have been used to allow an increase in non-current assets ($40) and to increase working capital ($20).

	$	
Cash flow		
From operations	30	
Loan	20	
Share issue	10	
Investment in non-current assets	(40)	**20**
Increase in working capital		
Increase in inventory	15	
Increase in investment	10	
Increase in cash	5	
Increase in receivables	10	
Increase in accounts payable	(10)	
Increase in tax	(10)	**20**

Presenting a statement of financial movements in this way helps to explain the sources and uses of cash flow and separates the investing activity and capital structure changes from those of working capital and liquid assets.

Cash flow statement

The cash flow statement provides an essential link between the income statement and the balance sheet. The detailed internal accounting records of a company are needed to prepare a statement of actual cash movements. It is not possible, as was the case with a funds flow statement, to prepare a cash flow statement yourself from the annual report. The statement provides information on the changes in a company's opening and closing "cash and cash equivalents". That is the cash balances and bank balances available on demand and any other highly liquid investments carrying no risk or uncertainty that are capable of quick conversion into cash

The aim of the cash flow statement is to allow an assessment of the company's ability to generate cash flows, their timing and strength, and to allow direct comparison with other similar businesses. IAS 7 governs it and requires that cash flow be shown under three headings of business activity – operating, investing and financing – which when combined can explain the change in cash position over the year. This provides the basis for a meaningful assessment and prediction of cash flow and facilitates comparison with other companies – accounting differences do not affect cash flow. In the United States the statement is called the statement of cash flows and the IASB is planning to adopt this title.

Operating cash flow comes from:

Income from sales of goods and services, interest and dividends received

Payments to suppliers, employees, operating expenses, and income taxes

The operating activities of a company can reasonably be expected to be the main source of its cash flows. The cash flow produced from running the business provides a basis for appreciating the quality of earnings and an assessment of the company's ability to continue to generate positive and strong future cash flows.

Investing activities include the acquisition of non-current assets and other long-term investments. Financing activities relate to changes in the financial structure of the company. Changes in equity – the issue or repurchase of shares and dividends paid – and changes in borrowings are dealt with here.

Cash flow from operating activities

The cash flow statement begins by detailing the cash generated from operations including:

Inflows	Outflows
Receipts from customers	Payments to suppliers
Sale of trading assets	Purchase of trading assets
Interest received	Interest paid
	Payments to employees
	Payment of taxes

Companies may choose between two formats in presenting their operating cash flow – the direct and indirect methods (sometimes referred to as net or gross). The indirect method is the most popular, but not necessarily the most informative. It does not always make clear where the money came from or where it went. The FASB and the IASC actively encourage companies to use the direct method of presentation.

The indirect method starts with the profit before tax, and then incorporates changes in working capital. The interest and tax shown represent the actual amount of cash paid during the year, whether or not any interest was capitalised.

The first step is adjusting the reported pre-tax profit figure for non-cash items that have been included in its calculation, such as depreciation or any investing or financing transactions. The profit or loss on sale of non-current assets and any foreign exchange differences are dealt with in the investing and financing activities sections of the statement. A loss on foreign exchange is added back and a gain deducted. Once this is done the changes in the elements of working capital are incorporated to arrive at the cash flow from operations.

When working capital increases the operating profit is greater than cash flow. When working capital decreases the cash flow from operations is less than operating profit. An increase in working capital is deducted from profit, and a decrease is added back to arrive at cash flow. The final adjustment is for tax to provide the net cash flows from operating activities. This final figure may be divided between continuing and discontinued operations if appropriate.

Profit before income tax
Adjustments for:
Depreciation and amortisation
Foreign exchange profit /loss
Profit /loss from sale of non-current assets
Interest paid/received

Increase/ decrease in inventory
Increase/decrease in receivables
Increase/decrease in accounts payable

Income taxes paid

Net cash flow from operations

The direct method gives the same net cash flow from operating activities as the indirect method but in a different way. It shows the gross cash in and cash out for each heading in the operating cash flow statement.

Cash from customers
cash paid to suppliers
cash paid to employees
cash paid for operating expenses

Cash generated from operations
interest paid
income taxes paid

Net cash from operating activities

Sales revenue can be assumed to be net of all sales taxes and after any bad debts. The cash flows for sales revenue and purchases are calculated in the same way as shown earlier in this chapter.

Cash inflow from sales revenue = sales revenue – increase or + decrease in receivables

Cash outflow for purchases = purchases – increase or + decrease in accounts payable

There may still be some allocation problems as it is impossible for any accounting standard to produce a set of rules tightly defining every possible event or transaction that a company might experience. For several items appearing in the cash flow statement a decision has been made as to within which heading they are to appear: is it an operating expense or an investment? However, the statement will show the impact of the transaction in cash terms.

Always remember when using the cash flow from operations that there is no provision made for the use or replacement (depreciation) of non-current assets such as plant and machinery. Operating profit can be expected to be greater than operating cash flow.

Cash flow from investing activities

The next section of the cash flow statement is that relating to the company's investing activities. Any increase in non-current assets resulting from their purchase will be shown here.

Inflows	Outflows
Sale of investments	Purchase of investments (not cash equivalents)
Sale of non-current assets	Purchase of non-current assets
Loans repaid	Loans made

Although a company may revalue some of its non-current assets, this has no impact on the cash flow statement as there has been no cash movement. The acquisition and sale of subsidiaries, associates and joint ventures together with any dividends received from these will be detailed in this section. The acquisition or disposal of long-term investments will also be shown.

> Receipts and payments for property, plant and equipment
> Purchase or sale of subsidiary companies
> Purchase or sale of associates and joint ventures
> Dividends received from associates and joint ventures
> Receipts and payments for intangibles

Net cash flow from (used in) investing activities

There is a difference between the change in a non-current asset shown in the balance sheet and that appearing in the cash flow statement. The cash flow statement identifies the actual amount of cash spent by the company during the year. The balance sheet figures are subject to timing differences. An asset may have been purchased but not paid for at the end of the financial year, so an increase in assets is shown in the balance sheet but there is nothing in the cash flow statement.

A crucial role of management is to make investment decisions allocating the available financial resources to appropriate parts of the business with a view to providing future profitable growth. The cash flow statement shows the cash outflows associated with the investing activities of the company and the cash inflows when assets are sold. It indicates the total amount spent on assets during the year but does not necessarily disclose in any detail precisely where or on what the cash was spent. The cash flow statement does not therefore provide a suitable basis for assessing the quality of the investments made.

Acquisitions and disposals

If a subsidiary is acquired or disposed of during the year, only the cash paid or received is included in the cash flow statement. A cash outflow is net of any cash gained from the subsidiary.

When an acquisition is made by the issue of shares, with no cash involved, the only impact on the cash flow statement is the receipt of the subsidiary's cash balances. The price paid may be different from that appearing in the cash flow statement. Where an acquisition has been made there may be only a single figure shown in investing activities. IAS 7 requires that this should be supported by a summary of the cash flow impact of the acquisition showing the fair value of net assets acquired and details of how the deal was financed. This offers more scope to assess the true viability of acquisitions as the actual cash outflows and the impact on financing requirements are disclosed.

For example, a company uses a combination of shares and cash to acquire a subsidiary.

Consideration paid ($)			Assets acquired ($)		
Shares issued	80		Assets	50	
Cash	20	100	Goodwill	20	
			Cash	30	100

The subsidiary has been purchased and the net cash result is to increase group cash balances by $10: $20 has been paid out to acquire $30. It is only this net cash movement of $10 that is recorded in the cash flow statement.

The way in which acquisition and disposal cash flows are considered depends on the nature of the group being analysed. Some companies trade or deal in businesses, buying and selling companies regularly throughout the year. For them the profit and positive cash flow generated from the sale of a business can be accepted as part of their operating activities. For most companies this is not the case; selling a major subsidiary may produce a substantial cash benefit, but only once.

If possible, a view should be taken on whether the sale of a subsidiary or major business investment is part of a carefully planned strategy or merely the result of painful necessity. It is not always possible to be certain of the reason for a disposal through reading the management statements in the annual report. It is unlikely that a company will admit that a subsidiary was sold because it was running out of cash. More commonly, the terms rationalisation, refocusing, re-engineering and suchlike are used to explain and justify major business disposals.

Cash flow from financing activities

The final section of the cash flow statement deals with the management of the financial structure of the company, showing any changes in borrowings and equity that have occurred during the year.

Inflows	Outflows
Issue of shares	Repurchase of shares
Debentures issued	Debentures repaid
	Dividends paid

Dividends paid to shareholders will be shown in this section. Interest payments may be shown here but are more likely to have been included in the operating activities section. Typically details will be provided for:

Equity dividends paid
Issue of shares
Share repurchases
Repayment of short- and long-term borrowings
Proceeds from short- and long-term borrowings
Capital and interest obligations under finance lease payments

Net cash flow from (used in) financing activities

The carrying value of assets held under finance leases is not normally separately identified in the balance sheet but included in the figure for total non-current assets. Finance leases do not involve any cash outflow for capital. Where an asset is acquired under a finance lease during the year the actual cash outflows will be shown in the financing activities section.

Apart from internally generated sources of finance, a company has only two options: it can raise additional funds from shareholders through the issue of shares (a rights issue), or it can go outside the company and borrow money from a bank or other financial institution. If any equity shares are issued or repurchased, the cash movement will be shown here. Remember that any shares issued without cash payment affect the balance sheet but not the cash flow statement.

The cash flow statement helps to identify how much money has been raised from shareholders and how much from short- and long-term external sources. Taken together with the internally generated cash flows, this gives a clear picture of the way in which the company has been financed during the year.

Management of liquid resources

For the purposes of the cash flow statement, cash or cash equivalents is defined as cash and bank balances (less bank overdrafts) plus any current asset investment that is readily convertible into cash. As part of its financial or treasury management aimed at getting some positive benefit from idle cash balances, a company may make a short-term investment which will be shown within current assets in the balance sheet. Surplus cash is used to earn interest, the investment having been planned to make sure that cash is available as and when required.

There will be a reconciliation linking the opening and closing cash and cash equivalents shown in the balance sheet with the cash flow for the year. This helps clarify the changes that have occurred.

A typical cash flow statement will show:

Opening cash and cash equivalents	XX
Cash flows from operating activities	
Net cash inflow (outflow) from operating activities	XX
Cash flows from investing activities	
Net cash outflow (inflow) from investing activities	XX
Cash flows from financing activities	
Net cash inflow (outflow) from financing activities	XX
Closing cash and cash equivalents	XX

There will be comparative figures for the previous year supported by detailed notes for each major item.

Exceptional and extraordinary events

Every business is likely at some time to experience an exceptional or extraordinary event. When this occurs a company would rightly wish to drawn analysts' attention to this item as not being part of the normal business activities. Until the revision of IAS 1 in 2005, such events were reported separately in the income statement and the cash flow statement. There was criticism of the way in which some companies were creative in their decision on what to include under the heading "extraordinary" in order to disguise operational shortcomings. This option is no longer open to them.

A major reorganisation by a company may result in significant cash outflows to cover redundancy payments or the cost of closing or relocating operating units. The cash outflow will normally be shown as a single figure within the cash flow from operations section of the statement with additional details in the accompanying notes.

Foreign exchange and cash flow

Most companies transact business in foreign currencies and many have subsidiaries in other countries. To prepare the financial statements all transactions must be translated into the reporting company's currency. When foreign assets and liabilities are translated into a holding company's currency at the balance sheet date exchange rate differences will occur. Foreign exchange gains or losses on operating activities will be included in the section of the cash flow statement dealing with the cash generated from operations – usually in the accompanying notes. The sections of the cash flow statement dealing with investing and financing activities will also have been adjusted for foreign exchange gains or losses. The effects of foreign exchange rates on the closing cash and cash equivalent figure will be shown as a separate item in the cash flow statement.

The treatment of exchange rate differences is complex. When looking at the cash flow statement all you need to remember is that it deals only with actual cash movements. Any exchange rate differences that have not had a cash impact during the year are ignored.

Summary

- To complete a full analysis and assessment of a company the cash flow statement must be used in conjunction with the income statement, which deals with the profit or loss made from running the business, and the balance sheet, which shows the financial position at the end of the year.
- The cash flow statement covers the same period as the income statement, setting out the changes in cash balances and borrowing that have taken place between the opening and closing balance sheets. It is extremely useful in assessing a company's liquidity, viability and financial adaptability. An increase in reported profit need not be supported by sound and positive cash flow.
- A reasonable starting point is to see if the company is showing a continuing and positive cash flow from its operations. Is there stability? Has the increase in cash flow over the previous year at least matched the rate of inflation?
- The cash flow statement shows whether a company is generating or consuming cash. Has it proved capable of producing sufficient cash from the business or has it used up all available liquid resources and had to raise additional funds?
- A change in the relationship between operating cash flow (cash flow statement) and net income (income statement) can act as a warning signal. If cash flow begins to lag behind income, ask why. One explanation may be that sales revenue is being massaged. Perhaps, to generate sales, customers are being given excessively generous credit terms. Net income increases in the year but, as receivables rise, cash flow does not follow.
- Remember, at any point in the cash flow statement, a company is free to create a subtotal and to highlight the figure. This does not mean that the figure is truly indicative of performance or position. Make sure your attention is not being distracted from more important evidence contained within the statement.
- If a business is absorbing large amounts of cash, this will be evident in the cash flow statement. A forecast can be made of how long the company could support the continuing cash outflow.
- The quality of a company's cash flow depends partly on management's competence and partly upon the nature of the business and its areas of operation. Even exceptional management may achieve only low profitability and poor cash

flows in a declining business sector. Its quality must also be judged on the basis of how much cash comes from continuing operations: the more the better.

- Study changes in cash balances and in each element of working capital. If, for example, inventory and customer credit levels are increasing, the company may be in trouble; the inducement of extra credit is not leading to additional sales. The company may be in danger of overtrading.

- Where is the cash flow coming from? In most groups, individual companies and business sectors have different cash flow patterns, but there should be at least one business capable of generating positive cash flows to help finance others with negative cash flows develop and survive. Showing cash flows as part of a company's segmental reporting would be useful.

- Other useful indicators of company performance are whether more or less cash is being held at the end of the year than at the beginning, or whether the company's borrowings have increased or decreased during the year.

- The cash flow statement can show whether the company has the necessary liquid resources to pay a cash dividend and whether it is likely to generate sufficient cash to meet its obligations, including loan repayments, as they fall due.

- The current year's cash flow statement can be used as a basis for forecasting future years' cash flow. Depreciation is simple to calculate and forecast for future years. Rates are known and assumptions about future investment in additional assets can be allowed for to provide a fairly accurate estimate for future years' depreciation charges.

- The profit contribution to cash flow is less easy to predict accurately. For most businesses, it is the least certain element in a cash flow forecast. However, an estimate can be made based on the trend shown for previous years.

2
ASSESSING THE FACTS

5 Guidelines for financial analysis

THIS CHAPTER GIVES SOME GENERAL GUIDELINES on the calculation and interpretation of the ratios covered later. Perhaps the most
important rule to remember is to keep it simple.

Comparability and consistency

The figures used in the analysis of a company or for the comparison of
a number of companies must as far as possible be truly comparable. In
calculating rates of return there is no point in taking the pre-tax profit of
one company and comparing it with the post-tax profit of another. A
company capitalising interest may appear to have a better profit performance than one that does not do so. If, rather than the interest figure
appearing in the income statement, the total interest payment for the
year is used for both companies, there may be no difference in their
profitability.

It is essential to make sure that consistent figures are used in the ratios
being developed. Companies may change the ways in which they present their financial data and define individual items in the financial
statements. Always check that the analysis has been adjusted to take
account of such changes; the notes to the financial statements should
give details of these as well as other crucial matters.

Never rely on a single ratio

It is inadvisable to judge a company on the basis of a single ratio. Either
the previous year's ratio should be calculated to gain an impression of
how what is being considered is changing and what is the trend, or the
ratio of one company should be compared with that of companies operating in the same business or of a comparable size. The tables of ratios
in Part 3 offer some benchmarks for the sector and country against
which individual companies may be assessed.

The more years the better

Do not judge a company on the basis of a single year's figures. Three
or, ideally, five years' figures should be analysed in order to get a
clear view of the consistency of a company's performance and to

highlight any movements in the ratios that require explanation or investigation.

The annual report should contain a five-year or ten-year history of the company. This can provide a useful start point in analysis. All the figures appearing in the history should be consistent and comparable. Any changes in the company's structure or operations will have been taken into account and all previous years adjusted as necessary.

The company history is a good source of financial statistics: employee numbers, dividend payments, earnings per share and share price. Sometimes companies present useful information on R&D or capital expenditure. Before starting an analysis check with the history to see what is immediately available – this may avoid some duplication of effort.

It does not require a great intellect to use creative accounting methods to produce a one-off high level of profitability for a company. The real art is in maintaining such an illusion. Once accounts are being manipulated a company is walking a tightrope, and each year more oscillations are generated, guaranteeing that at some time in the near future it is going to cry for help or fall off.

Year ends

One problem in comparing companies is that they are unlikely to have the same financial year end. In most countries there are three popular dates: March/April, September/October and December/January. A company's choice of year end depends on such things as the date it was founded, fiscal legislation, or the nature of its business. Companies involved in seasonal businesses are unlikely to want to prepare year-end accounts at the peak of their trading cycle, so few retailers have December 31st as their financial year end.

Differences in year ends and the timing of the publication of results often create problems in producing tables for cross-country and cross-company comparison. The best that can normally be done is to bring together companies reporting within the 12-month period, although this may span two calendar years. This may result in some distortions because of seasonality, but at least it provides an acceptable common time base.

How many weeks in the year?

Care should also be taken to make sure that the income statement is for a standard 52-week year. A company may have adjusted its year end and so have more or less than 12 months' trading contained in the accounts. For example, a change may follow a merger or acquisition where one company moves to bring its year end into line with the other. In such cases, the data used in the analysis can be adjusted back to 52 weeks or 12 months by dividing the data by the actual number of weeks or months covered in the income statement and then multiplying by either 52 or 12. However, bear in mind that such an adjustment may result in a distortion.

Average, median or mode?

It is often advisable to top and tail league tables of companies operating in a selected sector to provide some guidelines on average performance or position. Extremes of performance or position, although of considerable importance to the companies concerned, are best ignored when trying to determine averages or standards for a set of companies or a business sector. Otherwise an extreme case can distort any average being calculated.

In many cases, it is preferable to use the median rather than the average as the benchmark. If ten companies are being compared and the indicator being used gives a figure of 10 for nine companies and 100 for one company, the average (190/10) is 19. This results in nine out of the ten companies being below average.

A better guide may be the median or the middle or mid-point figure in a table showing the ranking of companies or ratios. Where there are odd numbers of items the median is the middle figure. In the example below the median of the first line is 7.

| 2 | 5 | 7 | 9 | 12 |
| | 6 | 8 | 10 | 11 |

The median can be calculated from the formula $(n + 1) \div 2$, where n is the number of items in the group. With five items this provides $(5 + 1) \div 2 = 3$, the third item in the list. With an even number of items the formula identifies the position of the median between the two mid-point figures $(4 + 1) \div 2 = 2.5$. The median is halfway between 8 and 10 = 9.

An alternative measure is to take the mode, that is, the figure that occurs most often in the table. The mode is best identified by eye rather than by calculation, and of course it is possible for a table to be bimodal (with two modes).

Investigate variations

When the ratios of a company cause it to stand out among others in the same sector it is important to try to discover the reasons for the variation. It may be that the company is unique and setting standards of performance or financial structure for the rest of the sector. However, care should be taken that its uniqueness is not merely the result of the application of accounting practices different from those of other companies.

Similarly, any sudden and dramatic shift in a company's performance or position should be investigated. A significant improvement in reported profit may be the result of a one-off sale of an asset or changes in the accounting treatment of items in the financial statements.

In financial analysis it is safest and usually most productive not to give the benefit of the doubt. When a company displays markedly different characteristics from others in the same sector, it is best to assume that this is not a positive signal until further investigation proves otherwise.

Graphs and charts

For most people a graph offers the best means of displaying a series of financial data and information. Setting out five years' turnover and profit or profit margin and the return on total assets in a graph provides an ideal way of identifying trends and annual movement and is certainly more effective than a table packed with figures containing the same data. Standard software packages make it easy to turn a set of figures into a graph, bar chart or pie chart.

Check the integrity

Companies have been making increasing use of graphic displays in corporate reports. But what kind of picture is being presented? It is a simple matter to disguise or distort a trend in, for example, profit growth by picking a scale for a graph that delivers the message you want to give. The two bar charts in Figure 5.1 on the next page display exactly the same annual profits. If you take the trouble to measure the bars with a ruler, both charts show the final year profit is four times that of the first year. However, for most people the one on the right appears to indicate the better performance.

Never rely on someone else's analysis

It is safest never to rely entirely on someone else's analysis, particularly if this is offered by the company being studied. Always base the company assessment and calculations on the original financial data available in the financial statements.

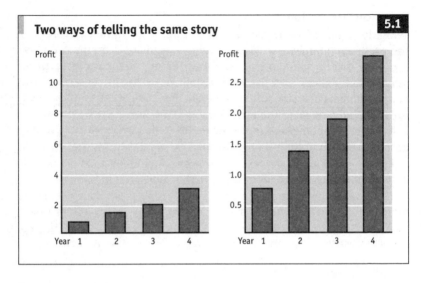

Two ways of telling the same story `5.1`

Percentage rules

A useful aid to interpreting a financial statement is to express the figures in percentage terms, particularly when studying one company's data for a number of years or data for several companies. Percentages simplify things wonderfully, reducing figures that may be presented in billions, millions or thousands to a single comparable measure. Furthermore, they make it easier to spot trends or differences, as the following example of a cash flow statement shows.

	$ m	$ m	%	%
Cash inflows				
Operating activities	885.2		90	
Financing activities	94.4	979.6	10	100
Cash outflows				
Investment and finance	197.6		20	
Tax	231.8		24	
Investing activities	279.6	709.0	28	72
Increase in cash		270.6		28

Common size presentation

Similarly, a percentage-like presentation approach, known as common size presentation, makes it easier to analyse and compare the contribution each source of finance makes towards the financing of the total assets employed by companies. Often it is useful to present all the important items in an income statement as percentages of sales revenue. An added advantage to the application of common size presentation is that where companies are reporting in different currencies all currency differences are automatically removed.

If total assets are expressed as 100, sources of finance can be shown in relation to this, as the following example shows.

($)	Year 1	Year 2	Year 3
Non-current assets	1,515	1,580	1,729
Current assets	1,573	1,704	1,692
Total assets	3,088	3,284	3,421
Equity	926	1,314	1,711
Non-current liabilities	618	656	343
Current liabilities	1,544	1,314	1,367
Total liabilities	3,088	3,284	3,421

The process is simple. Each source of finance is divided by total assets and multiplied by 100. For example, in year 3, capital and reserves of $1,711 divided by total assets of $3,421 and multiplied by 100 gives 50%. The balance sheets can now be represented as follows.

(%)	Year 1	Year 2	Year 3
Equity	30	40	50
Non-current liabilities	20	20	10
Current liabilities	50	40	40
Total assets	100	100	100

The three sources of finance can be clearly identified, and it is much easier to identify changes and trends from this presentation than from the three years' balance sheets.

Any changes in gearing can quickly be spotted when the common size presentation is used and debt/equity ratios can easily be calculated. This offers an alternative means of both calculating and interpreting gearing. From the first year's balance sheet, total debt of $2,162 divided by equity of $926 gives a debt/equity ratio of 2.3:1. The same calculation can be completed directly from the common size presentation. In year 1, total debt (70) divided by equity (30) produces the ratio 2.3:1 or 233%. By year 3 this can be seen to have reduced to 1:1 or 100%. The long-term debt ratio could be calculated in the same way, with long-term debt (20) divided by long-term debt and equity (20+30) giving a ratio of 0.4:1 or 40% in year 1 moving to 0.33:1 or 33% in year 3.

This presentation format can be used to explain how one side of the balance sheet, total assets, is being financed. For every $1 of assets employed in year 1 shareholders contributed 30¢, and by year 3 this had become 50¢. What remains of each $1 has been provided from external sources, debt and current liabilities; in year 1 this was 70¢ and in year 3 it was 50¢.

($m)	Turnover		Operating profit		Net assets	
	Year 1	Year 2	Year 1	Year 2	Year 1	Year 2
Class of business						
Consumer goods	956	998	65	71	408	421
Office equipment	488	532	15	22	188	201
Medical equipment	694	725	72	84	484	526
Electronic systems	355	501	−6	9	125	201
	2,493	**2,756**	**146**	**186**	**1,205**	**1,349**
Geographic analysis by location						
UK	860	877	61	63	451	434
Rest of Europe	485	498	32	34	274	255
North America	484	508	39	42	185	287
South America	307	486	−6	19	159	196
Asia/Australasia	259	333	19	26	136	177
Others	98	54	1	2	0	0
	2,493	**2,756**	**146**	**186**	**1,250**	**1,349**

(%)	Turnover		Operating profit		Net assets	
	Year 1	Year 2	Year 1	Year 2	Year 1	Year 2
Class of business						
Consumer goods	38	36	44	38	34	31
Office equipment	20	19	10	12	16	15
Medical equipment	28	26	49	45	40	39
Electronic systems	14	18	−4	5	10	15
	100	**100**	**100**	**100**	**100**	**100**

Geographic analysis by location

UK	34	32	42	34	37	32
Rest of Europe	19	18	22	18	23	19
North America	19	18	27	23	15	21
South America	12	18	−4	10	13	14
Asia/Australasia	10	12	13	14	11	13
Others	4	2	1	1	0	0
	100	**100**	**100**	**100**	**100**	**100**

This approach can also be used to analyse a five-year record, segmental report or one of a company's financial statements, as in the example.

Index numbers

The use of index numbers is another way of shedding light on the performance of a company. The result – a trend statement – offers a more reliable means of identifying trends in performance or position than a common size statement, as the following example of a company's five-year financial record shows.

($)	Year 1	Year 2	Year 3	Year 4	Year 5
Turnover	5,200	5,500	6,100	6,300	6,600
Pre-tax profit	350	400	475	490	520

If the figure for each year is divided by that of the base year and the result multiplied by 100, a series of index numbers is produced. The year 2 turnover ($5,500) divided by that of year 1 ($5,200) and multiplied by 100 gives 106.

	Year 1	Year 2	Year 3	Year 4	Year 5
Turnover	100	106	117	121	127
Pre-tax profit	100	114	136	140	149

In interpreting index numbers it must be remembered that they relate directly to the first year. Turnover in year 2 increased by $300 ($5,500 – 5,200), which was a 6% increase and was reflected in the index number movement from 100 to 106. However, it is incorrect to assume that the turnover increase in year 5 was also 6% (127 – 121). Turnover in year 5 increased by $300, which was less than a 5% increase on the $6,300 of year 4. The turnover in year 5 represents a 27% increase on that in year 1. Of course, if year 2 was used as the base (100) a different picture would be presented.

Growth rates and trends

Assessing the rate at which change is occurring can be useful in financial analysis. To measure the percentage change from one year to the next the calculation is:

$$100 \times [(\text{Year 2} - \text{Year 1}) \div \text{Year 1}]$$

Turnover and profit growth for the second and the last year are as follows.

	Year 1 − Year 2	Year 4 − Year 5
Turnover	$(5,500 - 5,200) \div 5,200 = 5.8\%$	$(6,600 - 6,300) \div 6,300 = 4.8\%$
Pre-tax profit	$(400 - 350) \div 350 = 14.3\%$	$(520 - 490) \div 490 = 6.1\%$

The company has an apparently steady growth in turnover. Where there is a significant level of inflation, growth patterns can be distorted. To overcome this problem an appropriate measure of inflation, such as the retail price index, can be used to adjust turnover. To express turnover for any year in year 5 dollars, that year's turnover is multiplied by the year 5 index divided by that year's index. For example, to express year 1 turnover in year 5 dollars the calculation is:

$$\$5,200 \times (140 \div 100) = \$5,200 \times 1.4 = \$7,280$$

The adjusted figures provide a better basis for interpreting the real underlying growth patterns. Based on the adjusted figures for the five-year period, profit increased by 6% and turnover decreased by 9%.

	Year 1	Year 2	Year 3	Year 4	Year 5
Turnover ($)	5,200	5,500	6,100	6,300	6,600
Inflation index	100	110	120	130	140
Adjusted turnover ($)	7,280	7,000	7,117	6,785	6,600

Compound growth rates

To assess the growth trend over a number of years the compound growth rate can be calculated. There are statistical formulas for calculating it, but as in most cases all that is required is a broad indicator of the rate, the table below can be used for most situations.

From the five-year financial record table appearing in an annual report it is possible to calculate growth over four years. If, using the figures in the example above, the final year figure is divided by that of the first year, the resultant factor can be read from the table to discover the approximate compound growth rate over the four-year period:

Turnover $6,600 ÷ $5,200 = 1.27   Pre-tax profit $520 ÷ $350 = 1.49

Looking at the four-year column in the table, the closest figure to 1.27 is 6% and to 1.49 is 10%. Thus over the period turnover has grown at the rate of just over 6% per year and pre-tax profit at just over 10% per year.

	2 years	3 years	4 years
1%	1.02	1.03	1.04
2%	1.04	1.06	1.08
3%	1.06	1.09	1.13
4%	1.08	1.12	1.17
5%	1.11	1.16	1.22
6%	1.12	1.19	1.26
8%	1.17	1.26	1.36
10%	1.21	1.33	1.46
12%	1.25	1.40	1.57
14%	1.30	1.48	1.69
16%	1.35	1.56	1.81
18%	1.39	1.64	1.94
20%	1.44	1.73	2.07
25%	1.56	1.95	2.44
30%	1.69	2.20	2.86
40%	1.96	2.74	3.82
50%	2.25	3.37	5.06
60%	2.56	4.10	6.55
70%	2.89	4.91	8.35
80%	3.24	5.83	10.00
90%	3.61	6.86	13.00
100%	4.00	8.00	16.00

If the growth for the last three years is required, the calculations would be $6,600 ÷ $5,500 = 1.2 and $520 ÷ $400 = 1.3. Moving down the three-year column, this indicates a turnover growth of just over 6% and profit growth of just under 10% over the last three years.

It should be noted that a compound growth rate is based only on the first and last years. The company providing the five-year record could have made a $600 profit or loss in year 3 and the compound growth rate would not be affected.

Foreign currencies

Analysing a number of companies based in the same country avoids any problems associated with currency. Making an international comparison is inevitably more difficult. There is little point in trying to compare a US company's $96,000 profit per employee with a French company's €90,000 and a UK company's £60,000. The best way to deal with this problem is to translate all the figures involved into one currency. However, there are potential difficulties in doing this, the most obvious being which exchange rate to use. Two alternatives are the exchange rate ruling at the balance sheet date of each company or the average exchange rate for the year. The simplest method, although by no means the most accurate or representative, is to take all the currencies involved and use the exchange rates of the day the analysis is being completed to translate the figures into a single currency base.

If the three example companies are being compared from a UK base, the figures can be adjusted to show the ratio in sterling equivalents.

	Rate	£
$96,000	1.6	60,000
€90,000	1.5	60,000
£60,000	1.0	60,000

The three companies can now be directly compared in a currency that the person preparing the analysis is used to working with. Thus international comparisons can be made of the size, efficiency and performance of companies. However, care must be taken in adopting this approach, particularly when the analysis is looking back over a number of years. The revaluation of one country's currency against those of others would almost certainly result in a dramatic shift in the translated values for any ratios being used in the year in which this took place.

Using databases

If a commercial database is available as the source of company data and information, this will offer not only ease of access to the financial statements but also the advantage that each one is set out in a standard format. This can be particularly attractive when companies operating in several countries are being compared. The figures will be in a consistent form and the accompanying text translated into a common language, considerably reducing the stress of analysis. Note, however, that commercial databases take the figures provided by companies in their financial statements at face value when producing ratios. If you suspect creative accounting has been employed, you will need to look at the information in the annual report.

It should be accepted that databases occasionally change the format of their financial data presentation. Adding or removing a line in the income statement or balance sheet can throw out any spreadsheet calculations if the raw data are imported directly into the spreadsheet. Always check to ensure that the data input is consistent before completing or using any form of analysis. (See Chapter 10.)

6 Measuring profitability

THIS CHAPTER IS CONCERNED with the analysis of company profitability. It starts by concentrating on the data contained within the income statement profit and loss account and then broadens out to include the balance sheet and other sources of financial data and relevant information.

What is profit?

One definition of profit is that it represents the surplus of income over expenditure. In accounting, where income is greater than expenditure a profit is produced, and where expenditure is greater than income a loss results. Hence in the UK the statement dealing with revenue and expenditure was termed the profit and loss account (P&L). Income statement is the name now used in all countries.

Defining and measuring profit provides one of several areas of argument between accountants and economists. Economists direct their attention to what may happen in the future – the present value of future income. Accountants are more concerned with what has happened in the past – revenue less expenses. An economist may prove to be accurate in forecasting *what* will actually happen but is less likely to be able to state precisely *when* it will happen. An accountant, however, might argue that in most cases an economist only has to define profit whereas an accountant actually has to quantify it each year as a single figure in a set of accounts.

Different perspectives
The term profit may mean different things, not only to economists and accountants but also to a company's various interest groups, each of which view the profit a company makes from a different perspective.

- **Shareholders** may be most concerned about the ability of a company to maintain or improve the value of their investment and future income stream. They look to the company to generate sufficient profit to provide for dividend payments and an increase in the market value of the shares they own. In most annual reports the company's shareholders are provided with a detailed statement of the changes that have taken place during the year in their investment in the company (see Chapter 2).

- **Lenders** of money may be expected to be most interested in evidence to support the company's ability to continue to pay the interest on borrowed funds as this falls due.
- **Customers** may be concerned to assess the levels of profit being made, particularly if there is regulation of the business sector intended to offer some level of customer protection. Now that increasing emphasis is put on high standards of customer service and satisfaction, there is little advantage in making excessive short-term profits at the long-term expense of the customer.
- **Competitors** are most interested in comparing their own performance and efficiency with that of other companies operating in the same business sector.
- **Management and other employees** are usually most interested in the profit being generated from their section of the business and in assessing their employment prospects. Senior executives are expected to focus on the overall levels of profitability being provided by the company's main operating units, its strategic business units (SBUs). Their interest should be focused on the future potential rather than the historic performance of the company.
- **Business and investment analysts** may be expected by their clients or employers to provide an indication of whether a particular company's shares are worth holding or buying for future gain, or are best sold immediately. They will study the current year's profit and compare it with previous years and that of other companies, and set this against their assessment for the future of the business sector to forecast profit trends.

The fundamentals of capital maintenance

Profit can be defined as the difference between the capital shown in the balance sheet at the start and that shown at the end of an accounting period. If this profit were distributed to shareholders as dividend, the financial capital of the company would be unchanged (financial capital maintenance). All companies are required to maintain their financial capital. It is also reasonable to expect a company to maintain its ability to produce the goods or services upon which its business depends by providing for necessary non-current assets replacement (operating capital maintenance).

Economists and accountants agree that in arriving at a figure for profit, account must be taken of the assets being used or capital employed by the company to generate that profit. Before a profit can be declared, the "using up" of part of the assets or capital employed in the business must be charged as part of the overall costs and expenses for the year. This, as discussed in Chapter 3, is fundamental to accounting theory and company law, and is normally achieved through the charging of depreciation. It can be seen as the setting aside of funds for the eventual replacement of the company's assets when this becomes necessary.

If a company were not to comply with the capital maintenance requirement and paid tax to the government on, and dividends to its shareholders out of, the amount it had not charged as depreciation, it would not be retaining sufficient funds to maintain the asset base of its operations. This would be reflected on the other side of the balance sheet in a reduction in the shareholders' stake in the business. As a result, the capital employed and potentially the ability to meet the liabilities of creditors and those lending money to the company would be eroded.

In short, a company that fails to make consistent and reasonable or prudent provision each year for depreciation will overstate its real profitability and store up trouble for the future. It is therefore important to ensure that not only the requirement of capital maintenance but also all the basic principles of income statement preparation (see Chapter 3) are followed by a company in arriving at its stated profit.

Starting considerations

The starting point for analysing and assessing profitability is most likely to be the annual report, which provides on a regular basis data on a company's activities. The income statement sets out the company's income and expenditure. The result will be a profit where total income is greater than total expenditure and a loss where the reverse is the case.

$$\text{Profit} = \text{total income} - \text{total cost}$$

This equation appears to offer a simple definition of profit. But how is cost calculated? It is worth remembering the story of the executive who, exasperated at never receiving a clear answer to any question he asked his accountant, demanded, "What is 1 plus 1?" The accountant smiled and replied, "Are you buying or selling?" Because it is rarely possible to provide a clear and unambiguous definition of the cost of any product or service, it is difficult to define profit and therefore to interpret the figure a company declares as its profit.

For the purposes of the ratios and analysis covered in this chapter, it is assumed that the income or sales revenue figures used exclude all sales taxes or equivalents. In the UK it is normal to give sales revenue exclusive or net of value-added tax (VAT).

Sales revenue during the year is often divided into income generated from continuing and from discontinued business operations. This division continues in the statement of profit for the year. The intention is to show consistently each year where the company has been generating income and profit, and to make it easy to see how much the businesses that will contribute subsequent profits (or losses) have contributed in the year being reported. A company that has sold a profit source and not reinvested in another one will not only report the monies received from the sale as part of its overall profit but will also be giving up the income that source would have contributed to future profits.

Measuring sticks

It is possible to prepare a table listing, in order of the monetary value of their profit for the year, companies operating within a business sector. This list, with the largest numerical profit at the top and the smallest at the bottom, would tell you which of the chosen companies was making the largest profit. It might also be useful in revealing the total profit made by the selected companies. However, such a list would not necessarily tell you which of the companies was the most profitable. To discover this, a number of ratios can help.

Profit margin ratios

In the income statement, the profit margin can be used to begin the analysis of a company's profitability. It is calculated by dividing profit by sales revenue and expressing the result as a percentage.

$$\% \text{ profit margin} = 100 \times (\text{profit} \div \text{sales revenue})$$

Gross profit margin

Working down the income statement, the first profit normally displayed is the gross profit, which is produced by deducting the cost of sales from sales revenue for the year. It is normally safe to assume that the cost of sales includes all the direct materials and services provided by suppliers, direct employee remuneration and all direct overheads. However, it is essential to read the notes providing additional details of the figures appearing in the income statement.

Unfortunately there is, as yet, little real consistency in how different companies present crucial information. For example, some companies deduct the remuneration of all shop-floor employees in arriving at gross profit and some do not. When several companies are being analysed, it will probably be necessary to make a number of adjustments to the figures provided in the accounts before it is possible to be confident that profitability ratios are truly comparable.

% gross profit margin = 100 × (gross profit ÷ sales revenue)

The gross profit margin, often simply referred to as the gross margin, offers a reasonable indication of the basic profitability of a business and is useful when comparing the performance of companies operating within the same sector. When one company has a totally different level of gross margin, it is worth trying to discover why.

Movements in the level of profit margins may be caused by many factors. For example, gross margin is influenced by changes in the mix of products or services being marketed by a company and is directly affected by price increases or decreases. Similarly, changes in production efficiency or materials purchasing affect the cost of sales, which in turn have an impact on gross margin. The potential for incorrect inventory valuation to distort profit, and thereby gross margin, was discussed in Chapter 2.

Operating profit margin

Operating profit usually follows gross profit in the income statement. It normally allows for all of a company's expenses of distribution, administration, research and development and general overheads.

Care must be taken to make sure there is a consistent treatment of any turnover and profit relating to joint ventures and associates. If the total turnover figure is being used, the total operating profit – including the share of joint ventures' and associates' profit – should be matched with this.

The operating profit margin offers an assessment of the profitability of a company after taking into account all the normal costs of producing and supplying goods or services and the income from selling them, but excluding financing costs, such as interest payments on bank loans, or investment income, such as interest earned on bank deposits.

% operating margin = 100 × (operating profit ÷ sales revenue)

If a company has a consistent level of gross margin but a declining operating profit margin, it is worth investigating why. One explanation could be efficient purchasing and basic cost control but poor control of general overheads, which are increasing without any compensating improvement in sales revenue.

At this stage you should turn to the notes that accompany the figures for sales revenue and operating profit in the income statement. As described in Chapter 3, these notes offer a valuable source of information on exactly where a company is generating revenue and, linked to this, what level of profit is being made in each business sector and geographic area of operation.

Because comparative figures are given for the previous year in the notes, it is possible to identify movements not only within a sector but also among the various geographic areas where a company has an interest. With some additional historic data any significant trends can be identified. Often it is possible to make comparisons with other companies operating in the same sector and location.

Pre-tax profit margin

Moving down the income statement, the next step is to deduct the remaining expenses and charges from operating profit to produce the pre-tax profit (PTP) for the year. When the pre-tax profit margin is calculated, this shows the level of profitability of a company after all operating costs and expenses except tax and dividends to shareholders have been allowed for.

% pre-tax profit margin = 100 × (pre-tax profit ÷ sales revenue)

A company maintaining a stable operating profit margin but a declining pre-tax profit margin may have raised finance for investment upon which it pays interest, but the investment has yet to be translated into either reduced costs or increased revenue. The interest charge is deducted in arriving at the pre-tax profit for the year, but no income has yet been generated from the investment of the finance raised.

After-tax profit and retained profit margins

It is possible to calculate both the after-tax profit margin and the retained profit margin from the income statement, but such ratios do not offer any significant additional help in the overall appreciation of a company's profitability.

The efficiency ratios

The next step in analysing a company's profitability is to combine information from the income statement and the balance sheet in ways that enable you to measure how efficiently a company is using its assets or capital employed.

($)	A	B	C
Revenue	100	100	100
Profit	20	20	27
Assets	100	125	150

For example, companies A and B have a 20% profit margin and C has a 27% profit margin. On the basis of this measure, C appears to be the most profitable company and it is impossible to distinguish between A and B. The following ratios can be used as part of a more detailed analysis.

Rate of return on assets or capital employed

The overall rate of return on capital or assets can be calculated by dividing profit, taken from the income statement, by assets or capital employed, as shown in the balance sheet, and expressing the result as a percentage.

$$\% \text{ rate of return on assets} = 100 \times (\text{profit} \div \text{assets})$$

$$\% \text{ rate of return on capital} = 100 \times (\text{profit} \div \text{capital})$$

If this ratio is produced for the three companies, their rates of return on assets are seen to be:

A	B	C
20%	16%	18%

Company C has the highest profit margin (27%), but it has a greater investment in assets than A or B. Company A has the same profit margin (20%) as B, but it has a lower asset base and so shows a higher rate of return. Linking the assets employed in the business to the profit being generated by them offers a more realistic measure of profitability than the use of profit margin ratios alone. Company A with a 20% return on assets is now identified as the most profitable of the three.

Which profit? What assets?
When dealing with profitability ratios it is important to recognise that there is no single method of calculating rates of return and that the same term may be used to refer to quite different things. A rate of return on assets (ROA) may have been produced using the gross, operating, pre-tax or after-tax profit. It is not usual to use gross profit in a rate of return measure, but there is no reason why this should not be done for a number of companies to provide the basis for performance comparisons and the analysis of a business sector.

Which profit measure to use?
As with any art, financial analysis is subject to fad and fashion. A ratio is adopted, rises in repute, declines and is replaced. One measure of profit currently enjoying favour is that of earnings before interest, taxation, depreciation and amortisation (EBITDA). It is argued that this measure strips out all the incidentals to highlight the "real" profitability of a business and is not biased by capital structure, tax systems or depreciation policies. It can be used to produce an EBITDA earnings per share figure (see pages 155–6).

The holy grail of financial analysis is the discovery of a single fool-proof measure of company performance. EBITDA can be useful as part of a detailed analysis of a company, but there are flaws in its claimed perfection. EBITDA ignores the cost of non-current assets employed in a business, yet surely these are as much an operating cost as anything else. As a measure of profitability it is a long way from the bottom line of the income statement, and so ignores not only depreciation but also interest and tax. A company delivering an after-tax loss from a huge investment in non-current assets financed by equally substantial borrowings could look quite healthy on an EBITDA basis.

Whichever profit is selected, the end result will be the return on assets, but each of the possible profits will produce a different level of return. For each ratio the denominator has remained constant but a different numerator has been used. Before making use of a pre-calculated rate of return figure always check which profit has been used to produce the ratio.

Similar problems can arise in selecting the denominator for the ROA ratio. This could equally well be the total, operating or net assets employed. Whichever figures are used, the end ratio is correctly described as a ROA for the company in question. If the three companies in the example on page 150 had used different definitions of profit and of assets, it would not be of any practical benefit to try to draw any conclusions by comparing their rates of return. For this reason, rate of return ratios given in annual reports or by analysts should not be taken at their face value.

In short, in calculating comparative rates of return it is essential that there is consistency in both the numerator and the denominator in the equation. In other words, you should ensure that each company's ROA is calculated in the same way.

Averaging assets

As soon as a figure for assets or capital is taken from the balance sheet for use in the development of a performance measure there is a problem. The balance sheet provides the financial picture of a company on the final day of its financial year. The income statement is a statement of the company's ability to generate revenue and profit throughout the financial year. The income statement is dynamic, covering the whole year; the balance sheet is static, showing the position only at the end of the year. The year-end balance sheet incorporates the retained profit appearing at the foot of the current year's income statement. Any finance raised during the year for investment in operating assets, even in the last few days of the year, appears in the balance sheet as a source of finance and an asset. For the purposes of rate of return ratios, there is a mismatch between the income statement and the balance sheet.

To overcome this, an average figure for assets or capital is often used in calculating rates of return. This clearly should produce a more accurate ratio, but, for most purposes, it is probably not worth the time and effort involved. Moreover, it may be difficult to get the necessary data for earlier years.

One instance where more detailed analysis is required, with perhaps an average asset or capital figure or other appropriate adjustment, is when a company has experienced major changes during the year. For example, it may have raised capital or made a major acquisition or disposal.

Rate of return on total assets

A useful ratio in analysing company profitability is the rate of return on total assets (ROTA). Total assets, as set out in the balance sheet, represent the total amount of physical and financial resources a company had available for use during the year to generate the profit shown in the income statement.

Irrespective of the way in which assets are financed (by using shareholders' funds, debt or short-term borrowing), or of how the total capital and debt is employed (in non-current assets, investments, intangibles or current assets), total assets represents the total resources available to a company to undertake its business. It is therefore appropriate to look at a company's ability to generate a profit on the basis of the total assets it has employed. Using an alternative to total assets as the denominator can make true comparisons difficult, as companies use different means of financing their business.

% return on total assets = 100 × (pre-interest and tax profit ÷ total assets)

When total assets is used, the numerator should be the pre-interest and tax profit (PITP) or earnings before interest and tax (EBIT). This is to find the true return on assets before the cost of financing through interest payments on borrowings used to finance any part of those assets is deducted. By the same logic, interest or income received from financial investments, which form a part of total assets, is included in this profit figure.

Return on total tangible assets

As intangible assets are often considered of less certain value than tangible assets, it is possible to argue that only the tangible assets employed in a company should be taken into account when measuring its rate of return. To arrive at a figure for tangible assets that can be used to determine the return on total tangible assets (ROTTA), deduct the intangibles set out in the non-current assets section of the balance sheet from total assets.

Return on (net) operating assets

To make further practical use of the segment details provided in the annual report, it is worth calculating the rate of return on operating assets (ROOA) or the return on net operating assets (RONOA). The figure for operating profit can be taken straight from the income statement or, for each business sector, from the segment notes. It represents the profit made by the company after allowing for all normal business costs and expenses but before interest and taxation.

Net operating assets

Net operating assets are the assets employed to support the running of a business, assuming that short-term creditors are used to finance short-term assets.

Some companies' balance sheets contain a separately identified figure of total assets less current liabilities (see Chapter 2). This presentation assumes that current liabilities have been used to finance current assets. The net current assets (or liabilities) when added to (subtracted from) non-current assets provide an indication of the total long-term capital and debt employed in the business. This figure can be used as the denominator for measuring the return on net operations assets.

Net operating assets = operating non-current assets + net current operating assets

Net current operating assets

In arriving at the figure for net current operating assets, cash and short-term investments within current assets are excluded as are any short-term borrowings or debt repayments appearing within current liabilities. These items are financial rather than operating assets. The intention is to show the profitability of the business excluding any financial asset or liability and allied income or expense.

Operating non-current assets

Within the non-current asset section of the balance sheet the tangible assets are shown at their carrying value – normally cost less accumulated depreciation. Intangibles and investments are separately valued and displayed. Intangible assets are included in this definition of operating non-current assets. However, because operating profit is before any interest or other non-operational items, any investments shown within the non-current asset heading should in theory be deducted. In practice, making such adjustments normally introduces as many problems as it solves. When in doubt keep the analysis simple and consistent.

NOA equals NOCE

The net operating assets (NOA) equal the net operating capital employed (NOCE) of a company.

Operating non-current assets	Equity
Inventory + receivables	Long-term borrowings and creditors
Less accounts payable	Less non-current asset investments
	$+/-$ net cash balances
Net operating assets =	**Net operating capital employed**

Breaking down RONOA

If the return on net operating assets is calculated using at least two years' figures this may be linked with the information provided on operating assets set out in the segment notes quantifying the investment in each sector and geographic area. From this analysis some indication is provided of how effective the company is in using its available operating assets in each sector. Comparison can be made with other companies and some benchmarks of performance can be developed.

The shareholders' return

So far the analysis of rates of return has concentrated on the operational side of a business in measuring the level of profit generated on the assets of a company. Shareholders are the principal stakeholders in a company; they own the company, and can be presumed to have invested their money with a view to receiving some benefits or returns. They want to profit from their investment.

Shareholders should use the profitability ratios described so far in this chapter to monitor a company's performance and to compare it with others in their portfolios or against business sector averages.

The after-tax profit should be used in developing measures of shareholders' return. After a company has covered all costs, expenses and tax, and provided for minority interests in the profit, what remains, often called profit attributable to shareholders, is available for dividends. The after-tax profit can be paid out in dividends to shareholders or retained to finance future growth and development.

It is possible to develop an after-tax rate of return on assets, which can be useful when considering the track record of one company but is of less value for comparing companies. As each company has its unique tax position – for example, one may own freehold property and another leasehold property, or they may be operating in different countries – it is difficult to draw any firm conclusions on performance in addition to those provided by the pre-tax profit ratios. But although after-tax profit may be of less interest as a basis for comparing companies' performance, it is crucial to every company's shareholders. It represents the end result of management's activities in running the company on their behalf throughout the year.

Which figure to take from the balance sheet to represent the shareholders' stake or investment in the business is more problematic. In most balance sheets the shareholders' total funds is set out as equity. Preference shares or other non-voting capital are often found within the figure for equity. Strictly, these should be removed in the calculation of shareholder returns, because it is only the ordinary shareholders, the owners of the company, that are being considered here, not other providers of long-term finance and capital.

The figure for shareholders' funds may have several different labels attached to it.

Net assets = total assets − (current liabilities + debt)
Capital employed = net assets
Equity = capital employed
Equity = capital employed = net assets

Once the shareholders' investment has been identified it is possible, using the after-tax profit, to calculate an appropriate rate of return. This rate of return may be defined as:

- return on capital (ROC)
- return on capital employed (ROCE)
- return on shareholders' funds (ROSF)
- return on equity (ROE)
- return on investment (ROI)
- return on net assets (RONA)

Earnings per share

Investors often make use of earnings per share (EPS) as a measure of the overall profitability of a company. EPS is normally to be found at the foot of the income statement (see Chapter 3). As with any pre-calculated ratio appearing in an annual report, care should be taken to discover precisely how it has been derived.

The basis of an EPS calculation is:

EPS = after-tax profit ÷ the number of shares in issue

This effectively links profit with a share. If you owned one company share, how much profit did the company earn – but not necessarily pay out – for you in the year? Inevitably problems can arise in defining what income was really available to shareholders and how to define a "share". IAS 33 (similar to FAS 128) deals with the calculation and presentation of EPS ratios. Earnings is defined as the after-tax profit (less any minority interests and preference dividends) for the year, and the number of shares as the weighted average of the number of equity shares – or common stock equivalents – in issue during the year. Where partly paid shares have been issued the equivalent number of fully paid shares is used in the EPS calculation. Where a company has treasury stock this is deducted from the denominator in the EPS calculation.

The weighted average is found by taking the number of equity shares in issue at the beginning of the year, adding this to the number at the end of the year and dividing by two. However, a more accurate timing weight may be called for. For example, a company has 1,000 ordinary shares in issue at January 1st. On June 1st it issues 250 fully paid shares. On December 31st there are 1,250 shares in issue.

$$\text{Weighted average} = 1{,}000 + (250 \times 7/12) = 1{,}146 \text{ shares}$$

The dilution factor

Two EPS figures are likely to be provided. Basic EPS is calculated as above. Diluted EPS is calculated using the same net profit but assuming all convertible securities have been converted into shares and all options and warrants have been taken up. When a loan is converted into shares there will be a saving in interest payments. Profit after tax increases, as does the number of shares used in the diluted EPS calculation. Diluted EPS will always be lower than basic EPS. The numerator and denominator for both will be shown in the notes to the financial statements.

Options and warrants

A share option gives the holder the right, but not the obligation, to acquire shares at an agreed price for a specified time period. Options may be offered to employees (see Chapter 3). If the share price rises above that of the option, it is beneficial to the employees to exercise their option (in the money). If it does not (out of the money), they have no obligation to part with any cash. IFRS 2 deals with share-based payment schemes. Sometimes a company raises finance and as an incentive it attaches a warrant to the debt to allow the future purchase of shares at an agreed price. Warrants are either detachable (they can be traded separately) or non-detachable (they cannot be traded).

A company with $500 after-tax profit has 1,000 shares in issue with a current market value of $5 each. It offers employees the option to purchase 200 shares at $4 – the exercise price. If the option is taken up, the company will receive $800. If it had sold shares on the market, it would have needed to issue only 160 shares ($800 ÷ $5). In effect it has issued 40 shares for free (the dilutive element in the EPS calculation) if the option is taken up. This is taken into account in calculating the diluted EPS.

Basic EPS	$500 ÷ 1,000	= $0.50
Diluted EPS	$500 ÷ (1,000 + 40)	= $0.48

Employee options are taken into account from the date of issue (grant date) in calculating the diluted EPS. Often these will form an important factor in arriving at the fully diluted EPS.

A put option is where the holder has the right to have the company repurchase shares at a specified price.

Comparing earnings per share

It is a mistake to assume you can compare profitability based on EPS. A difference in EPS can be brought about simply by differences in share capital structure. Two companies could have an identical after-tax profit of $100 and share capital of $1,000. But if one company had issued 25¢ shares and the other $1 shares, the earnings per share would be very different: 12.5¢ and 50¢.

A rights issue

When a bonus or rights issue is made all previous EPS figures are recalculated to allow comparison over time. A bonus issue provides shareholders with, for no payment, additional shares in proportion to their existing holding. A rights issue is an offer to existing shareholders to subscribe for additional shares. In 2008, as a result of the financial crisis, several companies made – or tried to make – rights issues to improve their debt/equity ratios. A company can communicate easily with existing shareholders and it is assumed that they will be positive towards the company and so provide a less costly means of raising additional capital.

How do shareholders know whether the offer is worthwhile? A value must be placed on the shares involved. A company with 1,000 shares in issue with a current market value of $5 offers shareholders the right to acquire one new share for every four held (250 shares) for $3.5 per share.

$$(1,000 \times \$5) + (250 \times \$3.5) = \$5,875$$
$$\$5,875 \div 1,250 = \mathbf{\$4.7}$$

The theoretical value of the rights issue shares is $4.7. With more shares in issue the price may drop, but this is potentially an attractive offer to shareholders when compared with the current share price of $5.

False conclusions

It is important to recognise that it is not possible to compare two companies' earnings per share and draw any useful conclusions.

	A	B
After-tax profit ($)	100	100
Share capital ($)	100	100
Number of shares	1,000	200
EPS	**0.10**	**0.50**

The two companies have an identical after-tax profit for the year and value of issued share capital. Company A has 1,000 shares of 10¢ each in issue and company B has 200 shares of 50¢ each in issue. It is wrong to assume by looking at the EPS that company B is more profitable or a better performer than company A. The difference in EPS may be simply because the companies have different share capital structures.

Useful conclusions

The only effective way to compare companies' earnings per share is to use the compound growth rate. Looking at the rate at which earnings have been growing over a number of years allows comparison of the ability of companies to improve their earnings.

Dividend cover

Having arrived at the after-tax profit for the year, the next step for the directors is to decide what dividend they intend to pay to their shareholders. The final dividend will not be paid until after the AGM at which the shareholders vote on the directors' proposal; it is unusual for the dividend to be rejected. Every major company should have a clear policy on dividend payments and dividend cover. This may be explained by the directors in their report.

To gain some appreciation of the safety of a company's dividend policy the dividend cover ratio can be calculated.

$$\text{Dividend cover} = \text{after-tax profit} \div \text{dividend paid}$$

A company paying a $10,000 dividend from $20,000 after-tax profit has a dividend cover of 2. It has $2 of after-tax profit available for every $1 of dividend distributed to shareholders; 50% of earnings are paid out in dividend. It can be a useful exercise to replace the figure for after-tax profit with that of the net operating cash flow – to be found in the cash flow statement – as the nominator in this ratio:

$$\text{Cash flow dividend cover} = \text{operating cash flow} \div \text{cash dividend paid}$$

The cash paid in dividends to shareholders will be found in the financing activities section of the cash flow statement. Using this ratio answers the question of how well operating cash flow covers any dividend paid. It can provide a much more acute appreciation of the safety of dividend payments to shareholders. The lower the dividend cover the more concern there is for shareholders' future income stream.

Mind the gap

If the dividend per share is deducted from the earnings per share, what remains is the per share retained earnings for the year. The cash flow statement can provide a similar measure.

$$\text{Earnings per share} - \text{dividend per share} = \text{retained earnings per share, or}$$

$$\text{Net operating cash flow per share} - \text{cash dividend per share} = \\ \text{retained cash flow per share}$$

The retained earnings per share is an important element in the assessment of the financial performance and position of a company. For any company it is to be expected that a continuing and significant source of funds is its current operations (the income and cash flow statements). A healthy and consistent level of retained earnings reinvested in the business is an indication that rather than relying on borrowed money, a company is generating the required financial resources internally.

The annual report will contain a typical five-year or ten-year history, where a company will show both the earnings and dividend per share for each year. It is worth bringing these two together to see the relationship. The gap – the difference between earnings and dividend per share – indicates how much each year the company is generating from its operations to plough back into the business for future growth. The larger this figure the better it is for the company. Net operating cash flow can also be used in the analysis. A company that is retaining little or no profit (operating cash flow) must inevitably be looking to its shareholders or outside sources of capital to finance any major investment programme or activity.

Benchmarks

It is not usual for a company to pay dividends from anything other than after-tax profit for the year, otherwise the capital maintenance requirement discussed at the beginning of this chapter would be breached. Thus a dividend cover ratio of 1:1 showing that a company is distributing all of its profit to shareholders and retaining nothing to support the future development of the business can be taken as a guide for the uppermost limit of prudent dividend policy. It would certainly be unusual, if not unacceptable, for a company consistently to operate on less than 1:1 dividend cover.

$$\text{Dividend cover} = \text{after-tax profit} \div \text{dividends}$$
$$= \text{earnings per share} \div \text{dividend per share}$$

Dividend politics

In most countries, when a company's profit declines it is expected that the dividend will be reduced; this is common-sense housekeeping. In the UK in the 1990s this rule did not appear to hold. The dividend cover for many companies declined rapidly as profits fell during the recession, but dividends were maintained.

There are at least two possible explanations for this. It could be claimed that company directors were taking a long-term view in deciding what dividend it was appropriate for their shareholders to receive, allowing for the inevitable fact of business life that as years passed there would be peaks and troughs in the actual profit generated. The possibility of short-term fluctuations in dividend cover was accepted to provide long-term regularity and security of dividend payment to shareholders. Alternatively, it could be that company directors, particularly chairmen and CEOs, were worried that if they did not deliver the level of dividend their major shareholders, the institutional investors, were relying on the share price of the company might fall, and they might be faced with personal job insecurity. Institutional shareholders rely on the dividend streams from their investments to support their own businesses.

The management of a company failing to perform with respect to dividend is likely, at least, to be open to criticism, and possibly the target for direct attention and action. Directors of family owned or controlled companies may find themselves under pressure to continue paying dividends that allow shareholders to maintain their lifestyle but may not necessarily be in the best long-term interests of the company. In the credit crisis that started in 2007, many companies reduced or ceased their dividend payments. This of course compounded the problems for the financial institutions which normally relied on the dividends as a regular and reasonably secure source of income.

The Du Pont pyramid of ratios

The use of the rate of return ratio as a measure of company profitability and performance is widespread and effective. If people had to opt for only one measure of a company's performance, most would choose the rate of return. Yet simply to take the profit for the year and express it as a percentage of the assets or capital employed in a business is a fairly blunt or broad approach to measuring profitability. A single figure from the income statement is linked to a single figure from the balance sheet. If this exercise is completed for two companies and the returns of both are similar, what conclusions can be drawn?

	A	B
Sales revenue ($)	300	100
Profit ($)	25	40
Assets ($)	125	200
Return on assets (%)	20	20

Both company A and company B have a 20% rate of return on assets.

To gain an understanding of the level of a company's profitability and how the profit is being made, there is much to recommend the use of the Du Pont approach, named after the US company credited with pioneering work in this area. Sometimes this is referred to as the construction of a pyramid of ratios, because all the ratios can be presented as a pyramid with the rate of return as the summit (see page 185).

Profit and cash flow measures in rate of return

In assessing the rate of return for a company, two separate questions are being addressed. First, the ability to make a profit from its operations; and second, the efficiency with which it is utilising its available assets and capital to produce that profit.

In all the following ratios, the net operating cash flow – from the cash flow statement – can be substituted for profit. This provides the basis for assessing the cash generating capability of a company, and makes a useful supplement to the profitability analysis.

Take the profit margin

To answer the first question, the level of profitability of a company's operations, the profit margin offers an appropriate and easily identifiable measure. If the profit margin is calculated for the two companies in the above example, for A it is 8.3% and for B it is 40%. On this basis company B is the more profitable with a profit margin almost five times greater than that of company A.

Introduce the asset or capital turn

A new measure, the asset or capital turn, must be identified to answer the second question and obtain a view of a company's efficiency in the use of its assets or capital. The only reason for a company to maintain assets is to support the conduct of its business and to assist the generation of current and future profits. The success of this intention, in accounting terms, can be measured through the level of sales revenue. The greater the level of sales revenue being generated from the use of the assets employed in the business, the greater is the level of effective utilisation of those assets.

$$\text{Asset turn} = \text{sales revenue} \div \text{assets}$$
$$\text{Capital turn} = \text{sales revenue} \div \text{capital}$$

If this ratio is calculated for the two example companies, it can be seen that they have quite different levels of ability to generate sales revenues from their assets.

A $300 ÷ £125 = 2.4
B $100 ÷ £200 = 0.5

Company A is turning over the assets employed 2.4 times each year, whereas company B manages to turn its assets over only once every two years. Company A has proved capable of generating $2.4 of sales revenue for each $1 of assets employed while company B has managed to generate only $0.50. If one company were a retailer and the other a heavy goods manufacturer, there would be little point in pursuing the comparison. However, if it is assumed that both the companies are operating in the same business sector, the conclusions of comparative performance and profitability would be justified and explanations for the differences sought through further analysis.

Bringing the two together

It is now possible to take these two companies and examine the differing means by which they have achieved an identical 20% rate of return. Company A has the lower profit margin but the higher asset turn. If the two ratios are brought together, it can be seen clearly how the rate of return is being produced.

$$\text{\% rate of return on assets} = \text{\% profit margin} \times \text{asset turn}$$

A $8.3\% \times 2.4 = 20\%$
B $40\% \times 0.5 = 20\%$

Now draw a chart

The combination of the profit margin and asset turn ratios to give the return on assets may be displayed in a chart, or pyramid of ratios. The use of the supporting ratios to those of a company's profit margin and asset turn is discussed in Chapter 7.

The presentation in Figure 6.1 of the rate of return as the combining of the two component ratios is a useful basis for the assessment and comparison of companies' performance. It is essential to calculate the overall rate of return of a company, ideally completing this for a number of years to see the trend and to allow direct comparison with other companies. It is also important to try to discover precisely how a company is achieving its level of profitability. What is the relationship between the profit margin and the asset turn? Is it consistent, and if not, why is it changing?

Return on assets

6.1

Using the ratios

The relationship between the two component ratios can be visualised as a seesaw with profit margin at one end and asset turn at the other (see Figure 6.2 on the next page). Company B in the example has a higher profit margin but a lower asset turn than company A.

Although both companies have an identical 20% rate of return, it is the result of a different balancing act between the two ratios. A company trying to improve its rate of return can do so only by adjusting either or both of the two component ratios. Can it improve the profit margin through improved cost efficiency or increased prices or a combination of the two? Is it possible to improve the ability to generate sales revenue from the same or fewer assets – for example, through lower inventory levels – or can investment be made to provide additional sales revenue at lower cost without harming the asset turn?

A company concentrating on only one of the two component ratios in an attempt to improve its rate of return is likely to run into difficulties. An example, based on a real-life situation, can illustrate the issues involved. If the average return on assets for the sector is 20% (10% profit margin and 2.0 asset turn), company X, at the bottom of the league table

The asset turn/profit margin seesaw — 6.2

for profitability for the sector, decides that performance must be improved. A small investment is made to increase capacity and, with a view to improving sales volume, the profit margin is reduced.

$	Average	Year 1	Company X 2	3	4
Sales revenue	1,000	800	825	850	850
Operating profit	100	60	52	48	44
Total assets	500	600	650	650	650
Profit margin (%)	10.0	7.5	6.3	6.6	5.2
Asset turn	2.0	1.3	1.3	1.3	1.3
ROTA (%)	20.0	10.0	8.0	7.4	6.8

Prices are cut – the easy bit – and the margin falls from 7.5% to 5.2%. One end of the seesaw has been pushed down, but what happens if the other end refuses to come up and there is not as great an increase in sales as anticipated? The result is a decline in profitability. If the asset turn remains at 1.3, with a profit margin of 5.2%, ROTA drops to under 7% in year 4. Maintaining the original 10% ROTA requires either a profit margin of 7.6% (7.6% × 1.3 = 10%), or an asset turn of 1.9 (5.2% × 1.9 = 10%).

League tables

Having calculated the profit margin, asset turn and overall rate of return for a selection of companies, a league table can be prepared. First, the companies can be ranked according to their rate of return. In most cases ROTA is as effective a measure as any for this purpose. This ranking highlights the most profitable companies within the chosen business sector.

Benchmarking

A ROTA table can help determine what should be taken as an acceptable or expected rate of return for a company operating within a particular business sector. The mid-point in the table provides an indication of the average or median rate of return for the sector. A benchmark for comparison is now available. Companies producing higher than the average rate of return can be identified, as can those that are trailing in the league. If at least three years' figures are used in the table, the trend whereby each company arrived at its current place in the ranking can be observed.

Deeper understanding

Separate tables can be prepared ranking the selected companies by profit margin and asset turn. These will help in interpreting the ROTA ranking. The two component ratios will also contribute to a deeper understanding of the way in which each company has generated its overall rate of return. Is the seesaw tipping the right way?

A food retailer can be expected to have a comparatively low profit margin but higher asset turn than most other types of retail companies. Discount retailers operate on the basis that low prices (low profit margins) result in more sales and produce a high asset turn: "pile it high and sell it cheap". In the ROTA listings the discount retailers, as is to be expected, are towards the top end of the asset turn ranking but lower down for profit margin. Similarly, a company manufacturing a simple unchanging product, for example nuts and bolts, may be able to edge its prices up in return for excellent customer service and quality, but as any other form of product differentiation is difficult it is likely to be operating on low profit margins.

A quality department store may be able to charge high prices to achieve a good profit margin, but it will also find it necessary to provide a pleasing environment for its customers (such as carpets, wide aisles and escalators) which requires capital investment and reduces the asset turn. A manufacturer of a premium product may be able to generate high profit margins but be forced to invest in expensive machinery and facilities necessary for its production.

The rate of return of a company may be viewed as resulting from its pricing policy as much as from internal efficiencies or levels of asset utilisation. Equally, it could be argued that rate of return is directly dependent on the quality of a company's financial management. If major assets are not purchased but rented, or just-in-time inventory control is introduced, the asset turn is improved. Although one factor may, at one time, be more significant than others, it is dangerous to take this in isolation as "explaining" rate of return. The two ends of the seesaw should be examined independently, but they should also be recognised as being directly and inseparably linked in the rate of return measure.

Like-for-like sales

Business sectors often use their own indices to prepare league tables, and these can be mistaken for profitability measures. The retail sector places considerable emphasis on "like-for-like" sales growth as an indicator of performance. The aim is to present a measure of year-on-year sales growth that is not distorted by sales from stores opened in the current year – these being excluded from the calculation. The assumption is that this truly indicates the underlying revenue growth, and so provides a comparative performance measure.

Immediately after the peak selling season like-for-like sales are given considerable emphasis in retail performance analysis – the higher the figure the better is the company rating. It is unwise to take too much notice of such analysis, and it is certainly a mistake to assume it has anything to do with profitability. A company selling at a loss is more likely to generate a higher like-for-like sales growth than one striving to maintain or increase profit margins.

Internally, the like-for-like sales ratio can be of great benefit to management. If calculated in a consistent manner it can indicate, period by period, how the business and its individual units are performing. However, it is unlikely that any two companies will calculate the ratio in exactly the same manner, so be careful in using it as the basis for comparison. There is no accounting standard or even firm guidance on presenting like-for-like figures. A soon as companies realise the importance analysts attach to a particular measure they do their best to deliver the right figures.

Value-added statement

Some companies provide a statement of value added in the annual report. Value added is produced by deducting from sales revenue or income all costs and expenses due to a company's suppliers of goods and services. The difference is the value the company has added to the goods and services it received.

Value added = sales revenue − purchases and services

If the annual report contains sufficient data, you can prepare a simple value-added statement, which can be used to reinforce the ratio analysis discussed earlier in this chapter. Having arrived at the total of the value added for the year, the next step is to see how this was divided up among the company's internal and external interest groups. If sales revenue is expressed as 100, representing 100 pence or cents or 100%, the proportion of revenue being allotted to each interest group can be shown.

Sales revenue		100
Suppliers	50	
Employees	20	
Interest	5	
Tax	5	
Shareholders	5	85
Retained profit		15

Presenting income and expenditure in this way is still popular with many companies as a means of explaining to their employees the quite complex financial information contained in the annual report. The value-added statement has proved to be a useful and practical means of communicating financial information to employees who find the annual report somewhat impenetrable.

A value-added statement can be displayed as a bar chart or pie chart. A pie chart can effectively represent the $1 or £1 coin and show how each unit of income or sales revenue received by the company in the year was shared out: how much went to suppliers, employees, shareholders and government, and how much was left as retained profit for reinvestment into the business at the end of the year.

Dispensing with profit

All the figures set out in the income statement can be incorporated in a value-added statement. For example, a single figure for profit for the year is sufficient in a value-added statement rather than the five or six years that appear in a typical published income statement. Companies often found that if they provided employees with the published income statement, one of the first questions that arose was which of the five or six profits shown should be used as a measure of profitability, and therefore as a basis for wage negotiations. Indeed, the word profit need not appear in a value-added statement. What is left after all interest groups have received their share of the value added (the retained profit) may simply be referred to as "amount retained for investment".

If a value-added statement is prepared for a number of companies operating in the same business sector, it may be used for comparison and the development of benchmarks.

Summary

- Profit is not the same thing as profitability.
- Profitability can only be measured using a ratio that combines profit with at least one other figure from the income statement, the balance sheet, or from somewhere else in the annual report.
- The preparation of profitability league tables comparing companies operating in the same sector makes it easy to see how companies are performing against the median benchmark.
- Never rely solely on one year's figures; three to five years' figures should be compared and an explanation sought for any big changes between one year and another.
- The most effective starting point in comparing the performance of a set of companies operating in the same business sector is to use the gross profit margin. This shows the level of a company's profitability after covering all the direct costs and expenses of running the business. For companies undertaking the same type of business, some common levels of gross profit margin are to be expected.
- Whichever profit figure is used, make sure that any "one-off" profits or losses are removed. It is a company's continuing and sustainable operating profit that should form the basis of any profitability assessment.

- Avoid using a company's own profitability indices, such as EBITDA. A company is free to be selective as to how a ratio is calculated and presented. Where a company uses non-GAAP measures this should be fully explained.
- To provide a comprehensive measure of profitability, you must determine how efficiently a company is using its assets to generate its profit. If only one measure of profitability is used, it should be that of rate of return. The rate of return on total assets (ROTA) ratio (profit before interest and tax expressed as a percentage of total assets) is the best to use. The figures needed to calculate it are easy to gather from a typical annual report. It can be used to make direct comparisons between companies as it is not subject to distortion resulting from differing forms of financial structures, the profit is before any financial charges and the denominator is not affected by the way in which the assets have been financed. The use of ROTA is particularly recommended when companies operating in different countries are being compared because it overcomes many of the problems of obtaining comparable figures.
- To understand a company better, see how it is achieving its rate of return by looking at the asset turn as well as the gross margin.
- Remember that RONA and ROTA measures are not affected by the financial structure of a company (gearing). Two companies with different capital structure can be directly compared as to their ability to generate profit from their assets.
- The segment notes in the annual report offer a valuable additional source of data to help assess a company's profit performance, as well as providing an appreciation of trends and shifts in the balance of its activities. Segment data are normally shown on an operating profit and operating asset basis. This allows the calculation of the return on operating assets for each business and geographic sector.
- Shareholders are obviously interested in the profitability of their company but can be expected to focus on the after-tax profit and the dividend they receive. A key measure for shareholders is earnings per share (EPS). This is calculated using the after-tax profit, with a few adjustments, as the numerator and the weighted average number of shares in issue as the denominator.
- Shareholders and analysts are interested in what remains after

the dividends have been paid out of the after-tax profit (the retained profit available for investment). This is an important indicator of the ability of a company to self-finance its operations. The more profit a company can reinvest in the business, after satisfying shareholder dividend requirements, the better.

■ Also of interest is the dividend cover ratio, that is, how many times the amount paid out in dividends the profit is. When the ratio is calculated for several years it gives a useful insight into a company's dividend policy and also how well a company has done in any particular year.

7 Measuring efficiency

THE EFFICIENCY OF A COMPANY can be defined as the relationship between the output of products or services and the input of resources necessary for their delivery. Quantified as a ratio of output to input, the efficiency of one company can be measured over time and compared with that of others. One of the main responsibilities of management is to make efficient use of the human, physical and financial resources available to a company. This chapter considers various means of measuring, assessing and comparing companies' efficiency of utilisation of each of these three categories of resources.

Practical control of efficiency in companies must be carried out internally. It is the focus of management accounting rather than financial accounting and external reporting. In most cases information about the internal control systems of companies is not available to outsiders.

Human resource management

The total employee cost and number of people employed for the current and previous year will normally be found in the notes in a company's annual report.

Problems of definition

It may seem unlikely that it should be difficult to define the number of employees of a company, but unfortunately it is true. In the annual report a company may define the number of employees as being any of the following:

- the average number employed during the year;
- the number employed at the end of the year;
- the total number of full-time and part-time employees;
- the number of full-time equivalent employees.

A full-time equivalent (FTE) is produced by dividing the total number of hours worked by all employees by the standard number of hours in the selected working period: a week, a month or a year. This definition is popular in the retail, hotel and catering sectors and in other organisations where large numbers of part-time workers are employed.

When a number of companies are being studied in order to assess the comparative efficiency in the use of human resources, it is important as far as possible to use a common basis for the definition of the number of employees. In most cases, the figure for employees given in the annual report will be either the average number employed during the year or the number employed at the year end. A straight comparison between two companies based on an analysis where one provides a figure for average employees during the year and the other for year-end total employees is potentially misleading. However, when comparing a number of companies, particularly if they are located in different countries, there is often no other option.

Average remuneration per employee

Most companies provide a figure for the total wages and salaries paid during the year – employee benefit expense. If total remuneration is divided by the number of employees, the result is the average remuneration per employee.

Average remuneration = total wages and salaries ÷ number of employees

Where there are significant variations in average remuneration between companies in the same sector, the first check (and this applies to all the ratios of efficiency in this section) is to see if there is a difference in the definition of the number of employees. If this is not the explanation, further investigation is required to discover the reasons for the variation. One company may be operating in a different segment of the market or be based in a higher- or lower-cost employment area than another. It is not appropriate to use this ratio as a measure of efficiency to compare companies in different countries, but it may be of use in deciding where to locate a business.

The figure given for the total employee costs can be assumed to include the remuneration of a company's directors since they are employees. Directors normally receive above-average pay, but it is unusual for this to result in the distortion of the average remuneration ratio for a major company – and you can subtract directors' remuneration as it is given separately (see page 180).

Interpreting the figures

A company seen to be offering its employees well below what appears to be the norm for the sector or the national average wage for the country in which it is based may be efficient in the control of employee cost, but whether such a policy will prove to be in the best long-term interests of all concerned is questionable. In recent years, many companies defending their executive remuneration packages have reaffirmed their belief that "if you pay peanuts you get monkeys". There is no reason to assume that this is not equally true for the shop or factory floor.

When a business sector is being investigated it may be useful to have some indication of the total numbers employed in it and the position of companies as employers. This can be achieved by preparing a table ranking the companies according to numbers of employees and calculating the total. From this the importance of an individual company as an employer within a sector, or of a sector as a source of employment within a country, can be highlighted. If employee figures for a number of years are available, then any employment trends by company or by sector can be identified.

The long-term view

Companies often choose to provide employee statistics as part of their five-year or ten-year record of financial performance. Where this information is available it can be used to study a company's record as an employer. Over a number of years a company can be expected to show some consistency in its number of employees. If a company increases the number one year and reduces it the next, it may be exhibiting weakness. Management may not be in control of the business and may be unable to plot and follow a medium-term, let alone a long-term, action plan. In a company that relies on highly skilled employees to deliver its products or services, a hire-and-fire employment policy usually has a negative impact not only on employee loyalty and productivity but also, eventually, on the company's financial performance.

Other sources of information

In addition to a company's annual report, newspapers, magazines and journals can be useful sources of information. Large changes, either up or down, in the employee numbers of a company are often the subject of informed comment. Trade journals that cater for the business sector a company is in can also be helpful.

Sales revenue per employee

Having looked at the number of employees and their average remuneration, the next step is to consider employees' contribution to the generation of sales revenue and profit. If sales revenue is divided by the number of employees, the ratio of sales revenue per employee is produced. This is a measure of the ability of a company to generate sales revenue on the basis of its employees.

$$\text{Revenue per employee} = \text{sales revenue} \div \text{number of employees}$$

This ratio should be calculated for a number of years to see the trend for a selected company. It is particularly useful when used to compare a number of companies operating in the same business sector. Companies can be ranked in order of their sales per employee, and, if the data is available for a number of years, their relative and changing positions in the league table can be assessed.

Interpreting the figures

Differences between companies in the sales per employee ratio can often be explained by differences in their focus within a sector. A discount food retailer is likely to have higher sales per employee than a department store, and the rate for a fashionable boutique may be even higher. A labour-intensive goods manufacturer will have lower sales per employee than one with a highly automated plant. A construction company that subcontracts much of its work to other companies rather than undertaking this itself will have a much higher sales per employee ratio than one that does not subcontract. When studying a business sector, it is important to look at variations among companies in the level of this and other ratios and to try to explain any trends exhibited, both for individual companies and for the sector as a whole. A company may then be seen in the context of its business sector to be setting, following or matching the general standards of performance and trends.

A company that cannot generate sales revenue per employee of at least double the average wage applying in its country of operation can be assumed to be if not already in trouble then certainly heading for it. A company only just managing to earn enough revenue to cover its wage bill and associated employment costs will not be producing exciting rates of return.

Profit per employee

Most businesses can be expected to strive to produce the highest level of revenue per employee possible, but it is profit rather than revenue that may be seen as the only true measure of efficiency. There is little point in generating revenue if this does not in turn produce profit. The ratio of profit per employee is a measure of the ability of a company to produce profit based on employees.

Profit per employee = profit ÷ number of employees

Chapter 6 discussed the importance of the selection of an appropriate profit from the income statement to produce a meaningful profit margin. The same issues are involved in the decision about which profit to use in the ratio of profit per employee. It is probably most effective to concentrate on the gross and operating profits per employee as measures of how efficiently a company is using its employees and the employees' contribution to its overall performance and success.

Interpreting the figures

As with the ratio of sales per employee, the trends for both individual companies and the business sector should be studied. Individual company performance in profit per employee can be compared with the average or standard for the sector and year-by-year movements assessed. Significant one-off shifts in this ratio should be investigated to discover if they are the result of a change in the efficiency of a company or some other action or event – such as an acquisition or disposal of a labour-intensive subsidiary. Where possible, it is most effective to concentrate on the continuing business operations of a company and to ignore any exceptional profits.

Value added per employee

Chapter 6 dealt with the use of a value-added statement to investigate a company's cost and expense structure and the way in which the corporate cake is divided among various interest groups. Value added can be defined as the difference between the revenue received by a company and the amount it paid for goods and services. It is easy to produce a figure for the value added per employee, and, as with profit per employee, the higher the ratio the better is a company's performance.

Value added per employee = value added ÷ number of employees

Employee cost per unit of revenue or unit of value added

A third measure relevant to efficiency in the utilisation of employees can be produced by dividing the total employee cost by sales revenue and presenting it as a percentage. This produces the employee cost per unit of sales revenue.

Employee cost per unit of revenue = 100 × (employee costs ÷ sales revenue)

Value added may be used in place of sales revenue to produce a ratio of employee cost per unit of value added to indicate the proportion of value added of a company being devoted to employees.

The employee cost to sales ratio shows what proportion of each unit of sales revenue generated during the year was taken up by employee remuneration and allied expenses. Broadly, the lower the ratio the better it is for the company. If less of each unit of revenue is devoted to employee remuneration, there will be more available for other purposes.

	$	$
Sales revenue	100	100
Employee cost	30	20
Employee cost per unit of revenue	**0.30**	**0.20**

Interpreting the figures

For every $1 of sales revenue generated during the year, company A puts 30¢ and company B puts 20¢ towards employee remuneration and allied expenses. If the amount set aside for employment expenses is taken as a measure of efficiency, company B appears to be performing better than company A. There may be a number of reasons for the variation between the two. Company B may employ fewer people or pay a lower rate to its employees, or it may be operating in a different segment of the market and be able to charge a higher price for its products or services.

Relating employee cost to revenue is a useful way of comparing companies operating in the same business. If the ratio is calculated for a representative number of companies, an average or median can be found for the sector against which individual companies can be measured and compared over time.

Where the ratio of employee cost to sales revenue is used for international comparison, major variations can be expected because wage levels differ and social security and other benefit charges may be included in the total employee cost. It is therefore not recommended that too much weight be placed on this ratio for comparison of companies operating in different countries.

Tangible non-current assets per employee

In many businesses the investment in tangible non-current assets provided to assist employees is an important factor in gaining an overview of the efficiency of a company's activities. If heavy engineering companies or car manufacturers are being analysed, it is useful to assess their ability to generate sales revenue and profit per employee and to maintain control over total employment costs; but measurement of investment in assets used in the production process to support employees' activities is equally important in assessing each company's efficiency in human resource management.

If the total of tangible non-current assets shown in the balance sheet is divided by the number of employees, the ratio of tangible non-current assets per employee is produced.

Tangible non-current assets per employee = tangible non-current assets ÷ number of employees

Interpreting the figures

This ratio provides a basis for comparing companies with respect to the investment they have made in assets necessary for their production activities. For example, a car manufacturer can be expected to require continued and substantial investment in robotics to maintain the quality and level of output and, perhaps, to allow a reduction in employee numbers. This will be reflected in the asset per employee ratio. A company undertaking the necessary investment can be expected to display a higher figure for the ratio than one that is not.

The use of this ratio may also be appropriate when analysing some service organisations. For example, when studying the passenger transport sector the amount of non-current assets per employee may be used to compare one company with another to assess the supporting investment in trains, planes, ships, buses or coaches. The ratio can also be employed to highlight for further investigation the variation between companies operating in the same line of business but in different countries.

Inevitably there will be problems of comparison, as some companies may own their factories and plant and machinery and others may rent or lease these assets. However, when the non-current asset per employee ratio is prepared for a number of companies operating in the same business, it provides a useful measure of the comparative levels of investment in assets used in the production process. The average or median ratio for all of the companies being studied gives a base against which to assess individual companies and, over a number of years, to observe any trends that are developing in a business sector.

Operating or net assets per employee

If a company provides detailed segmental information that includes the allocation of employees between sectors and geographic locations, the ratios described above can be adapted to provide measures for each unit. It should also be possible to calculate the operating assets or net assets per employee from the segmental information provided. If it is possible to prepare these ratios for a number of years, movements in the allocation of a company's employees between businesses and countries, as well as the supporting investment in productive assets, can be observed.

Directors' remuneration

There has been widespread criticism of what have been described as "fat cat" remuneration packages given to some directors. The annual report contains details of the remuneration or emoluments of a company's directors. The figure for directors' remuneration or emoluments can be taken to cover all of their salary, profit share, bonus payments and other benefits. Include in directors' remuneration not only bonuses for good performance but also any one-off payments for redundancy, contract severance or "golden goodbyes". Whether a board member takes the money as a result of competence or incompetence, it is an expense to the shareholders. Shareholders appear to be becoming increasingly irritated by payments made to directors that bear no relationship – except inverse – to company performance or investor returns.

The fact that the US government had to use taxpayers' money to fund the $700 billion pledged to reduce the shock created by the 2008 banking crisis revitalised calls for curbs on executive pay. Even when their companies failed, or shareholders lost their investment when they were taken over, some executives walked away with multimillion-dollar pay-offs. In the UK the collapse of Northern Rock and several other banks in 2008 required government intervention. Some £500 billion of taxpayers' money was pledged to the financial sector and public feelings concerning executive pay became evident, pushing the government towards legislation or at least much tighter oversight of executive remuneration packages.

As a contribution to showing how well directors are doing for shareholders, a performance graph – ideally for the last five years – is included in the report on directors' remuneration. This illustrates the trend in total shareholder return against a selected index – for example, the FTSE 100. Total shareholder return consists of the change in the market price of shares together with all income (dividends) which is assumed to have been reinvested in additional shares.

Plus dividends

It is important to remember that this figure does not include any dividends received by directors on shares they own in the company. To gain a fuller picture of the total income that flows to directors from the company, the number of shares they own should be multiplied by the dividend paid. This can be done quite easily, as the annual report should contain a table listing directors' names and the number of shares owned or in which they have a beneficial interest.

The cost of the board

It is worth calculating the cost of the board of directors as a whole. The total remuneration package of each director, consisting of salary and fees plus any bonuses or other benefits, should appear in the annual report. If the total of these is added to the total number of directors' shares multiplied by the dividend paid, a reasonably accurate figure of the cost of the board of directors is produced. This figure can be expressed as a percentage of sales revenue or profit, as was suggested for the total employee cost, to produce ratios that can be used to compare the practice of different companies. Where one company is seen to provide much higher directors' remuneration than similar companies, you may want to find out why this is the case.

Average director's remuneration

If the total figure for directors' remuneration shown in the accounts is divided by the number of directors, a figure for the average director's remuneration is produced. The current year's figure can be compared with that of previous years to test for consistency and trends. It can also be compared with that of similar companies.

Share options

Directors and other employees of a company are often given share options. Share option schemes are considered a standard means of motivating and rewarding a company's management. An individual is offered the right to purchase a company's shares at some time in the future at a predetermined price. For example, a director may be offered the right to purchase 1,000 shares in two years' time at $2 each. If in two years the share price reaches $4 and the director exercises the right to purchase, a "profit" of $2,000 is made (although if shares are then sold there may be a capital gains tax liability). Shareholders have a right to expect a company to inform them not only of what share option schemes are in operation but also of what options have been taken up by executives and at what prices. Where this information is available it can be incorporated in the analysis of directors' rewards suggested above (see Chapter 3).

Who controls the board?

Ultimately, shareholders – although in practice this means the institutional investors who have substantial shareholdings – can overturn the directors' remuneration policy. Indirect pressure from government, public opinion, professional bodies and stock exchanges may also influence board policy. However, there are many instances where boards have shown themselves to be thick-skinned when it comes to the remuneration of board members.

Of course, if media reports of the remuneration of a company's directors do not tie up with the information given in the annual report, further investigation is required. If the media have their facts correct, and the board is not being straight with shareholders on directors' remuneration, can you trust other information in the annual report?

Physical resource management

The decision of how to measure the efficiency of a company's use of its available physical resources – the assets employed – must be based on an understanding of the nature of its business. Different types of businesses demand different measures.

Starting point

A useful first step towards such understanding is to turn to the income statement to discover the broad cost structure of the company being analysed. The income statement provides outline details of a company's costs and expenses. The way the information is set out depends upon the nature of the business. For example, retail and manufacturing companies may set them out as follows.

Retail	Manufacturing
Cost of sales	Cost of sales
Staff costs	Distribution expenses
Occupancy costs	Administration expenses
Maintenance and renewals	Research and development

If each cost and expense heading is expressed as a percentage of sales revenue for the year and a number of years are considered or a number of companies are compared, trends and variations can quickly be highlighted for further investigation.

Sales revenue		100	
Cost of sales		<u>65</u>	
		35	% gross profit margin
Distribution	12		
Administration	8		
Research & development	1		
Other expenses	<u>4</u>	<u>25</u>	
		10	% operating profit margin

Analysing the rate of return

A single overall measure of a company's efficiency can be taken as the rate of return it produces on the assets employed. Rate of return ratios were discussed in Chapter 6. The target for almost any business is to make efficient use of assets to produce sales revenue from which profit is made. Dividing sales revenue by the assets employed in the business produces the asset turn ratio (see page 163). This ratio is for most companies an eminently suitable measure of their efficiency in managing their assets.

Asset turn = sales revenue ÷ assets

A company displaying a low asset turn when compared with similar companies may be assumed to have some unproductive assets, some overvalued assets or inadequate management skills, or a combination of the three. The asset turn ratio is simple to produce, combining sales revenue from the income statement with the denominator – total assets, net assets, capital employed or whichever one is chosen. (Chapter 6 discussed the selection of an appropriate asset or capital employed figure from the balance sheet.) If calculated for a number of years, it offers some insight into the continuing efficiency of a company. When a number of companies operating in the same business sector are being studied, this ratio is an excellent basis on which to make judgments of comparative efficiency in the use of assets to generate sales and profit.

The overall rate of return of a company is produced from the combination of profit margin and asset or capital turn. The one multiplied by the other provides the ratio.

% rate of return = % profit margin × asset or capital turn

The use of the Du Pont or pyramid approach to presenting rates of return is discussed on pages 163–6. The two main component ratios of profit margin and asset turn can be further subdivided to offer insight into the way in which the rate of return is produced and the efficiency of a company at various stages of its production activities.

This pyramid of ratios can be helpful in analysing a company and in identifying which aspects of a business most affect its overall profitability. For example, it enables you to assess the impact on the rate of return of a decline in the inventory turn.

Ideally, it is the continuing business operations of a company that should be the focus of this analysis. In practice, however, where several companies operating from various country bases are being studied it is probably easier to take the total of both continued and discontinued operations for a year-by-year comparison.

For any company, the act of adding or removing businesses from its portfolio of operations can be significant, as can when in the financial year this is done. The accounting treatment of acquisitions, in particular, can influence the profit displayed for the year. Whether a proportion of the full year's profit or the total profit of the acquired company is brought into the income statement can have a direct influence on apparent profitability.

Once the figures have been translated into a table, it is easy to see whether there is a consistent approach by which a company is, over a number of years, managing to achieve its profit margins. If similar data

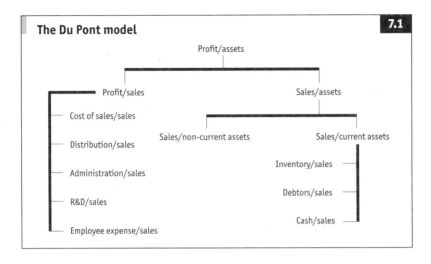

The Du Pont model 7.1

can be collected for similar companies, benchmarks can be selected for the measurement of comparative performance (see Chapter 9).

Additional measures

A company may, in its annual report, provide additional information on the company's operations and performance. Needless to say, a company that has nothing to boast about will not often provide anything beyond the minimum required.

In the case of companies that provide more information than that stipulated by legislation or accounting rules and practice, note that they may adopt any form of presentation they wish and the figures published are not necessarily subject to the normal independent check and verification by an auditor. Furthermore, the provision of additional operating details in one year's annual report does not commit a company to provide the same details in other years or, if it does, to ensure that the figures are presented on a consistent and therefore comparable basis.

Many retail companies give details of the number and size of their outlets and total sales area. These provide a basis for calculating ratios of sales and profit per square foot or square metre of selling space. For any retailer, a practical measure of its efficiency is that of its ability to generate sales and profit per unit of sales space, and operating targets are often set to try to improve both of these ratios.

Such measures are an excellent means of assessing one company's performance over a number of years and of comparing several companies. But differences between companies may be explained partly because they are in different sectors of the business. For example, a food retailer can be expected to sell more per square metre than a department store but to be operating at a lower profit margin and therefore probably a lower profit ratio.

Output or level of service ratios
Other businesses may provide statistics on their output or levels of service. A transport company may publish the number of passengers carried or the passenger miles travelled in a year. These figures can be used as the denominator in ratios to assist the study of a company's historic performance and to compare one company with another.

The cost and profit per passenger or per passenger mile can be calculated in a similar way to provide another measure of how efficiently companies deliver transport services. The staff cost of one company can be linked to the number of passengers, or ideally passenger miles, to allow comparison with previous years and with other transport companies. Transport companies in other countries may usefully be included in the analysis to produce the average amount paid by a passenger.

An electricity generating or supply company may provide details of the amount of electricity (mw) produced during the year. A motor manufacturer may disclose how many cars or tractors were produced during the year. Whenever a suitable common denominator for a business sector can be determined, this should be used as the basis for the preparation of a series of ratios to measure efficiency and performance.

Other sources of information
Additional information on a company or business sector can usefully be obtained from sources other than annual reports. Newspapers, journals, magazines and government and trade publications may offer data and information that can effectively be incorporated in performance and efficiency measures.

It is often possible to obtain national statistics relevant to a business sector – for total retail sales, total amount of electricity generated, number of cars and trucks manufactured and sold, for example. Even if the financial year end of a company does not match the calendar or fiscal year on which the statistics are based, it is still worth estimating the market share of a company to see how this has changed over the years.

Declining assets

Some indication of the age of assets employed in the business may help in the assessment of the efficiency of a company. Details may be provided in the notes accompanying the balance sheet; there should at least be a statement on when the assets were last valued. A general guide to the expected future effective working life of assets can be arrived at by dividing the balance sheet value of the tangible non-current assets by the depreciation charged for the year in the income statement. The resulting figure indicates how many years it will be before the assets are completely written off and may be taken as a measure of their estimated future useful working life.

Estimated life of assets = tangible non-current assets ÷ depreciation

If tangible assets are shown in the balance sheet at $100 and the income statement includes $10 for depreciation, this implies a ten-year useful working life for the assets. Of course, there are many factors and events that can render this ratio ineffective. A company may acquire a major asset at the end of the year and decide not to make any depreciation charge for it in the accounts. It may revalue all or part of its assets, or it may change its depreciation policy. But this quick and simple ratio provides a starting point for more detailed analysis of tangible non-current assets.

In the income statement notes a company should provide details of its depreciation policy, giving for each class of asset the rate and method of depreciation being charged. The most common depreciation methods were discussed in Chapter 2. Depreciation policy can have a significant impact on reported profit.

Asset replacement rate

The rate at which a company is replacing its assets can provide an indication of its ability to keep pace with technological change – an important factor for most companies and crucial for many. One means of determining the rate is to divide the tangible non-current assets shown in the balance sheet by the amount of capital expenditure for the year.

Asset replacement rate = gross tangible non-current assets ÷ capital expenditure

The figures for the gross, undepreciated value of tangible non-current assets and capital expenditure are given in the notes in the annual report. Alternatively, although it is not ideal, the capital expenditure figure in the cash flow statement can be used. A company with gross tangible assets of $1,000 and capital expenditure for the year of $125 can be assumed to be replacing its assets approximately every eight years. Ideally, this ratio should be calculated for a number of years so the trend and consistency can be studied, and one company can be compared with others to see whether it is above or below the average or standard levels for the business sector.

Capital expenditure turnover

The way a company's capital expenditure is maintained or moving in relation to sales revenue can be measured by dividing sales revenue by capital expenditure to produce a ratio of capital expenditure turnover.

$$\text{Capital expenditure turnover} = \text{sales revenue} \div \text{capital expenditure}$$

If the ratio is decreasing, this may indicate that a company is increasing its investment in tangible assets to support the continuing generation of sales revenue. An increasing ratio may indicate a reduction in investment owing to a lack of available funds or a lack of confidence in the business's prospects.

The asset ownership ratio

In studying the tangible assets of a company, it is worth seeing what proportion of the non-current assets is owned and what proportion is leased. Is the foundation of growth to be on owned or leased assets? What may be the implications of this policy and what is the practice of other companies in the same business sector? The notes in the accounts give details not only of the division between owned and leased assets but also of that between long and short leases and operating and finance leases. This additional information may be of use when looking at the trend exhibited by a company over a number of years as it grows and develops.

$$\text{Leasehold proportion} = 100 \times (\text{leased assets} \div \text{total tangible non-current assets})$$

Research and development

A crucial function that often acts as a direct link between a company's physical and human resources is research and development (R&D). The successful and profitable move from basic research to the development of commercially viable products and services is normally achieved through the application of the talents of highly skilled employees using sophisticated machines and instrumentation.

As described in Chapter 3, for most companies in most countries the total amount of R&D is written off in the year in which the expense is incurred; it is not usual to capitalise all or part of the R&D expense. If a company incurring an R&D expense of $100 follows the generally accepted accounting practice of writing the total amount off through the income statement, a loss may be disclosed as in company A below.

	A	B
Income statement		
R&D	100	10
(Loss) profit	(Loss)	Profit
Balance sheet		
R&D	n/a	90

The income statement is charged with the total $100 of R&D expenditure and none is capitalised into the balance sheet. If the company were allowed to spread the R&D expense over a ten-year period, arguing that this was the time period over which the benefits from the investment would be gained, the position would be that of company B. Nothing has really changed, but a loss has been turned into a profit of $10 and the balance sheet value of the company is $90 larger because a new asset of R&D has appeared reflecting the capitalisation of the balance of the expense, which will be written off over the next nine years. This might be acceptable if there was no uncertainty about the survival of the company over the nine years, but were the company to run into problems immediately after the publication of its annual report, it is debatable whether the R&D asset in the balance sheet could be sold for $90. R&D is an intangible asset and accountants generally consider that its real value is too subjective for quantification in the accounts. Referring to Chapter 2, the rule of "when in doubt write it off" applies.

A simple test of the effectiveness of a company's R&D investment is to see whether or not it produces results. There is no commercial benefit to a company in investing resources in interesting research projects if these do not result in products and services reaching the marketplace. There is equally no point in a company investing large sums in R&D when there is no call for this from its customers. For retail companies only a limited amount of R&D is worthwhile, but for their suppliers more substantial investment in this area may be essential. Sectors in which sizeable and continuing investment in R&D is crucial include pharmaceuticals, defence and information technology.

A company's annual report contains details of the amount spent on R&D and may also provide information on new products developed and launched, together with details of any breakthroughs that have taken place. All this is of at least some help in assessing the effectiveness of a company's R&D programme.

R&D to sales ratio

One way of determining the consistency of a company's policy on R&D is to divide the amount spent on it by sales revenue. The result multiplied by 100 gives the R&D to sales ratio.

$$R\&D \text{ to sales} = 100 \times (R\&D \text{ expense} \div \text{ sales revenue})$$

For most companies, a reasonably constant level of investment in R&D is to be expected. A decline in the ratio may be because R&D expenditure is constant but sales revenue is rising, but a sudden reduction in the ratio may be an indication of corporate malaise. An easy way to "improve" profit when business is tough is to cut expenditure on things like R&D. As discussed in Chapter 10, such action may bring short-term profit, but it may also damage long-term prospects.

Problems with percentages

Although this ratio removes any necessity for currency conversion where international comparisons are being made, it does not overcome the size differences of companies. If two companies invest 1% of their sales revenue in R&D, the ratio would not distinguish between them. However, if one company had sales of $10m and the other had sales of $1m, the amounts being invested in R&D by each are very different. For example, a big computer company may spend more on R&D than the total sales revenue of some of its smaller competitors.

Another problem is that many companies set their R&D budget as a regular percentage of sales revenue. This has the merit of consistency, but it may lead to difficulties. If revenue is declining, owing to a lack of competitive edge in a company's products, reducing spending on R&D in line with the set R&D to sales ratio is likely to exacerbate the decline.

Additional sources of information

Well-informed media coverage and reports from analysts who are experts in the relevant sector will help in assessing a company's R&D performance. However, a simple but effective rule for anyone thinking of investing in a company is: "If you can't see it, don't buy it." Before investing money in a company, try to get some first-hand knowledge of its products or services. Are the company's products and the range offered as good as, if not better than, those of competitors? Do the company's staff give the impression of competence and enthusiasm? If you are not impressed, why should anyone else be?

When you have invested in a company, regular physical checks on its products and services are as important as the financial analysis suggested in this book. This may seem like hard work, but it can be interesting and it is definitely a safer approach.

Financial resource management

Chapters 8 and 9 deal with many aspects of financial management efficiency, but there are some that are properly covered here.

The treasury function

The role of a company's treasury department has increased in importance in recent years, mainly as a result of the increase in international business and the complexity of cash flows. Not long ago, a finance director might have spent a few minutes now and then considering the implications of currency movements for a company. Today, every major company has full-time professional staff overseeing the management of finance and cash flows.

For a company with its head office in the UK and a subsidiary operating in the United States, a shift in the exchange rate between the pound and the dollar can have a dramatic impact on group profitability. If the subsidiary has a profit of $100 and this is "sent" to head office when the exchange rate is $1.55, £64.52 is incorporated into the group accounts. If the exchange rate was $1.65 or $1.45, the profit would become £60.60 or £68.96. Thus the equivalent of a 10% change in the apparent profits of the subsidiary can be brought about simply by fluctuations in the exchange rate. The accounting treatment of international transactions is discussed in Chapters 2 and 3. Any company should do its best to avoid undue exposure to the risks of exchange rate movements. In recent years, there have been some notable examples of companies that have lost large amounts of money because they were in effect betting on how currencies would move in relation to each other rather than hedging their risk from exchange rate fluctuations. Managing currency transactions is a core responsibility of the treasury department.

Interest cover ratio

One financial efficiency measure for a company is its ability to pay the interest on its borrowings from operating profits. When profit before interest and tax (PBIT) or earnings before interest and tax (EBIT) is divided by the amount of interest paid, the resulting interest cover ratio shows how many times a company's profit covers the interest payments it has to make.

$$\text{Interest cover} = \text{pre-interest and tax profit} \div \text{interest}$$

The higher the figure the safer is the company. A company with an interest cover ratio of 2 could suffer a 50% drop in profit and still meet its interest payments. A company with a ratio of less than 1 would have to dip into its cash reserves or sell assets or raise additional finance to meet its interest payment commitments if there was any reduction in profit.

Summary

- Efficiency is normally associated with the control of costs and expenses and with the productive use of all the available resources of a company to deliver its products or services to the marketplace at a competitive price.
- The efficiency of a business can be measured in various ways. It can be argued that the acid test of efficiency is profit. The development of a suitable set of performance measures linked to profitability is described in Chapter 6. However, a company may be highly efficient in managing its costs and expenses but face factors beyond its control that limit its ability to generate profitable revenues. There may be a recession or oversupply, or there may be a price war within the sector. In such circumstances, the lower profitability of the company may not indicate a lack of efficiency.

After you have gathered relevant data for as many years as possible, a useful first step is to reduce the income statement to a common factor basis by expressing costs and profits as a percentage of sales revenue (see Chapter 5).

	Year 1 ($)	Year 2 ($)	Year 1 (%)	Year 2 (%)
Sales revenue	7,200	8,500	100	100
Cost of sales	4,680	6,125	65	72
Gross profit	2,520	2,375	35	28

Using this approach makes it much easier to pick out changes and trends, either from year to year for one company or when comparing one company with another, particularly if they are operating in different countries. The profit margin ratio strips out problems of size and currency.

- Profit per employee is probably the best measure of the efficiency of use of the human resource element of a company.
- The rate of return ratio is the best single ratio to use as a measure of the overall efficiency of a company (see Chapter 6). An efficient company is more likely to produce a profit than an inefficient one, and is thus more likely to produce consistently higher rates of return.
- In assessing the ability of a company to make use of its available resources, the asset turn ratio is ideal. It is quick and simple to calculate. Sales revenue is taken from the income statement and a figure for assets taken from the balance sheet; one divided by the other produces the asset turn for a company. If each time a company makes a sale it takes a profit, the more sales are generated the more profit is produced. The higher the asset turn the better is the productive use being made of the assets employed in the business and the better is the eventual overall rate of return.
- Financial management can be encapsulated in the interest cover ratio. This displays the cost of a company's external borrowings as a proportion of pre-interest and tax profit for the year. The more a company finances operations from external sources on which interest is paid or the higher the interest rates being charged the lower is the ratio.

8 Working capital and liquidity

THIS CHAPTER CONCENTRATES on the ways of assessing the short-term financial position and health of a company. Although the terms solvency and liquidity are often used to refer to the same thing, each focuses on a different aspect of financial viability. Solvency (discussed in Chapter 9) is a measure of the ability of a company to meet its various financial obligations as they fall due, whether they are loan repayments or creditors' invoices. Liquidity is directly related to cash flows and the nature of a company's short-term assets; that is, whether there is an appropriate amount of cash on hand or readily available. You may have $1m invested in stocks and shares but not enough cash in your pocket to buy a bus ticket. You may be solvent but far from being liquid.

A simple check on the short-term financial viability of a company might be first to make sure a profit was made for the year, and then turn to the balance sheet to see if there was a large cash balance at the end of the year. If the company made a profit and shows positive cash balances, you might think all is surely well. Unfortunately, you might be wrong; positive cash balances at the year end, even when combined with profit, do not guarantee corporate survival in the short term, let alone the long term.

The balance sheet is a snapshot of a company's assets and liabilities at the end of the financial year. It does not claim to be representative of the position during the rest of the year. The income statement matches income and expenditure for the year. Income and therefore the profit for the year includes credit sales income and credit expenditure as well as cash transactions. A company might show a profit for the year but have numerous creditors, perhaps its major supplier of raw materials, requiring payment in cash within the next few weeks. It is also possible for a company to manipulate the year-end cash position. If towards the end of the financial year the company puts more emphasis and effort into collecting cash from customers and slows payment to creditors, this will result in an increase in cash balances.

Creditors provide finance to support a company and debtors tie up its financial resources. A company extending more credit to its customers than it, in turn, can take in credit from its suppliers may be profitable, but it is also running down its cash resources. This is called overtrading and is a common problem among small and rapidly growing companies. It is crucial for any business to maintain an adequate cash balance between credit given to customers and credit taken from suppliers.

Working capital and cash flow

The relationship between short-term assets and liabilities was discussed in Chapter 2. Current liabilities are set against current assets to highlight net current assets or net current liabilities. The net current assets figure is often referred to as the working capital of a company to emphasise the fact that it is a continually changing amount.

Current assets and liabilities change not only from day to day but also from minute to minute as a company conducts its business. Cash is used to pay the invoices of suppliers for the production of goods that are then sold, usually on credit, to customers, who in return pay cash to the company. The cash cycles around the business on a continuing basis (see Figure 8.1 on the next page). On each turn of the cycle the company makes a profit, the goods or services being sold for more than the cost of their production, resulting in more cash available to expand the business and for the purchase or production of goods for sale.

The key to a company's short-term financial viability is to be found in the study of working capital. Current assets consist of cash or near-cash items listed under four main headings: inventory (or stock), pre-payments, receivables and cash. In the standard balance sheet presentation these are set out in order of liquidity, with cash being the ultimate form of liquidity:

- Inventory: finished goods, work in progress, raw materials
- Prepayments: advance payment of expenses
- Accounts receivable (debtors): trade and other
- Cash: cash and bank balances, short-term deposits and investments

Current liabilities are the total amount of creditors due for payment within one year, indicating how much the company will have to pay in cash in the near future. Short-term borrowings also appear as part of current liabilities. Typically, five items appear in the balance sheet under this heading:

- Accounts payable (creditors): trade and other

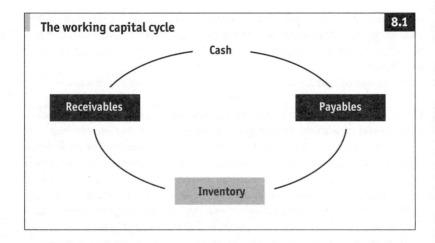

The working capital cycle 8.1

- ☑ Accruals: expenses not paid at the end of the year
- ☑ Bank loans: short-term loans and other borrowings
- ☑ Tax: amounts due for payment with the coming year
- ☑ Dividends: dividends declared but not yet paid to shareholders

Inventory

The least liquid current asset is inventory (or stock). When inventory is sold to customers, it moves up the current asset liquidity ranking to become part of debtors and lastly to become completely liquid as a part of cash and bank balances when customers pay their invoices.

For many companies the total figure for inventory in the balance sheet is further subdivided in the notes to give the amounts held as raw materials, work in progress and finished goods. For practical purposes it is safe to assume that finished goods represent a more liquid asset than work in progress, which in turn is likely to prove easier to turn quickly into cash than raw materials.

Most companies can be expected to sell their inventory and turn it into cash at least once each year. If this is not the case, there should be a good reason for the company to hold that item or amount of inventory. If inventory is not turning into cash, valuable financial resources are being tied up for no profitable return.

Receivables

After inventory, the next most liquid item appearing within current assets is receivables. These are divided into receivables where the cash is expected to be received by the company within 12 months of the balance sheet date and those where the cash is expected later. Often it is necessary to refer to the notes to discover the precise make-up of the total figure.

If a group of companies is being analysed, the amount disclosed for receivables may include amounts owed by subsidiary companies. These are also divided into the amount due within one year of the balance sheet date and the amount due later.

It is reasonable to assume that receivables due within one year are mainly trade receivables; that is, customers owing money for goods or services provided during the year and expected to pay the cash due to the company under the normal terms of trade. If customers are offered 30 days' credit, they are expected to pay cash to the company within 30 days of accepting delivery of the goods or services provided.

To give the impression of income growth, a company may pursue a creative approach to sales revenue recognition – for example, counting future income in the current income statement. That something is amiss will be indicated by the much greater growth in trade receivables than in turnover. A company may opt to push inventory out to dealers on a sale or return basis and treat this as sales revenue for the year. In effect, the company is turning inventory into receivables. The income statement will show revenue and profit increasing, but there will be a mismatch evident when the growth trends of inventory and debtors are compared.

Faced with an unacceptably large level of credit extended to customers, a company may factor or securitise trade receivables. This will result in a reduction in the level of receivables shown in the balance sheet – the true level is disguised. Always read the notes provided in the accounts for trade receivables. For a normal, healthy company, the growth in levels of turnover, inventory and trade receivables can be expected to be compatible. Any significant differences should be studied.

Receivables shown in the balance sheet may be assumed to be good debts. Customers owing the company money are expected to pay their bills when they fall due. Any known or estimated bad debts will have been written off through the income statement. Bad debts can be either deducted from sales revenue to reduce income for the year or charged as an expense in arriving at the profit for the year. Almost every type of business experiences bad debts. Customers may become bankrupt, flee the country or otherwise disappear; or there may be fraud.

Bad debts may be written off individually as they are incurred or there may be a regular percentage of sales revenue written off each year. Often a percentage charge is made, based on historic experience for the particular company and the sector in which it operates. If there is a substantial or material bad debt, the company may make reference to this in the annual report. If a major customer is declared bankrupt, this should be drawn to shareholders' attention in the annual report, even if the company hopes eventually to recoup all or most of the debt.

Prepayments and accruals

Sometimes a company will show prepayments or payments in advance as an item within current assets. Prepayments are money the company has paid in the current year for goods or services to be received in a future year. For example, a company may pay the rent on property three months in advance. For most forms of analysis, prepayments are treated as being as liquid as debtors.

Current liabilities often contain an amount for accruals. These may be considered the reverse of prepayments. Accruals are expenses relating to the current year that have yet to be settled in cash. Trade payables are the suppliers' outstanding invoices for goods and services delivered during the year. Accruals relate to other operating expenses, such as power and light, paid in arrears rather than in advance.

Cash

Cash is as liquid as it is possible to be. It consists of money in the company's hands or bank accounts. Cash is immediately available to provide funds to pay creditors or to make investments.

Why do companies need to hold cash? Cash as an asset is worthless unless it is invested in productive assets or interest-bearing accounts. Companies hold cash for the same reasons as individuals. John Maynard Keynes, a successful investment analyst as well as a notable economist, identified three reasons for keeping cash rather than investing it in other assets:

- Transaction
- Precaution
- Speculation

The transactions and the precautionary motives should, ideally, dictate the appropriate size of a company's cash and bank balances. A company with no cash cannot continue in business. It would be unable to pay suppliers or employees. Cash is essential to fulfil the everyday routine transactions of the business. A company with insufficient cash in hand has no cushion to cover unbudgeted costs. Just as individuals try to keep some cash readily available, so companies need cash at short notice for the equivalent corporate experience.

Speculation, the third reason for holding cash, is generally less relevant to companies, since directors are on the whole not encouraged to gamble with shareholders' money. For individuals, surplus cash used for investment with a view to the longer term, perhaps planning for retirement, can be said to be precautionary, whereas that used to buy lottery tickets, back horses or play poker is definitely for short-term speculation – money that may be lost but life can still continue.

One important aspect of the internal financial management of a company is to achieve the delicate balancing act of having precisely the right amount of cash available at any time. To have too much is wasteful; to have too little is dangerous.

How much money a company needs depends on what it does. A company that can confidently look forward to regular cash inflows, such as a food retailer, has less need to maintain substantial cash balances than a company with more discrete or uneven cash inflows, such as a construction company or a heavy goods manufacturer.

The only way to assess whether a particular company's cash balances are adequate is to compare them with those of previous years and those of other companies in the same kind of business. The ratios described later provide useful measures by which you can make comparisons.

In assessing a company's liquidity, it must be remembered that the timing of the balance sheet may have significant implications for the level of cash balances. A retail company producing accounts in January, following the Christmas sales period, might be expected to show little stock but a high cash balance. The company would be more liquid at the end of January than in December.

Cash and cash equivalents

Companies often invest cash which is not immediately required for running the business in short-term marketable securities or even overnight on money markets. Such investments appear as part of current assets in the balance sheet and are assumed to be readily turned into cash. For financial analysis purposes they are treated as being as liquid as cash.

Current liabilities

Many of the ratios that measure and assess a company's liquidity and solvency use the total figure for current liabilities. For most purposes this is perfectly acceptable, but it will produce somewhat cautious results.

Loans and other borrowings that fall due for repayment in the coming year are correctly shown as part of current liabilities in the balance sheet. Other short-term bank borrowing may also appear within current liabilities. Often, as with an overdraft in the UK, this is because they are repayable on demand. It may be argued that it is overcautious to include them among "creditors falling due within one year" when calculating liquidity or solvency ratios.

Intra-group trading

Intra-group trading by subsidiary companies may give rise to debtors and creditors appearing in current assets and liabilities at the year end. If a more sophisticated and refined analysis is required, these might be either netted off to produce a net debtor or creditor figure, or excluded completely. For most purposes, they may be treated in the same way as trade receivables and payables.

Measuring liquidity

Cash and receivables are defined as the liquid or quick assets of a company. A liquid asset is already cash or capable of being turned into cash within a fairly short time. To look only at the total of current assets in the balance sheet is not a sufficient guide to the liquidity of a company.

($)	A	B	C
Inventory	50	25	25
Receivables	25	50	25
Cash	25	25	50
	100	100	100
Current liabilities	80	80	80
Operating profit	40	40	20
Depreciation	10	10	5

Although the three companies in the example have identical current assets of $100, their liquidity is quite different. Company C is the most liquid. At the year end it has $50 in cash and can expect to receive $25 in the near future from customers. Although company B has the same amount of liquid assets as C ($75), it is not as liquid as it has less cash immediately available. Company A is the least liquid with 50% of current assets being held as inventory, which will probably take much longer to turn into cash than debtors.

Current ratio

A simple guide to the ability of a company to meet its short-term obligations is to link current assets and liabilities in what is commonly termed the current ratio. This appears to have been developed by bankers towards the end of the 19th century as one of their first and, as it proved, one of their last contributions to financial analysis. It links total current assets and total current liabilities.

$$\text{Current ratio} = \text{current assets} \div \text{current liabilities}$$

Current assets consist of cash balances, short-term deposits and investments, receivables, prepaid expenses and inventory. Current liabilities include payables, short-term bank borrowing and tax due within the coming year. The combination of the two in the current ratio provides a somewhat crude guide to the solvency rather than the liquidity of the company at the year end.

For the three companies in the example there would be no difference in the current ratio. As each company has $80 total current liabilities the ratio is:

$$\$100 \div \$80 = \$1.25$$

For every $1 of current liabilities, each company is maintaining at the year end $1.25 of current assets. If the company paid all its short-term creditors, it would have $0.25 left for every $1 of current asset used. As a rough guide, for most companies, to exhibit at least a 1.5:1 relationship between current assets and liabilities can be taken as an indication of the ability to meet short-term creditors without recourse to special borrowing or the sale of any assets, except those appearing as current in the balance sheet.

Liquid ratio

However, its inability to distinguish the short-term financial positions of the three companies highlights the comparative uselessness of the current ratio. A stricter approach is to exclude the year-end inventory from current assets to arrive at what are called liquid assets – those being cash or as near cash as makes no difference. This ratio is sometimes called the acid test, but it is more often termed the liquid or quick ratio.

$$\text{Liquid ratio} = \text{liquid assets} \div \text{current liabilities}$$

For the three companies the liquid ratio is as follows.

($)	A	B & C
Liquid assets	50	75
Current liabilities	80	80
Liquid ratio	**0.62**	**0.94**

The liquid ratio is easy to calculate from the balance sheet and there are two reasons to support its use. First, it is difficult to know precisely what physically is included in the figure for inventory disclosed in the balance sheet. Second, even good inventory often proves difficult to turn quickly into cash. Where inventory consists mainly of finished goods ready for sale, valued at the lower of cost or net realisable value, a company trying to turn such inventory quickly into cash would be unlikely to achieve this value; potential buyers can usually sense when a seller is desperate to sell and will hold out for the lowest possible price. Thus a prudent approach to assessing the ability of a company to meet its short-term liabilities assumes inventory will not provide a ready source of cash.

Company A is now identified as being potentially less liquid than companies B and C. There is still no revealed difference between B and

C. Both have an identical liquid ratio of 0.94:1. For most businesses, to have $0.94 readily available in cash or near cash for every $1 of current liability would be seen as very safe. Such a company could, without selling any inventory or borrowing money, immediately cover all but 6% of its short-term liabilities. A potential supplier, having first checked that the previous year's accounts disclosed a similar position, might justifiably feel confident in extending credit to such a company.

Whether the fact that company A has a liquid ratio of 0.62 would make suppliers unwilling to deal with it would depend on further knowledge and analysis. But clearly, through the use of the liquid ratio, company A is now isolated as being in a different short-term financial position from B and C.

Current liquidity ratio

Although the liquid ratio appears to be an improvement on the current ratio, it has still proved impossible to distinguish between companies B and C in the example. A further refinement is to consider current liabilities not only with current and liquid assets but also with a company's cash flow generating capability.

The simplest definition of cash flow is profit without any deduction for depreciation. Depreciation is merely a book-keeping entry and does not involve a physical movement of cash. If depreciation is added back to the trading or operating profit shown in the income statement, the resulting figure provides a rough indication of the cash flow being generated by the company during the year. On this basis, the cash flow for A and B is $50 and for C is $25.

A company wishing to pay creditors will first make use of its liquid assets. If it is assumed that inventory is not capable of being turned rapidly into cash, then, before borrowing money to pay creditors, the company will rely on cash being made available from its operations. The current liquidity ratio calculates how many days, at the normal level of cash flow generation, would be required to complete the payment of creditors.

Current liquidity ratio = 365 × (current liabilities − liquid assets) ÷ cash flow from operations

For the three companies in the example:

($)	A	B	C
Current liabilities	80	80	80
Less			
Liquid assets	<u>50</u>	<u>75</u>	<u>75</u>
	30	5	5
Divided by			
Cash flow	<u>50</u>	<u>50</u>	<u>25</u>
	0.6	0.1	0.2
x 365			
Days	**219**	**36**	**73**

If the only sources of finance other than liquid assets proved to be cash flow from operations, it would take company A 219 days, more than seven months, to complete payment of its current liabilities, whereas company B would require 36 days and company C 73 days. Assuming all three companies were operating in the same business sector, creditors assessing them would rightly feel least confident of company A.

Ratios in perspective

To explore further how the short-term financial position and viability of different companies can be analysed and compared, here is another example.

($m)	Department store group (D)	Food retailer (E)	Heavy goods manufacturer (F)	Restaurant chain (G)
Inventory	75	38	193	10
Other	30	20	80	40
Trade receivables	80	5	162	30
Cash	<u>120</u>	<u>15</u>	<u>215</u>	<u>190</u>
Current assets	305	78	650	270
Trade payables	35	76	70	75
Other creditors	<u>165</u>	<u>104</u>	<u>300</u>	<u>285</u>
Current liabilities	200	180	370	360
Operating profit	130	60	160	300
Depreciation	20	25	35	20

From this the ratios covered so far in this chapter can be calculated.

	D	E	F	G
Current ratio	1.53	0.43	1.76	0.75
Liquid ratio	1.15	0.22	1.24	0.72
Current liquidity ratio	−73	601	−163	114

Companies D, F and G show a current ratio of close to, or better than, 1:1. For every $1 of current liability at the year end they have $1, or more, available in current assets. The food retailer (E) and the restaurant chain (G) can be expected to operate with a lower current ratio than the department store group (D) or the heavy goods manufacturer (F). Their business is based on the sale of food with lower investment in inventory than for the other businesses represented in the example; nor do they normally offer long credit terms to their customers.

The differences between companies' financial positions are reinforced by the use of the liquid ratio. The manufacturer (F), with $1.24 in liquid assets for every $1 of current liability, shows the highest level of short-term solvency. As a potential creditor, possibly considering becoming a supplier, to company F, the 1.24:1 cover would provide reasonable confidence that invoices would be paid in full and on time.

However, before committing to a working relationship with F it would be necessary to compare this company with others in the same business to discover if 1.24:1 was typical. If a potential supplier to company E studied other food retailers, it would be seen that between 0.10:1 and 0.50:1 is typical. Thus on the basis of this ratio alone dealing with company E would appear reasonably safe.

As both the department store (D) and the manufacturer (F) have liquid ratios of more than 1:1, they will show a negative current liquidity ratio. They could pay all of their short-term liabilities from liquid assets and still have some left over. In practice, having seen the negative values for the liquid ratio, potential creditors would not find it worth calculating the current liquidity ratio for these companies since this would not give them a better appreciation of their likely financial exposure in dealing with the companies.

The food retailer (E) discloses the highest figure for the current liquidity ratio. If the company used all its readily available liquid assets to pay current liabilities and there were no other immediately available sources of cash, it would require a further 20 months (601 days) of operating cash flow to complete payment. Before drawing any conclusions about the acceptability of this and any other ratio, it is necessary to obtain some benchmarks for comparison. If the food retailer's 601 days is compared with the department store's –73 days, it is clear that they have different short-term financial positions, and that, although they are both retailers, they are in completely different businesses.

The food retailer can confidently expect a more consistent and regular pattern of future daily sales than the department store. Customers make purchases more regularly in food supermarkets than in department stores. A creditor to company E can be reasonably confident that the next day some $2.7m, the average daily sales figure (see page 208), will pass through the cash tills in the supermarket. The sales of the department store, although also averaging $2.7m per day, are more likely to be skewed in terms of their cash impact towards Christmas or other seasonal events.

Creditors of the food retailer need not be concerned about the 601-day current liquidity ratio. In the UK and the United States, current liquidity ratios of up to 1,200 days (four years) for food retailers are not unusual. In continental Europe, largely because of different working relationships with suppliers, ratios two or three times greater than this are to be found.

The key to interpreting this ratio, as with all others, is to obtain a sound basis for comparison. Different countries, as well as different business sectors, often have different solvency, liquidity and cash flow experiences and expectations.

Working capital to sales ratio

A useful indicator of the adequacy and consistent management of working capital is to relate it to sales revenue. For this measure, working capital, ignoring cash and investments, is defined as follows.

Working capital = inventory + trade receivables − trade payables

For the four companies in the example the figures are as follows.

($m)	Department store group (D)	Food retailer (E)	Heavy goods manufacturer (F)	Restaurant chain (G)
Inventory	75	38	193	10
Trade receivables	80	5	162	30
Trade payables	35	76	70	75
Working capital	120	−33	285	−35
Sales revenue	1,000	1,000	1,000	1,000
Working capital to sales revenue (%)	**12.0**	**−3.3**	**28.5**	**−3.5**

A negative figure for working capital denotes the fact that the company had, at the year end, more trade payables than inventory and trade receivables. This is acceptable, providing creditors have confidence in the continuing ability of a company to pay its bills when they fall due. Normally, such confidence is directly linked to the company's business sector and its proven record of cash flow generation. What is acceptable for the food retailer and the restaurant chain is not acceptable for the heavy goods manufacturer, because its cash inflow over the next few days is much less certain.

As a general rule, the lower the percentage disclosed for this ratio the better it is for the business. If the department store group were to increase turnover by $1m, this ratio suggests that an additional $120,000 of working capital would be required. For the heavy goods manufacturer, an additional $285,000 would be required to support the same $1m sales increase. However, for the food retailer and restaurant chain, for which the ratio is negative, an increase in sales revenue would appear to lead to a decrease in their working capital. This might well be the case for a company experiencing steady growth and maintaining creditors' confidence.

Receivables to payables ratio

More detailed analysis can be completed using specific ratios focusing on particular aspects of the working capital management and structure of companies. For example, the relationship between credit given to customers and credit taken from suppliers can be assessed and compared by linking trade debtors and creditors.

Trade receivables ÷ trade payables

For the four companies in the example the figures are as follows.

	D	E	F	G
Receivables ÷ payables	2.3	0.1	2.3	0.4

This ratio shows that for every 100 units of credit taken from suppliers, company D, the department store, and company F, the heavy goods manufacturer, were extending 230 units of credit to their customers. Company G, the restaurant chain, gives only 40 units of credit to its customers for every 100 units of credit it receives from suppliers. Further evidence of the aggressive use of suppliers' finance by company E, the food retailer, is provided as this ratio shows that for every 100 units of supplier credit the company extends only 10 units to its customers.

In normal circumstances, this ratio should remain reasonably constant from year to year. Large and erratic shifts either way may signal a change in credit policy or business conditions.

Average daily sales and costs

Another useful indicator of a company's short-term cash flows and financial position is its average daily sales (ADS) and average daily costs (ADC). You can divide the total sales and cost of sales by 240 to more closely represent the number of working days in the year, but, given the broad nature of the analysis, it is as effective to use 365 days as the denominator.

The cost of sales is found in the income statement in most annual reports. The figure normally includes purchases but not always staff wages and associated expenses. If there is difficulty in obtaining a truly comparable cost of sales figure for all the companies being analysed, then, by deducting the operating or trading profit from sales revenue, you will get an approximation of cost of sales.

($m)	D	E	F	G
Turnover	1,000	1,000	1,000	1,000
Average daily sales	2.74	2.74	2.74	2.74
Cost of sales	650	920	840	620
Average daily cost	1.78	2.52	2.30	1.70

Although comparing the ADS and ADC gives a broad idea of how much more a company receives than it spends each day, the reality is that companies whose trade is seasonal will spend much more than an average amount to build up stock before their peak periods for sales. They will also receive more than average from sales during peak periods.

The cash cycle

When combined with other information from the balance sheet, ADS and ADC can help you understand the way in which the cash is flowing around the business in the cash cycle or working capital cycle ratio.

Inventory

To discover how long a company's cash is tied up in inventory, the balance sheet figure for inventory is divided by ADC to give the number of days that inventory appears to be held on average by the company. The ADC figure is used because inventory is valued at the lower of cost or net realisable value so there is no profit element involved. To use ADS would result in the number of days being understated.

($m)	D	E	F	G
Inventory	75	38	193	10
ADC	1.78	2.52	2.30	1.70
Days' inventory	**42**	**15**	**84**	**6**

The longer inventory is held, the longer financial resources are tied up in a non-profit-generating item; the lower the number of days' inventory shown, the faster is the turnover of the inventory. Each time inventory is turned the company makes a profit and generates cash.

In the example, the companies hold, on average, 37 days of inventory. As you would expect, the heavy goods manufacturer (F) has the highest level and the restaurant chain (G), with fresh food, the lowest. The crucial factor is how these levels compare with those of other similar businesses.

An alternative way of looking at the efficiency of inventory levels is to calculate the inventory turnover for the year; this can be done by dividing the annual cost of sales by year-end inventory. The higher the resulting figure the more effective is a company's management of inventory. However, a company with a high inventory turnover may be maintaining inventory levels too low to meet demand satisfactorily, with the result that customers go elsewhere.

($m)	D	E	F	G
Cost of sales	650	920	840	620
Inventory	75	38	193	10
Inventory turnover	**9**	**24**	**4**	**62**

These figures provide an alternative view of how effectively companies are managing inventory.

Trade receivables

To discover the level of credit being offered to customers (trade receivables), average daily sales (ADS) is used as the denominator. The figure for trade receivables is usually found in the notes to the accounts and not on the face of the balance sheet.

($m)	D	E	F	G
Trade receivables	80	5	162	30
Average daily sales	*2.74*	*2.74*	*2.74*	*2.74*
Days' receivables	**29**	**2**	**59**	**11**

In the example, the average figure for what is sometimes called the credit period is 25 days. In effect, the companies are lending customers money for that period until cash is received, and they must provide the necessary finance to support this.

In the case of the department store group (company D), it can be assumed that cash is used to purchase inventory, which is displayed for 42 days before it is bought by a customer, who does not actually pay for it for another 29 days. The time from taking the cash out of the bank to receiving it back, plus a profit margin, is 71 days. The faster the cycle, the better it is for the company.

For example, if the ADC for the department store is $1.8m and it proved possible to reduce the level of inventory by one day, the cash cycle would speed up, the profit margin would be achieved one day earlier and more profit would be made in the year. Also the assets employed in the business would decrease by $1.8m, being one day's less inventory. If the time taken to collect cash from its customers could be reduced by one day, there would be a reduction of assets employed in the business of $2.7m and a corresponding increase in rate of return.

Cutting inventory or receivable levels reduces the assets employed in the business and increases profit, thus raising the return on total assets (see page 153). There is a direct link between the efficient management of cash flows and the overall profitability of a business.

Trade payables

Trade creditors represent the amount of money the company owes its suppliers for goods and services delivered during the year. These are normally found, as are trade receivables, not on the face of the balance sheet but in the notes to the accounts. As trade payables are shown at cost in the balance sheet, they are divided by average daily cost (ADC).

($m)	D	E	F	G
Trade payables	35	76	70	75
Average daily cost	*1.78*	*2.52*	*2.30*	*1.70*
Days' credit taken	**20**	**30**	**30**	**44**

In the example, the average length of credit the companies are taking from their suppliers (the reverse of credit given to customers) is 31 days.

Calculating the cycle

Cash flows out of the bank into inventory, from inventory into customers' hands then back into the bank. The suppliers of the inventory are paid cash and the cash cycle is complete. The three ratios can now be combined to give the cash cycle or working capital cycle.

Cash cycle = days' inventory − days' trade payables + days' trade receivables

	D	E	F	G
Days' inventory	42	15	84	6
Less				
Days' credit taken	20	30	30	44
	22	−15	54	−38
Plus				
Days' credit given	29	2	59	11
Days' cash cycle	**51**	**−13**	**113**	**−27**

The average cash cycle is 31 days. The two extremes are the heavy goods manufacturer (F) with a cash cycle of 113 days and the restaurant

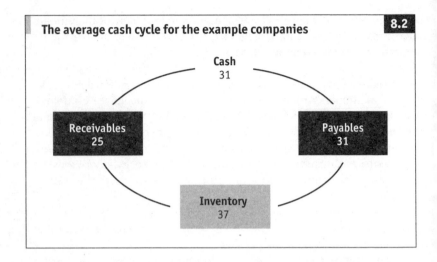

The average cash cycle for the example companies 8.2

Cash
31

Receivables
25

Payables
31

Inventory
37

chain (G) with –27 days. It is possible now to return to the simple representation of the cash flow cycle shown earlier in this chapter and apply the average figures produced from the analysis (see Figure 8.2).

The average cash cycle experienced by the companies was for cash to be tied up in inventory for 37 days; after goods had been sold to customers it took a further 25 days for the cash to be received. The average company therefore required 62 days' finance to cover inventory holding and credit extended to customers. As the average company took 31 days' credit from its suppliers, it had to finance only 31 days of the cash cycle itself. Suppliers provided 31 out of the required 62 days' finance for the average company's investment in working capital.

The cash cycle can provide an indication of the short-term financial implications of sales growth. If the average cash cycle of 31 days is used this suggests that for every $100 of sales $8.5 working capital is required.

$$31 \div 365 \times 100 = 8.5$$

If it was planned to increase sales by $1m, some $85,000 additional working capital must be found to support the growth.

Using creditors for finance
The use of creditors to finance this operating cycle is normal. The degree to which short-term creditors' money is used depends partly on what is normal or acceptable within a business sector, and so acceptable to

suppliers, and partly on the financial management policy of the individual company. In retail companies, particularly food retailers, it is not uncommon for trade creditors to be used to finance the business to the extent that a negative number of days is disclosed for the cash cycle.

A negative figure for the cash cycle indicates an aggressive and positive use of suppliers' money to finance the operations of the company. A cash cycle of -10 days could be interpreted as the company taking cash out of the bank, holding it for 10 days as inventory and selling it to customers who pay within 1 day: a total of 11 days. Then the company retains the cash, including the profit margin, in the business, or invests it for interest, for a further 10 days before paying suppliers the money owed.

However, most businesses do not have negative cash cycles. Food processing companies supplying retailers, for example, can be expected to have comparably high cash cycles.

Manufacturers can be expected to hold much more inventory than retailers. In the case of company F, there is some 84 days' inventory including raw materials, work in progress and finished goods. Manufacturers are not cash businesses like many retailers, and they are unable to collect cash from their customers as quickly. Company F, on average, is offering customers 59 days' credit, twice as long as the department store group (D). This fact is supported by the average days' credit being taken by the retailers. The credit taken by the retailer is often the credit given by the manufacturer. Lastly, manufacturers are unlikely to be able to take much more credit from their suppliers than can retailers. The heavy goods manufacturer (F) takes some 30 days' credit from its suppliers, as does the food retailer (E).

The heavy goods manufacturer therefore experiences a cash cycle of 113 days, representing the finance the company must provide for working capital. Different types of businesses produce different standards of ratios.

It could be argued that the cash cycle should be produced by taking the average of opening and closing inventory, receivables and payables. This is found by adding the current and previous year's figure for each item and dividing the result by two. Given the broad nature of the analysis being undertaken, it is probably just as effective to use the year-end figures set out in the most recent balance sheet.

Assessing the cash position

Current assets include the year-end cash balances of the company. At the same time, current liabilities may show some short-term bank borrowing. It may seem odd that a company can have positive cash balances on one side of the balance sheet and short-term bank borrowing on the other. Such a situation is quite normal, particularly when dealing with a group of companies. If subsidiary companies are, while under the control of the holding company, operating independent bank accounts, one may have a short-term bank loan and another may have positive cash balances. In the assessment of liquidity, short-term bank borrowing should be set against positive cash balances to provide a net cash figure.

It is not normally possible to gain detailed information concerning a company's banking arrangements from the annual report. Moreover, the level of short-term borrowing shown at the year end as part of current liabilities may not be representative of the rest of the year.

What constitutes a good cash position?

Too little cash might indicate potential problems in paying short-term creditors. Too much cash, as an idle resource, may indicate poor financial management. Cash itself is no use unless it is being used to generate additional income for the company. Cash balances may produce interest when deposited in a bank, but a company should be able to generate more net income by investing the money in its own business.

Too much cash may make a company an attractive proposition to a predator. A company that is profitable and well regarded in the marketplace, with an appropriately high share price, may not have substantial cash balances. All available cash may be reinvested in the business to generate more profit. Such a company may regard a less profitable but cash-rich company as an attractive target for acquisition.

Various ratios can be used to gain some indication of the adequacy of a company's cash position. It is useful to have some idea of what proportion of current assets are being held in the form of cash and short-term investments. Short-term investments may be treated as the equivalent of cash.

For the example companies, the percentage of cash to total current assets is as follows.

	D	E	F	G
Current assets ($m)	305	78	650	270
Cash ($m)	120	15	215	190
Cash holding (%)	**39**	**19**	**33**	**70**

The more liquid a company is, the higher is the proportion of current assets in cash or near-cash items. The restaurant chain (G) held almost twice as much cash, represented as a proportion of current assets, at the year end as the department store group (D). The heavy goods manufacturer (F) and food retailer (E) maintained lower levels of liquidity.

It might also be of interest to see what proportion of a company's total assets is held in liquid form either as cash or as short-term investments.

	D	E	F	G
Cash ($m)	120	15	215	190
Total assets ($m)	850	600	980	1,130
Cash holding (%)	**14**	**2**	**22**	**17**

Under this measure, there is little difference to be observed between D, F and G. For every $1 of total assets, company F had more than 22¢ retained in very liquid assets. Company E is the least liquid, holding just over 2% of total assets as cash or short-term investments.

The speed with which cash circulates within a company can be assessed by linking sales revenue for the year with year-end, or average, cash balances.

	D	E	F	G
Sales revenue ($m)	1,000	1,000	1,000	1,000
Cash balance ($m)	120	15	215	190
Cash turn	**8.3**	**66.7**	**4.6**	**5.3**

The higher the figure for cash turn the faster the cash circulation and the better it is for the company; each time it completes the circuit the company's profit margin is added. Once again, different levels of cash turn are expected and acceptable for different types of business. The food retailer has the most rapid cash turnover (66.7 times in the year) and the heavy goods manufacturer the slowest (4.6 times).

Defensive interval

Another useful measure of the adequacy of liquid resources is the defensive interval. If an extreme position is taken and it is assumed that a company, for whatever reason, ceases to have any cash inflows or sources of credit, its survival would be limited to the length of time that existing cash balances and short-term investments could support operations before the company was forced to rely on another source of finance to meet its obligations. This ratio, the defensive interval, is calculated by dividing cash and investments by ADC.

Cash and cash equivalents ÷ average daily cost

The more liquid a company the longer is the defensive interval.

	D	E	F	G
Cash ($m)	120	15	215	190
Average daily cost ($m)	1.8	2.5	2.3	1.7
Defensive interval	67	6	93	112

The previous ratios showed the restaurant group (G) to be the most liquid company, so it should come first when the defensive period is calculated. If all other sources of finance were closed to company G, it would theoretically be able to maintain its basic operations for almost four months (112 days) before running out of liquid resources. The food retailer (E) would, on the basis of a similar calculation, have cash flow problems within one week.

Another way of calculating the defensive interval is to use the average daily operating cash outflow of a company. If operating profit is deducted from sales revenue and depreciation is added back, a rough indication of total operating cash outflows is produced. Alternatively, the cash flow statement can be checked to see if it provides details of cash payments to suppliers and employees' remuneration.

Lastly, when assessing liquidity, the figure for cash shown in a company's balance sheet will truly reflect the cash in hand or in the bank at the end of the year. It does not necessarily provide information on what currencies are involved or where the cash is actually held.

Profit and cash flow

There need be no short-term relationship between the profit a company displays in the income statement and the amount of cash it has available at the year end. There are a number of reasons for this. For example, a charge is made each year in the income statement for depreciation that does not affect cash balances. Differences between changes in cash position and reported earnings normally result from the following:

- Operating activities. There may be timing differences between the impact of cash flowing in or out of the business and that of transactions appearing in the income statement. Non-cash expenses such as depreciation are recognised in the income statement.
- Investing activities. Capital investment – purchasing fixed assets – or corporate acquisition or disinvestments may be contained within the balance sheet but not the income statement.
- Financing activities. Raising capital or repaying loans will change the cash position but not the profit in the income statement.

The working capital cycle discussed earlier can be disrupted if it is necessary for a company to use financial resources outside the current asset and current liabilities area. When a company makes capital investments, or pays dividends to shareholders, interest on borrowings or tax, the amount of cash within the working capital area is reduced.

Cash flow measures

Cash flows are difficult to manipulate and so the cash flow statement offers a valuable source of information about the financial management of a company (see Chapter 3). It can be helpful to express the figures in the cash flow statement in percentage terms, especially when comparing several years or several companies. It also helps to highlight trends (see Chapter 5).

Chapter 6 discussed how substituting operating cash flow for profit in some of the ratios of profitability and rates of return can assist the appreciation of a company's performance.

($m)	D	E	F	G
Sales revenue	1,000	1,000	1,000	1,000
Operating cash flow	150	85	195	320
Total assets	850	600	980	1,130
Cash flow margin (%)	15.0	8.5	19.5	32.0
Cash flow rate of return (%)	17.6	14.2	19.9	28.3

For any company, the main source of cash is its normal business activity. The way in which a company finances its operations depends partly on the type of business and partly on its stage of growth and maturity. The restaurant chain (G) has the highest cash flow margin (32%) and cash flow rate of return (28.3%). A high level of internally generated cash is to be expected of a mature and successful company, whereas a younger and rapidly growing company is likely to have a different balance between sources of cash inflow.

The cash flow margin and cash flow rate of return on assets (CFROA) provide a useful supplement to the cash flow statement in showing the ability of a company to generate cash flow from operations. They also offer an insight into how successful a company is in converting sales revenue into cash. For every $1 of sales revenue company D produces 15¢ of cash flow and G produces 32¢. The higher this ratio the better it is for a company.

A further area for exploration within the cash flow statement is to assess what a company is doing with its available cash. Is the cash being used to pay tax and dividends or for reinvestment in the business in non-current assets? A comparison with previous years' figures will reveal whether the company has a consistent policy on the level of investment (see Chapter 11).

The cash flow statement can also be used to spot signs of potential problems. Companies suffering from growth pangs or overtrading can be expected to show an increase in the level of receivables linked to sales revenue as more customers are offered extended credit terms. At the same time, credit taken from suppliers increases to an even greater extent as the company finds it difficult to make the necessary payments on time. During this process cash balances and short-term investments decline rapidly as cash is used up. Any major changes observed in the levels of inventory, debtors, creditors and liquid balances shown in the cash flow statement may reflect either the careful management of working capital or a lack of control by the company.

Lastly, the cash flow statement can be used to help decide whether the costs of capital and borrowings are consistent and of an appropriate level. Each year the proportion of cash flow being used to pay dividends to shareholders and interest on borrowings should be checked.

Summary

- Reading the annual report and discovering that a company made a profit for the year and has several million in cash in the bank at the year end is not sufficient evidence that the company is safe.
- The balance sheet and cash flow statement offer the key to understanding the short-term financial position of a company. The year-end short-term assets and liabilities are set out in the balance sheet; details of the major sources of cash inflow and the uses made of these during the year are to be found in the cash flow statement. This statement also shows, normally as its starting point, the amount of cash generated from the company's operations during the year through the income statement.
- The liquid ratio (quick ratio) is the simplest and probably most effective measure of a company's short-term financial position. It is assumed that inventory will not prove an immediate source of cash so it is ignored. It is easy to calculate this ratio for the current and previous year directly from the balance sheet. The result gives a simple indication of the liquidity of a company and to what extent this is consistent between the two years. The higher the ratio the greater confidence you can have in the short-term survival of the company. A 1:1 ratio indicates that for every $1 of its short-term creditors and borrowings the company is maintaining $1 in cash or assets that can realistically be turned into cash in the near future.
- As with all ratios, before interpreting the figures, it is essential to compare the subject company with others either in the same industry sector or of similar size or business mix. A low liquid ratio may be perfectly acceptable for a food retailer but not for a construction firm.
- The liquid ratio is no guide to the profitability or cash flow generation of the company. A profitable company with a healthy cash flow is less likely to suffer short-term financial problems than one with a less positive performance. Yet both companies

might have an identical liquid ratio. The current liquidity ratio provides a useful means of combining a company's liquidity with its cash flow generating capability. The lower the number of days in the current liquidity ratio the safer the company is likely to be from short-term liquidity and solvency problems. As a rough rule for most businesses, warning bells should sound if the ratio is seen to be moving to over 1,500 days (four years).

◪ The liquid and current liquidity ratios provide a fairly straightforward indication of the short-term position of a company. But to gain real insight into a company's liquidity and financial management the cash flow statement should be carefully studied for at least the two years provided in the latest annual report. If the cash inflow from operations (profit plus depreciation) is not consistently the major source of funds for the company, try to find out why and then decide whether it is reasonable to assume that this state of affairs can continue.

◪ The cash cycle helps you see how a company is managing cash flows through investment in inventory, credit provided to customers and credit taken from suppliers. The faster the cash circulates through the business the lower is the amount of the capital tied up in operating assets and, as every time the cash completes the circuit a profit is taken, the higher is the rate of return achieved.

9 Capital and valuation

ANOTHER IMPORTANT ASPECT in the overall assessment of a company's financial position is its capital structure and the way this is viewed by providers of finance. This chapter analyses sources of finance and the performance measures applied by investors.

A useful first step in the analysis of a company's financial position is to use the balance sheet as a basis for seeing how the company is financed: the proportions of the total capital employed provided by shareholders and other sources of finance.

Equity and debt

A balance sheet has three broad classifications of liabilities: equity (shareholders' funds), non-current liabilities (long-term creditors) and current liabilities (short-term creditors). These reflect the three potential sources of finance open to any company. Finance can be raised from shareholders, through long-term or short-term borrowing, or through the management of working capital. The raising of any form of finance – debt or equity – is completed by means of a "financial instrument".

The shareholders' contribution to the finances of a company may be given a variety of names:

- equity
- net worth
- net assets
- capital and reserves
- shareholders' (stockholders') funds

Equity is the term most commonly used to identify the ordinary shareholders' investment in a company. The balance sheet figures for equity may include preference shares or other non-voting shares a company has in issue, but such shares should not be included in the definition of equity. Equity represents the "residual interest in the assets of an entity that remains after deducting its liabilities".

Any finance other than equity is referred to as debt, which can be divided into long-term and short-term borrowings and creditors. Borrowings with a life of less than one year appear within current liabilities and are short-term. Long-term borrowings appear as part of non-current liabilities. A note will detail their date of repayment and interest rate.

Equity shares provide a company with long-term finance. They are not normally redeemables and have no guarantee of income, through the payment of dividends, attached to them. Debt is normally borrowed for a fixed term with a fixed rate of interest. With debt, interest charges have to be paid and at some time the money borrowed will have to be repaid. With equity there is no expectation of capital repayment and any dividend paid is under the control of the company. The relationship between debt and equity is crucial to an appreciation of the financial structure of a company and its viability.

Gearing or leverage

Raising finance from external sources increases risk because, in the case of loans, there is a cost (interest) and an obligation to repay the loan. If it is a convertible loan, it can result in a reduced degree of control that existing shareholders have over the company when new shares are issued.

The relationship between debt and equity is referred to as gearing or leverage. Management should make sure that the balance between debt and equity finance is appropriate for the business being conducted. Too much debt and a company is said to be highly geared; a low-geared company is financed mainly by its shareholders. The higher the level of debt in relation to equity the greater is the potential risk to shareholders of not receiving a dividend or getting back the capital they have invested. Interest on debt must be paid before any dividends, and all borrowings must be repaid before anything becomes available for shareholders.

Debt/equity ratio

The relationship between internal (equity) and external (debt) sources of finance can be expressed as a percentage or a ratio: the debt to equity ratio.

($)	A	B	C
Equity	250	500	1,000
Non-current liabilities	500	500	500
Current liabilities	250	250	250
Interest charge	50	50	50

Debt/equity ratio = (non-current liabilities + current liabilities) ÷ equity

For the three companies the debt/equity ratios are:

	A	B	C
%	300	150	75
times	3	1.5	0.75

The debt/equity ratio is the most commonly used measure of the relationship between internal and external finance. Company A with equity of $250 and debt of $750 has a debt/equity ratio of 3 or 300%. This can be interpreted as indicating that for every $1 of shareholder investment in the company, outside borrowings and creditors provide $3. Company C has only $0.75 of debt for every $1 of equity. Thus company A is the most highly geared company.

An alternative approach is to take the long-term borrowings – to be found in non-current liabilities – as the numerator and add it to the equity as the denominator to provide a long-term debt ratio.

Long-term debt ratio = long-term borrowings ÷ (long-term borrowings + equity)

	A	B	C
%	66.7	50.0	33.3

Defining debt and equity

There is no standard definition of gearing, and there are often considerable practical difficulties in making the distinction between equity and debt. Although a debenture or bank loan is clearly part of debt, how do you classify a convertible loan, which carries a fixed rate of interest and is capable of being repaid on an agreed future date or of being converted into equity shares?

Using the balance sheet and its notes it is possible to identify all long- and short-term borrowings of a company. What remains are other non-current liabilities – including taxation and provisions – and other current liabilities – including trade payables, taxes payable and provisions. You may use these refined figures of debt and equity in any analysis. A sound rule in financial analysis is to be conservative; when in doubt treat an item as debt.

The time for which debt is scheduled for repayment is an important factor influencing the interpretation of any gearing ratio. Any borrowings not scheduled for repayment within one year are included in debt. A company not required to repay loans for five years may be viewed differently from one where repayment will take place in two years. The gearing ratios of the two companies may be identical, but the underlying implications are different. The notes accompanying the financial statements will provide details of debt repayment terms and their interest rates.

Off-balance-sheet items

When a company raises finance or acquires assets and there is no identifiable change in the balance sheet, it is referred to as an off-balance-sheet transaction. There is nothing new in off-balance-sheet items: just because a transaction is not reflected in the balance sheet does not make it automatically suspect. Off-balance-sheet items caused considerable concern in the 1990s. A whole range were offered by financial experts to assist companies reduce disclosure of costs and the risks of finance. They followed precisely the requirements of GAAP and accounting standards but failed to show the real picture.

Joint ventures provided a good example of the potential for off-balance-sheet financing. Two companies (X and Y) set up a joint venture, and each invests $100 in the new company (Z) for 50% of the equity. They jointly act as guarantors for a bank loan of $1,000 to set Z up in business. The balance sheets of X and Y show only the $100 investment in the joint venture. The liability for the loan of $1,000 does not appear; it is an off-balance-sheet item. The figure of $100 will increase under the equity method of valuation as X and Y make more investment in Z or the joint venture begins to make a profit. Each company takes 50% of Z into its balance sheet.

The greater the assets and the lower the liabilities in a company's balance sheet, the happier everyone is. A bank lending money to a company will want to minimise the risks involved; it may stipulate a maximum level of debt-to-equity (gearing) for the company. If the company exceeds this level, the bank can require the loan to be repaid immediately. Similarly, analysts, as a simple measure of credit-worthiness, may set "safe" levels of gearing that the company should not exceed. In such cases there is pressure on management to minimise liabilities appearing on the face of the balance sheet. For companies X and Y, in effect their level of debt has increased by $500, but there is no evidence of this in their balance sheet gearing ratios.

Accounting standards have significantly limited the scope for off-balance-sheet manipulation. Legislation has also played a part. The United States has the Sarbanes-Oxley Act, and from 2008 UK companies were required to disclose the potential impact of off-balance-sheet items (Companies Act 2006). Where such items are found to exist they should be included in the definition of a company's debt for the purpose of analysis.

Debt ratio

A simple measure of a company's gearing is provided by the debt ratio.

$$\text{Debt ratio} = \text{total debt} \div \text{total assets}$$

	A	B	C
%	75	60	43
times	0.75	0.60	0.43

The debt ratio can be calculated either directly from the balance sheet or from a common size statement. The higher the ratio the higher is the gearing. A ratio of 50%, commonly viewed as the limit for accepting without question a company's level of gearing, indicates that for every $1 of assets 50¢ has been financed by long-term and short-term debt. Using this guideline, company A is highly geared with 75% of total assets financed by debt, whereas company C is low geared at 43%.

Interest cover ratio

Interest paid on debt is charged as an expense before arriving at the profit for the year attributable to shareholders. An increase in external borrowings brings higher gearing and a greater interest charge in the income statement. Once a loan is taken, the interest payments must be made in cash and the capital sum repaid on the agreed date. A company not generating enough profit to cover interest payments or having insufficient cash available to repay the loan faces serious difficulty.

An effective ratio for combining profitability with the impact of gearing is interest cover. This measures the ability of a company to generate sufficient profits to allow all interest on borrowings to be paid. It is calculated by dividing the profit before interest and tax (PBIT) by the interest charge for the year. The figure for PBIT should exclude any exceptional or extraordinary items, and so represent the profit being generated from regular trading operations.

Interest cover = profit before interest and tax ÷ interest paid

The figure for interest used in the ratio should be that due for payment during the financial year, and care should be taken to add back to the figure appearing in the income statement any interest that has been capitalised or interest received that has been deducted. This information will be found in the notes accompanying the income statement or the cash flow statement.

	A	B	C
Profit before interest and tax ($)	200	100	400
Interest ($)	50	50	50
Interest cover	**4**	**2**	**8**

The higher the interest cover the lower is the risk that there will be insufficient profit available for payment of dividends to shareholders. Company C has the highest interest cover; profit could decline by eight times before it would be unable to cover the interest due on borrowings. The comparatively high interest cover of C is partly because of its profitability and partly its gearing: C has the lowest gearing.

Interest cover can be used to assess the impact of changes in profitability on the risk of shareholders not receiving a dividend. For B a 50% decline in profit would result in there being nothing available for the payment of dividends; every $1 of PBIT is required to pay interest. In the same circumstances and ignoring tax, B would have $25 and C would have $150 available for the payment of dividends.

($)	A	B	C
Profit before interest and tax	100	50	200
Interest	50	50	50
Profit before tax	50	0	150

Attractions of high gearing

Simple arithmetic supports a decision by a company to take advantage of outside sources of finance. Shareholders will clearly benefit if a loan bearing a 10% interest charge is invested in the business where it is expected to generate a 20% rate of return. For no increase in their investment shareholders' return improves, through either increased dividends or capital growth, or a combination of the two.

The situation where there is a 50% decrease in profits has been considered, but what happens when profits double? Profit, subject to tax, becoming available to the shareholders of B increases by 300% and interest cover moves from 2 to 8 times ($400 ÷ $50).

($)	A	B	C
Profit before interest and tax	400	200	800
Interest	50	50	50
Profit before tax	350	150	750

When a company is confident that the costs of external borrowings can be covered through the increased profit flowing from the investment made in the business, it makes sense to increase gearing. An added incentive for debt is that interest is normally tax deductible but dividends are not. High gearing increases the risk associated with the investment, but it can provide shareholders with high returns.

Asset gearing and return on equity

In Chapters 6 and 7 we used the Du Pont Chart – developed in 1919 – to analyse profitability and efficiency. The profit margin and asset turn were combined to generate a rate of return on assets employed. The same approach, using after-tax profit, can be used to calculate return on equity (ROE) – a key performance indicator for any company.

Return on equity = (after-tax profit ÷ assets) × (assets ÷ equity)

($)	A	B	C
After-tax profit	75	25	175
Total assets	1,000	1,250	1,750
Equity	250	500	1,000
Return on equity (%)	**30.0**	**5.0**	**17.5**

With a little expansion this model can be very effective in assessing the impact of gearing on a company's ROE. How a company's assets are financed can be reviewed with the asset gearing ratio – sometimes referred to as the equity multiplier. This is directly linked to the debt ratio and identifies what proportion of the assets or capital employed is provided by shareholders. Assets may be defined as total assets or in any manner you intend to use consistently in your analysis – tangible operating assets (ROTOA) or net operating assets (RONOA).

The impact of gearing can clearly be seen; the higher the gearing the higher this ratio.

Asset gearing = assets ÷ equity

($)	A	B	C
Total assets	1,000	1,250	1,750
Equity	250	500	1,000
Asset gearing	**4**	**2.5**	**1.75**

Company A's shareholders are supporting only one-quarter of the total assets employed in the business. For each $1 of equity in company A there is $3 of debt and creditor finance ($750 ÷ $250). Company C shows only $0.75 ($750 ÷ $1,000). This can be viewed as the multiplier working for shareholders to increase the profitability of their investment. Any interest payable has been deducted in arriving at the after-tax profit. If two companies have the same total assets and after-tax profit, the one with the greater asset gearing will show the higher ROE.

Financing a business with debt can increase shareholder returns. For every $1 of equity in company A there is $4 of assets. This acts to increase the profits available to shareholders. If the after-tax profit margin (7.5%) is multiplied by the asset gearing ratio (4), the result is ROE of 30%. Company C has a higher profit margin (8.75%) but a lower asset gearing (1.75) producing a 17.5% ROE.

Return on equity can be seen to be the end result of three ratios.

$$\text{ROE} = (\text{profit} \div \text{assets}) \times (\text{revenue} \div \text{assets}) \times (\text{assets} \div \text{equity})$$

Assuming that sales revenue for all three companies is $2,000 ratios are:

	A	B	C
Profit ÷ assets	3.75	1.25	8.75
Revenue ÷ assets	2	1.6	1.14
Assets ÷ equity	4	2.5	1.75
Return on equity (%)	**30.0**	**5.0**	**17.5**

If companies B and C increased their gearing level to that of A (4), ROE would rise to 8% for B (1.25 × 1.6 × 4) and 40% for C (8.75 × 1.14 × 4).

This illustrates the impact of gearing on shareholder returns.

This combination of ratios offers an effective tool to aid the analysis of a company's rates of return and financial structure. Capital structure measures are combined with the ability to produce profit (profit margin) and to use assets to generate revenue (asset turn). It can also be used to assess the implications of any likely changes in the business – what happens if profit margin declines and gearing increases?

Dangers of high gearing

The more a company relies on debt the less control is has over its finances and the more it is at risk. A highly geared company may find bankers are less likely to accept changes in the terms of a loan agreement than shareholders are to accept a lower or even no dividend as the company runs short of cash or needs money to invest in assets.

High gearing can bring high volatility in the level of profit available to equity shareholders. For a highly geared company, a small movement in profit can have a dramatic influence on equity earnings. A small decline in profit may result in the company having to use all of the profit to service debt rather than pay dividends.

When business is booming, a company may regard an increase in gearing as not only attractive but also essential. It can be seen as a sign of poor financial management not to borrow more to achieve returns greater than the cost of the borrowing. During times of inflation, when the real cost of debt decreases, the pressure can be irresistible. However, if the boom slows and/or ends in recession, the highly geared company faces difficulties as profits decline, interest rates rise and the loans fall due for repayment.

The problems that many banks encountered in the credit crisis that started in 2007 provide a further illustration of the potential problems associated with high gearing. Suppose company A found that 10% of its total assets – sub-prime mortgages – had become valueless. The assets' carrying value becomes $900 and shareholders' funds are reduced to $150. The debt ratio moves from 75% to 83% ($750 ÷ $900) and the debt/equity ratio from 4 to 5 times ($750 ÷ $150), now showing the company in a somewhat different light.

A further danger inherent in high gearing is that as the providers of debt see gearing rise they may, to reduce their own exposure, insist that certain restrictions are built into the loan agreement – for example, an upper limit for gearing or tougher levels of interest cover or liquidity. The company loses some degree of control and flexibility of approach in its financial management. If it breaks the loan restrictions, it may be held in default and forced to make immediate repayment.

Share price and value

In the UK, shares are normally issued at a par value. The par value of a share is the nominal value at which it is issued and appears in the balance sheet. A company may issue 25p or £1 shares and this, rather than the market price, is the value consistently used in the balance sheet. When shares are issued at a price higher than par value the difference is shown in equity as share premium or capital in excess of par value. The par value of a share has no relevance to financial analysis. In the United States, it is common for companies to issue shares of no par value.

In general, share prices reflect views of the future rather than the mainly historic perspective presented in an annual report. A balance sheet should not be expected to reflect the market price of shares. It is the share price quoted on the stock exchange that determines the value of an investment. Share prices and price movements of the previous day are given in the press together with the high and low points for the year.

Many factors can influence a company's share price. Some are clear and quantifiable; others are more esoteric and ephemeral. A company issuing a profit warning can expect a drop in share price. Rumours of a takeover, a technological breakthrough, changes on the board, a big order or a lost one can all influence share price. Share price will partly reflect the general mood of the market, which is in turn linked to the national and global, economic, political and social environment. General optimism produces a bull market (one in which share prices are rising) and pessimism a bear market (one in which share prices are falling).

There can be only one indisputable answer to the question: Why did the shares go up by 5% yesterday? That, as any market trader knows, is: Because there were more buyers than sellers.

The prime trigger for a movement in share price is a change in investors' confidence in the ability of a company to produce profits in the future. Shares may have been purchased on the basis of the past performance of a company, but they are held in expectation of future returns: income and capital gain.

The sector in which a company operates can also influence share price. If it is one that is seen as being static, this will hold back the share price, whereas the reverse is true for a dynamic or glamorous sector.

Each stock exchange has its own share price indicator. In the UK, the FTSE 100, commonly referred to as the Footsie, includes the share prices of the largest 100 listed companies. This is a good real-time indicator of the market; a rise in the FTSE can be taken to indicate a general upward movement in share prices. The United States has the Dow Jones and NASDAQ, France the CAC General, Germany the DAX and China the Shanghai Composite.

Betas

For any given period, movements in both a company's share price and a selected stock exchange index can be plotted to give an indication of the sensitivity of the company's share price to general movements in the market. In the UK the FTSE 100 or the FT All-Shares index is used; in the United States it is the NYSE Composite (all stocks on the exchange). The statistical analysis supporting the calculation of betas is complex. Both income and capital gains from each share are compared with the return from the selected market index over a number of years. Betas are incorporated into the capital asset pricing model (CAPM), which can be used to quantify the cost of a company's equity. If a share moves precisely in tune with the market it will have a value of 1 – which, by definition, is that of the average company. This is called a company's "beta" – the beta rating or beta factor. This gives a measure of the volatility of a share relative to the market.

If it was found that for every 1% move in the stockmarket the company's share moved 1.5%, applying the 1.5 factor to the market index should provide an indicator of the likely price of that company's shares. A beta of 1.5 suggests that for every 1% move in the market the share will move 1.5%. If the buoyancy of the market is directly linked to expectations for the economy, companies with high betas are likely to be directly affected by boom or doom. With a sound economy high-beta companies can be expected to generate extremely good returns, but in recession they will probably be poor performers. A company with a low beta is likely to be little affected by changes in the economic environment. Government stocks or gilts have a beta of 0; the interest received is not affected by stockmarket fluctuations.

The higher the beta – the higher the volatility – the higher will be a company's risk premium. A risk premium may be seen as the extra return an investor can be expected to require to invest in the share.

Low-risk – low-beta – shares will attract little or no risk premium. If the average risk premium – market risk premium (MRP) – is 5% and the company has a beta of 1.5, its shares can be expected to have a 7.5% (5 × 1.5) risk premium.

Net asset per share and market to book ratios

If a company is wound up and the assets are sold for their balance sheet values, after all external liabilities are settled what remains – net worth or net assets – is all that is available to repay equity shareholders. It is therefore worth calculating the net asset per share ratio to get an idea of the value of the assets supporting the share price. The higher the assets per share the lower is the shareholders' risk.

Asset backing = net assets ÷ number of shares in issue

($)	A	B	C
Sale of total assets	1,000	1,250	1,750
Less			
Debt	500	500	500
Current liabilities	250	250	250
Net assets	250	500	1,000
Number of shares	250	500	1,500
Net assets per share	1.00	1.00	0.67
Share price	3.00	1.00	1.50

For most companies, net asset backing per share is lower than the current share price for the simple reason that there should be more to a company than just the book value of its assets. The same will apply when the total stock exchange value – the market capitalisation or book value – of a company is set again the balance sheet value of net assets. This will provide the "market to book" or "price-to-book" ratio, which will normally be greater than 1. If this is not the case, it means that little value is being placed on expectations of growth or improved performance.

For major US companies before the financial crisis that started in 2007, the ratio was close to 5:1 with only $1 of assets in the balance sheet to support $5 of stock exchange value. Intangibles are an important factor in this ratio. Typically, internet or dotcom companies have a low net asset per share but high market to book ratio.

Where the share price is lower than the net asset backing, this can be interpreted in a number of ways. It may be that the company has not been performing as well as others in the same sector and there is general agreement that this is likely to continue, with the result that there is little demand for the shares. Where the net assets per share are much higher than a company's share price it may be seen as past redemption, and almost certainly a target for takeover by someone who has spotted the chance to acquire assets cheaply. The financial crisis that started in 2007 offers many examples of this occurring.

Smoothing earnings

A popular means of measuring company performance is earnings per share (EPS). This ratio is produced by dividing the after-tax profit for the year, after deducting minority interests and any non-voting share dividends, by the weighted average of the number of equity shares in issue during the year (see Chapter 6). It is also a ratio often used as a performance target as part of management incentive schemes.

There is an understandable tendency among directors to prefer to show a smooth profit growth over a number of years rather than a series of volatile shifts. It makes it appear they are in control of the business. Investors also are usually calmed by such a trend being achieved.

Companies X and Y might have achieved the same level of profit. Company X shows a steady profit growth whereas Y has a volatile pattern of earnings. Investors will prefer company X. Although profitability may be identical, there appears to be more certainty (less risk) with an investment in X. This is often said to be because of the "quality of earnings" of one company compared with another.

It is generally accepted that a smooth upward profit trend is better than a track record similar to the skyline of the Swiss Alps. Given the choice, most companies would prefer to see their profits increase gradually over a number of years. Smoothing profits is attractive. A smooth profit trend indicates that management has firm and effective control of the business.

Creative profits

Directors can be tempted to become creative in their financial statement presentation. This is particularly true if they have a personal interest in their company's performance – share options, commission, or bonuses for achieving performance targets.

Profits can be smoothed in many creative ways, for example by

Different ways of making the same profit `9.1`

Company X — Profit / Years

Company Y — Profit / Years

changing depreciation policy or capitalising expenses. The time at which a transaction is recognised in the financial statements can be an important consideration. If a major event producing large profits is not brought into this year's accounts but moved to the following year, reported profit can be effectively smoothed; this is not uncommon for German companies.

It is much more difficult to produce a profit immediately than to shift profit from this year to next. There is a temptation for a highly profitable company, uncertain of the future, to set aside some of its current profit for a rainy day. A reserve might be created. A cash sale of $100 is not taken into the income statement but placed in the balance sheet as "deferred revenue". Next year the $100 revenue is brought into the income statement and the reserve disappears. A variation is to pre-pay expenses: pay some of next year's expenses in cash and include in the current year's cost of sales.

It is to be hoped that auditors will catch any such tricks. To date the most extreme example of manipulating reserves was WorldCom, resulting in a overstatement of profit in 2000 of some $3 billion.

Pension fund accounting, off-balance-sheet financing, the manipulation of reserves and provisions, year-end inventory valuations and the treatment of bad debts have all, in their time, helped to smooth profits and influence balance sheet valuations. The steady flow of IFRS and various "watch-dog" organisations have improved matters considerably, but always be on your guard.

Always use your own analysis of a company as the basis for assessment. Never rely on ready-made analysis provided in the annual report. Many commercial databases which offer financial analysis take all the figures in the financial statements at their face value. The arithmetic may be good but the quality rotten.

Risk and the payback period

A simple and popular means of taking account of risk is to be found in the payback period. Payback is used in investment project assessment and provides an indication of how long it will be before a project generates sufficient income to recover the capital investment. The shorter the payback period the better. An investment of $1,000 offering an annual income of $100 has a payback period of ten years. An alternative option might be to invest the $1,000 in a project offering a $200 annual income stream. A payback period of five years is likely to be more attractive than the first option.

Price/earnings ratio

A company's earnings per share can be incorporated in an equivalent to the payback measure: the price/earnings (P/E) ratio. Share price is dependent upon investors' opinions of a company's future earning potential as much as anything else. Earnings per share (as last reported) can usefully be linked to current share price to provide some indication of expectations for future performance.

Price/earnings = share price ÷ earnings per share

	A	B	C
Share price (¢)	300	100	150
Earnings per share (¢)	30	5	11.7
Price/earnings	**10**	**20**	**12.9**

For company A a P/E of 10 can be interpreted as showing that when a share is purchased for 300¢ this represents the equivalent of ten years' earnings of 30¢ a year – in other words, a payback period of ten years.

The higher the P/E ratio the greater the confidence investors have in the future prospects and performance of the company. A high P/E ratio indicates investors have confidence that the company will maintain and probably improve its current performance in the coming year.

High or low price/earnings?

The only way of deciding whether a company has a high or a low P/E ratio is to compare it with other companies. Companies are listed in the financial media by their sector of operation. The company with the highest P/E ratio is considered, on that day, to be the sector's best future performer for investors.

As earnings per share is dependent upon share price, the P/E ratio is influenced by forecast trends, rumours or myths of the moment. It is not unusual for the company with the highest ratio one year to be the first in the sector to succumb to recession or mismanagement. By definition, a high P/E ratio indicates that it is probably too late to invest in the company since the price to be paid will be too high. It may also indicate that a company is already overvalued. Experience suggests that the only way for a high P/E to move is downwards.

It can be useful to compare a company's P/E ratio with the average for the sector or with that of a selected competitor. If the average P/E for the sector is 15, the relative position of the three example companies is indicated.

	A	B	C
Actual P/E	10	20	12
Average P/E	15	15	15
Relative position	67	133	80

Prospective price/earnings

If a forecast is made of a company's likely future profits, this can provide a figure for likely future earnings per share. If company A is forecast to have a profit growth of 20% in the coming year, after-tax profit will rise to $82.5 and EPS to 33¢. If current share price is divided by forecast earnings (300 ÷ 33), a prospective P/E ratio of 9.1 is produced. This prospective P/E is the product of arithmetic and is not influenced by real life.

If any item is left as unknown in the equation below, it is easy to discover its value.

Share price = earnings per share × price/earnings ratio
$$300 = 30 \times 10.0$$
$$330 = \mathbf{33} \times 10.0$$
$$\mathbf{300} = 33 \times 9.1$$

For company A, where only one variable in the equation is adjusted, earnings per share are forecast at 33¢ and share price rises to 330. If share price were held at 300¢, with 33¢ earnings per share the P/E ratio moves to 9.1. Prospective P/E ratios can only be estimated, but once some forecast is obtained for profit and P/E these can be used to indicate likely future share price movements. If for company A earnings per share is forecast at 33¢ and it is considered that the company should command a P/E ratio of 12, the likely future share price can be calculated as follows.

Future share price = forecast earnings per share × prospective price/earnings
396 = 33 × 12

Problems with price/earnings ratio
In most cases, the P/E ratio being used in analysis is that provided by a newspaper, not one calculated by the user. This can cause a number of problems. The profit used as the basis for a published P/E ratio is normally that shown in a company's income statement and may therefore have been arrived at creatively. Furthermore, one side of the equation is historic profit, which is not guaranteed to be a guide to future performance, and the other side is current share price, which changes from minute to minute on the stock exchange. A rumour of takeover or a major technological breakthrough in product development will not alter historic earnings, but it will certainly have an effect on share price.

Dividends
Companies normally make two dividend payments per year: an interim payment based on half-year profits and a final payment at the end of the year. These will appear in the statement of shareholders' equity and the cash flow statement.

Investors see dividends as an indicator of current performance and future profits. An increased dividend signals that a company's directors consider prospects to be good. Dividends also act as a signal to the market. Good news, indicated by an increase in dividend, usually triggers a rise in share price and bad news the reverse.

Dividend per share
The dividend per share (DPS) can be calculated using the same denominator as earnings per share (EPS). The total dividend for the year is divided by the weighted average of the number of shares in issue.

Dividend per share = dividend ÷ weighted average number of shares in issue

	A	B	C
Dividend ($)	25	20	87
Number of shares	250	500	1,500
Dividend per share (¢)	**10**	**4**	**5.8**

Remember, as with EPS, it is not possible to directly compare different companies' DPS. Companies with an identical dividend but different share structures will not show the same DPS.

Retained profit per share

When the profit for the year attributable to equity shareholders is known, the next step is to decide what the dividend should be and how much of the profit should be retained for use by the company. If the dividend per share is deducted from the earnings per share, what remains is the retained profit per share for the year (see page 160).

Retained profit per share = earnings per share − dividend per share

(¢ per share)	A	B	C
Earnings	30	5	11.7
Dividend	10	4	5.8
Retained earnings	20	1	5.9

Dividend cover

If after-tax profit attributable to ordinary shareholders is divided by the dividend, the result is the number of times the dividend was covered. As with interest cover, the higher the dividend cover ratio the better or safer is the position of a company. However, levels of what is considered acceptable vary across business sectors. If a company is operating in a sector that is reasonably unaffected by economic downturns, such as food manufacturing and retailing, a lower dividend cover ratio is more acceptable because the risk is lower.

Dividend cover = after-tax profit ÷ dividend
= earnings per share ÷ dividend per share

	A	B	C
After-tax profit	75	25	175
Dividend	25	20	87
Dividend cover	**3.0**	**1.25**	**2.0**

Payout ratio

Another way of looking at the safety level of dividend payments is to show what proportion of profit is being distributed to shareholders.

$$\text{Payout ratio} = 100 \div \text{dividend cover}$$

	A	B	C
Payout (%)	33	80	50

The higher the payout ratio the lower is the dividend cover; the level of profit cover for dividend is just being expressed in a different way. A company with a high payout ratio is not retaining profit to reinvest in the business. You should always try to discover why. Is management not confident about the future prospects of the business, or are they taking a short-term view of keeping shareholders happy with a dividend payment rather than providing for future long-term growth?

Gross dividend

Companies deduct tax and make a net dividend payment to shareholders. To allow comparison with other investment opportunities, tax should be added back to produce the gross dividend per share. Company A has a dividend of 10¢ per share. If the tax rate is 20% the gross dividend is 12.5¢; 2.5¢ covers the basic rate tax and 10¢ is paid to shareholders.

$$\text{Gross dividend} = \text{dividend} \div (1 - \text{tax rate})$$

Earnings yield

To obtain some indication of the return flowing from an investment, the current share price and earnings per share can be combined to give the earnings yield.

$$\text{Earnings yield} = 100 \times (\text{earnings per share} \div \text{share price})$$

	A	B	C
Earnings per share (¢)	30	5	11.7
Share price (¢)	300	100	150
Earnings yield (%)	**10**	**5**	**7.8**

Earnings yield is not an indicator of the actual return on investment. It is based on earnings per share not the dividend received by shareholders. If the P/E ratio is known, it is simple to calculate the earnings yield. Company B with a P/E ratio of 20 has an earnings yield of 5 (100 ÷ 20) and company C 7.8 (100 ÷ 12.9).

Dividend yield

Dividend yield links the current share price to the dividend received.

$$\text{Dividend yield} = 100 \times (\text{dividend per share} \div \text{share price})$$

	A	B	C
Dividend per share (¢)	10	4	5.8
Share price (¢)	300	100	150
Dividend yield %	**3.3**	**4.0**	**3.9**

Changes in share price bring about a change in the dividend yield. As share price changes there is an automatic adjustment in dividend yield, as illustrated below for company A, whose share price moves between 150¢ and 600¢.

Dividend (¢)	10	10	10
Share price (¢)	300	150	600
Dividend yield (%)	**3.3**	**6.7**	**1.7**

Shareholders' return

The return shareholders expect from their investment in shares is a combination of the capital gain flowing from an improvement in share price and income from dividends – total shareholders' return (TSR). A change in share price is part of the total return from their investment. If the shares in company A increase in price by 10%, the total return to shareholders, ignoring tax, in the period is 30%: the dividend yield (20%) plus the capital gain (10%). If the share price of C falls by 5% in the period, the total return to shareholders is –1%.

To calculate the current or the likely future total return on investment, these two can be combined. If A's share price is forecast to rise to 396¢ and the dividend per share to 12¢, then the likely future return can be estimated as follows.

Capital return	$= 100 \times$ (share price change ÷ opening share price)
	$= 100 \times (96 \div 300)$
	$= 32\%$
Dividend yield	$= 100 \times$ (dividend per share ÷ share price)
	$= 100 \times (12 \div 300)$
	$= 4\%$
Total return	$= 32 + 4$
	$= \mathbf{36\%}$

Valuing companies

There are many ways of arriving at a value for a company. The annual report can be used as a basis for valuation; the balance sheet offers comprehensive details of the assets and liabilities. However, it is not intended to offer a valuation so it is best used only as a rough guide. The only time there can be an accurate and indisputable value for a company is when it has just been bought or sold. At other times its value is an estimate based partly on science and partly on art.

Capitalisation

If a company's shares are quoted on a stock exchange, there is a ready source of data upon which to base a valuation. Multiplying the current market price of a share by the number of shares in issue provides an indication of the company's current stock exchange value. This is its market value, or the capitalisation of the company.

	A	B	C
Share price (¢)	300	100	150
Shares (number)	250	1,000	1,500
Capitalisation ($)	**750**	**1,000**	**2,250**

Company A has a capitalisation of $750. If you wanted to acquire the company, $750 is probably a better guide to the price to be paid than, say, total assets ($1,000) or equity ($250) in the balance sheet.

The financial media publish capitalisation figures for companies daily or once a week. This provides a basis for the comparison of the size of companies according to current stock exchange values. In practice, if you decided to acquire A, as shares began to be purchased market forces would bring about a price rise. The capitalisation of $750 offers a guide to the minimum likely price for the company.

Earnings multiple

Another way of calculating a company's capitalisation is to multiply after-tax profits by the P/E ratio. Company A has a P/E ratio of 10 and after-tax profit of $75, the product of which is the $750 capitalisation.

Capitalisation can be readily produced only for quoted companies. To calculate the value of a non-quoted company, you can use the P/E ratios of stock exchange listed companies operating in an appropriate business sector. A practical source in the UK is the *Financial Times*, which has a daily list of companies by sector. The P/E ratio of three or four comparable companies or the sector average can be used as a basis for valuation.

Armed with an appropriate benchmark P/E ratio, it is possible to calculate share price. For example, a company operating in a sector with an average P/E ratio of 16.6 has earnings per share of 5¢ and no quoted share price.

Price earnings ratio	= share price ÷ earnings per share
Share price	= price/earnings ratio × earnings per share
83.3¢	= 16.66 × 5¢

Using the average P/E ratio for the appropriate sector produces a suggested share price for the company of 83.3¢. In most cases it should be possible to identify one or two quoted companies that reasonably match the activities or spread of business of the company being valued.

After-tax profit versus earnings per share

The shares in the company were valued at 83.3¢ using the sector average P/E ratio of 16.66. The basis of the valuation is the after-tax profit generated by the company and attributable to equity shareholders. This is not affected by the number of shares in issue or, ignoring tax implications, by dividend policy. It is therefore better and much simpler to use this as the basis for valuing non-quoted companies.

If the after-tax profit of $25 is multiplied by the 16.66 P/E ratio the result is $416, which when divided by the number of shares in issue (500) gives the same share price of 83¢. It is easier and more practical to use $416 as a value for the company, but the individual share price may be important if shares are being transferred between family members in a private company.

Investing in a small private company is usually considered more risky than buying shares in a quoted company. To compensate for this, the P/E ratio used in valuing a private company may be adjusted by an appropriate amount, referred to as the risk premium. If the P/E ratio selected is 16.66 and a 35% risk premium is considered applicable, the multiple to be applied to value a company is 10.8 (16.66 – 35%). If the company has after-tax profits of $25, applying the 10.8 multiple gives a value of $270 and a share price of 54¢ ($270 ÷ 500).

Further problems are encountered if only a proportion of a company's equity is being valued. In this situation the method detailed above can be used with discount factors applied to the multiple according to the quantity of shares involved. A 5% block of shares might be discounted by 60%, but if 51% of a company's shares are being acquired the discount might be only 10–20%.

The average for a sector can be used, but in most cases it should be possible to find at least one suitable company to use as a basis for direct P/E comparison. If you have access to the *Financial Times*, a simpler alternative is to use the FTSE Actuaries Share or Sector Indices. If there are no obvious sources of P/E ratios, experts suggest that a multiplier of 10 should be applied to after-tax profits to provide an indication of company value.

Dividend valuation method

If it is assumed that the value of a share is the present value of its future dividends, dividend can form the basis for valuing a company. The basic formula is:

$$\text{Value} = (\text{dividend} \times (1 + \text{dividend growth}) \div (\text{required return} - \text{dividend growth})$$

An appropriate discount factor can be applied to give the present value of the anticipated dividend stream. If the current dividend of a company is 6¢ per share, dividend growth is expected to be 5% per annum and shareholders require a 15% rate of return, a share in the company can be valued at 63¢.

$$\text{Value} = (6.0 \times 1.05) \div (0.15 - 0.05) = 6.3 \div 0.1 = 63¢$$

Government bonds and rates of return

Investors can be assumed to look for different rates of return linked to the risk of a given investment opportunity. The lower the risk the lower is the required rate of return. The rate of return investors require has a direct influence on the cost of a company's capital. The higher the risk the higher is the rate of return required, and the more it costs a company to service through dividend and interest payments the finance provided. A good starting point is to look at returns from risk-free investments.

It is generally accepted that lending money to the government is risk free, as the interest rate and maturity date are fixed and certain. Thus the return from government securities can be regarded as that required from a risk-free investment. Investors in other securities, such as equities, require an additional return to compensate for the additional risk. This is called the risk premium. Using non-redeemable bonds, the interest yield can be calculated in a similar way to that of dividend and earnings yields.

Bond value ($)	100	100	100
Price paid ($)	100	50	200
Interest rate (%)	5	5	5
Interest yield (%)	**5**	**10**	**2.5**

If investors see that the returns from alternative sources are greater than 5%, they may sell their bonds to take advantage of the opportunity. The sale of bonds brings about a reduction in their price ($50) and their yield increases to 10%. When bonds are seen as a better investment, the price rises to $200 and the yield falls to 2.5%.

The base bank rate of interest, quoted daily in the media, can be used as an alternative to government securities to provide an indicator of the risk-free rate of return.

Equities risk premium

As well as the risk-free rate of return, investors can reasonably expect a premium for the risk involved in investing in equities. The equity risk premium has normally been 5–10% on both the UK and US stock exchanges.

An additional premium is required when considering investment in private, non-quoted companies, which are generally assumed to be a more risky investment than quoted companies. As a general rule, a minimum of an additional 25% premium should be added to compensate for the risk of unlisted company investment. Many valuation experts, however, suggest that the premium should be 30–40%

Cost of capital

The view investors take of the risk associated with buying shares in a company determines its cost of capital. The higher the risk the higher are the expected returns and the higher is the cost of raising finance. Before a company returns a profit it must cover the cost of capital. Interest on borrowed funds will have been charged before arriving at the profit for the year, but the company will not necessarily have made an appropriate allowance for the cost of equity capital provided by shareholders.

The cost of debt can be estimated from the financial statements. There will be notes providing details of the interest rates applying to loans. The after-tax cost of borrowing $500 at 10% interest with a tax rate of 50% is 5%; at a tax rate of 40% the after-tax cost of borrowing would be 6%. Inflation reduces the real cost of debt financing. With a currency decreasing in value over time, the true rate of interest adjusts and so does that repaid at the end of the loan period. Calculating the actual cost of borrowings for loan or convertible stock not issued at par is complex. For most purposes, it is adequate to take the interest rate quoted as being an approximation of the actual real cost.

There are many ways of estimating the cost of equity. One is to use dividend yield adjusted for the impact of tax. This is only an approximation as it does not take account of the fact that dividend rates may change and, of course, that share prices change from day to day. A simple adjustment to allow for some rate of growth could be applied to the dividend yield or the earnings yield could be used. The higher the P/E ratio the lower is the earnings yield. A high P/E assumes that investors have confidence in the future performance of the company so raising finance is cheaper; of course the reverse also applies.

Investing in new and untested technology can offer huge returns if it is successful, but there is also the possibility of the investment having to be written off, so a high risk is involved. If investors are to be attracted to the investment, they must have some incentive. The cost of equity is the return required by investors to provide capital to a company; the higher the perceived risk of the company the higher is the cost of capital.

The capital asset pricing model (CAPM) offers an approach to calculating the cost of equity for a company.

$$\text{Cost of equity} = \text{risk-free rate} + \text{beta (market rate} - \text{risk-free rate)}$$
$$18\% = 5\% + 1.3\,(15\% - 5\%)$$

With a risk-free rate of return of 5% and a market rate of return of 15%, the "equity risk premium" is 10%. A company with a 1.3 beta has an estimated cost of equity of 18%. If the company had a beta of 2, the cost of equity would rise to 25%.

Another way of arriving at an approximation of the cost of capital is to take a simple weighted average for equity and debt. The cost of debt is taken as the interest rate applying to each item and the cost of equity as the dividend yield.

Summary

◪ The debt/equity ratio is a well-tested and simple measure of the balance between the finance provided by equity shareholders and that derived from external borrowings (debt). Although the ratio may be subject to manipulation, it still provides the best starting point for an assessment of capital structure. The content of the denominator and numerator can be refined as appropriate. The lower the ratio the greater is the proportion of finance being provided by shareholders. A company with a low debt/equity ratio is said to be low geared.

◪ The debt ratio is helpful in interpreting the structure of a balance sheet. It shows what proportion of total assets has been funded by external sources of finance. For most businesses, when more than 50% of assets are debt financed it is advisable to complete a detailed analysis of the company and its likely future prospects before considering an investment. If only one measure of gearing were allowed, this would be the most attractive.

◪ Notes in the annual report will provide details of a company's debt, showing for the next five years the amount, rate of interest and date when the borrowings mature or are to be repaid. At first glance these notes may appear overwhelming, but they are worth studying. A simple indicator of the likely demands to be made on a company's future cash flow is created by taking the total annual interest charge and adding to it any capital repayments to be made for each of the next two or three years. Based on previous experience, does it look as if the company can meet these expected cash outflows without having either to sell assets or to initiate new borrowing?

◪ For shareholders, the efficiency of a company in making debt work for them is an important consideration. Shareholders' return is a combination of profitability and gearing. Two ratios can be combined to highlight how return on equity is being achieved.

◪ The interest cover ratio is an effective way of linking the level of gearing with profitability. A company borrowing money to finance its operations must pay the agreed interest in cash each year. The greater the interest cover provided by pre-interest and tax profit the safer is the company's position. A high-geared company must guarantee to maintain a safe level of interest cover. A combination of high gearing and low interest cover is not a healthy sign.

◪ Similarly, the extent to which dividend is covered by profit is a useful indicator of the comfort or safety level for shareholders. The higher the dividend cover the greater is the proportion of retained profit being ploughed back into the company.

◪ A useful measure is to use cash flow as the basis for cash flow dividend cover. All interest, tax and non-equity dividends are deducted from operating cash flow and the result divided by the equity dividends. This ratio identifies the proportion of cash flow, after all external financing charges, that is available for equity dividends.

◪ Dividend per share should be combined with earnings per share in studying the historic record of a company. If earnings per share and dividend per share are plotted, the difference is the amount per share being retained in the business each year. Some consistency in the three figures should be evident.

◪ The financial media provide daily calculations of dividend yield and P/E ratios. When studying a listed company it is possible to make a direct comparison with the P/E ratios of similar companies, and to obtain some indication of the ranking given by investors. The higher the P/E ratio the higher are investors' expectations of that company's future performance.

■ A company with a high P/E ratio is not necessarily a good investment. A high ratio indicates that the market has already taken into account the future prospects of the company and that it is probably already too late to buy.

■ Published P/E ratios can be used to provide a valuation for non-listed companies. If the average ratio for the appropriate sector is found and applied as a multiplier to the after-tax profit of the company, the result is an indicator of total value.

10 Strategy, success and failure

WHEN ANALYSING A COMPANY three key areas should be examined: management, operating performance and financial position. Using annual reports and other published information to analyse the past and forecast the future in two of these three areas has been covered in earlier chapters. This chapter goes over some of that ground again, considers approaches to assessing the strength of management and discusses the unavoidable mix of the quantifiable and the qualitative necessary to make an overall assessment of a company's performance and its future prospects.

Sources of information

XBRL

Recent moves towards the standardisation of financial reports should soon bring significant further improvements in the quality, value and accessibility of corporate financial information. This is to be based on the adoption of Extensible Business Reporting Language (XBRL). Do not be put off by the name. In all probability this is where the future of both corporate reporting and analysis lies. There will be a standardised form of presentation and national language will no longer be a barrier to analysis. You will be able to import company data easily into your own spreadsheet and with little trouble make comparisons with other companies. There will be certainty of reliable and consistent financial definition of each item used.

The US Securities and Exchange Commission (SEC) accepted XBRL filings in 2005 and in 2006 provided $5m to assist in the development of common electronic definitions for every accounting transaction. This involves "tags" or "tagging" individual items of information appearing in financial reports. This will eventually allow investors, using the internet, to access and compare the accounts of any company, or all companies within a chosen sector. Visit the SEC website to discover more – "interactive data (XBRL)".

The internet

The internet is now recognised as a primary vehicle for corporate communications. All companies operate a website. You can access general business information, financial statements and annual reports with little trouble – just enter the company's name in a search engine. All listed companies have an "investor relations" section in their website which is where annual reports are normally found as well as up-to-date financial information.

Using a webcast for the annual general meeting (AGM) or a statement from the chief executive officer (CEO) is becoming increasingly popular – particularly with regard to institutional investors and analysts. Expect corporate communications to become more interactive in the near future.

The media

Newspapers, journals, magazines, TV and radio, and professional or trade publications provide further information that may help interpret the facts given in the annual report or on developments since the report was published. Media reports may provide technical analysis of the company, its current and likely future markets and operating environment, or they may give more qualitative impressions with reports of lawsuits or gossip column pieces about directors. However, bear in mind that Enron was "America's most innovative company" between 1996 and 2001 according to *Fortune*, and in 2000 was voted "energy company of the year" by the *Financial Times*.

Appearance may matter

The annual report should not be underestimated as a visual presentation of the company and its directors. A dull report may indicate a dull company; an overglamorous report may indicate a company too concerned with impressive presentation, perhaps in order to disguise poor performance – "never mind the quality, feel the width".

Photo opportunity for the board

The way in which the board is presented reflects the changing trends in corporate reporting. From the 1960s to the mid-1970s, the classic "oil painting" profile of the chairman gazing into the far distance thinking deep strategic thoughts was considered appropriate to show the company was led by a tough but fair father figure. There was little detail, beyond the statutory minimum, of the other directors.

In the late 1970s, it became important for the board to be seen to be managing the company as a team. It was recognised that a team was needed to support a dynamic leader to ensure success. The result was often a photograph of the CEO sitting in the boardroom surrounded by all the other directors (standing). Positive statements were made concerning the "diversification" policy the board was adopting.

The mid-1980s showed directors actively running the business. They were shown walking around a shop or factory and talking to employees. Typically, the director was named and looking at the camera, while the employee was anonymous and stacking a shelf or working a machine. The annual report explained the importance of "unbundling" or restructuring the group.

By the end of the 1980s, with the growth in empowerment of employees, annual reports increasingly included photographs of employees working alone or in happy groups, with no directors in sight. The board was once more relegated to a single page in the annual report.

The early 1990s saw directors back as a group at the boardroom table or a selected site, not necessarily doing anything but looking quietly confident and in control. It was often difficult to identify the leader.

In the 2000s there has been more emphasis on corporate responsibility, ethical practices and environmental reporting. The terms "global", "value", "environmental issues" and "sustainable development" are common. New chairmen and CEOs are taking advantage of the chance to explain their strategy and key performance indicators to investors. If things are proving difficult for a company sometimes the annual report can appear somewhat funereal, but as things improve colour returns. Marks and Spencer's 2004 report cover was a wash of colour. A new CEO and a fight to avoid takeover resulted in a plain black cover in 2005.

Famous last words

Perhaps a more enjoyable, but possibly masochistic, pastime for the immediate future may be collecting the "last words" of chairmen and CEOs appearing in the media as they try to explain their disastrous performance and their company's collapse. As an example, an analyst neatly summed up his and the market's experience with the collapse of a UK bank as "at least we've learnt not to put a grocer in charge of a bank" – the bank's CEO had previously worked for a major food retailer. In *Little Dorrit* Charles Dickens created the swindling banker – "that illustrious and great national ornament" – Mr Merdle, who defrauded investors with a pyramid or Ponzi scheme. His last words were: "Could you lend me a penknife?" Some 150 years later Bernard Madoff, using exactly the same scam as Merdle but on a much greater scale, delivered the less memorable: "It's all just one big lie."

The most significant change in the 2000s is the importance being given to a company's website as a means of corporate communication. Xerox was one of the first companies to publish its interim statements online rather than mailing them to shareholders, saving some $100,000 per year. Publishing an annual report online is now acceptable practice in the UK – shareholders must expect to request a hard copy. Some companies have already gone "interactive" with their reports. Do make a company's website the first place you look to see what information is available.

Corporate governance

Corporate governance embraces not only the way in which a company is managed and its dealings with shareholders but also every aspect of its relationship with society. Emphasis on corporate governance was stimulated partly by apparent fraud and mismanagement in some major UK and US companies and partly by the increase in corporate failure rates during the recession years of the 1980s and early 1990s. Shareholders and others dealing with a company wanted assurance that it was being well and correctly managed. In 1992 the Cadbury Committee established a code of best practice for UK companies. It contained 19 points and required that the reasons for non-compliance with any of these should be given in the annual report. Several other committees followed, leading to the publication of the Combined Code in 1998 and its revision in 2003. "The principles on which the Code is based are those of openness, integrity and accountability"; it is now mandatory for all listed companies (see Chapter 1).

The code requires the board to present a balanced and understandable assessment of the company's position and likely prospects in the annual report. The introduction of the Combined Code for UK companies has substantially improved the quality and quantity of information on directors and their effectiveness in running a company. There has been similar experience in other countries. The OECD published *Principles of Corporate Governance* and in 2003 the European Commission issued *Modernising Company Law and Enhancing Corporate Governance in the EU – A Plan to Move Forward*. In the United States, following the collapse of Enron and WorldCom, the Public Accounting Reform and Investor Protection Act – normally referred to as the Sarbanes-Oxley Act (SOX) – was passed to improve investor confidence and encourage full and transparent corporate reporting.

The board and its roles

The prime role of the board is to satisfy shareholders through the successful implementation of the chosen corporate strategy. Ideally, the annual report should contain an organisation chart to show the reporting lines and areas of individual authority and responsibility. At least the direct business responsibilities of each member of the board should be identified.

Who are the directors and how good are they?

The annual report should contain sufficient information on directors to enable an assessment to be made of their competence and experience. At least each director's age and length of service should be recorded. A simple aid to assessing the board is to calculate the average age of the directors. If it is the late 50s for executive directors and over 60 for non-executive directors, the board may be getting past its sell-by date, with directors more concerned with serving their time than the shareholders' interests.

The age of directors can also indicate when succession is likely to be necessary. A board changing only as a result of death or retirement may be doing a good job, but are the directors capable of innovation or facing rapid and challenging change?

To be effective, directors must have real business experience in dealing with both hard times and good times. Investors need to be confident that the top team is capable of sure-footed management whatever the business environment.

Financial analysts assess companies in three main ways: by studying the financial statements to discover underlying strengths and expose weaknesses; through general background research into the business sector and its future; and by visiting the company and talking to the executive team. Face-to-face meetings are extremely important; if senior management fails to inspire confidence support for the company will drop, even if there was a record profit in the previous year.

One person, two jobs

It can be argued that every company needs someone, particularly in its early growth period, in firm control offering effective leadership and direction. As a company grows and becomes a more complex organisation, it becomes more difficult if not impossible for one person to manage single handed. There is eminent sense behind the separation of the roles of chairman and CEO, and this is required by the Combined Code.

Sainsbury, until the mid-1990s the UK's foremost food retailer, provides an example of the potential problems that can arise. In 1996, after profits fell for the first time in the company's history, there was immediate media comment. *The Times* (May 6th 1996) ran a headline "Sainsbury's decline is blamed on arrogance and complacency" and drew attention to the fact that David Sainsbury was both chairman and CEO. In 1998 the final act took place, with the Sainsbury family being separated from the management of the company. Marks and Spencer, another major UK retailer, suffered similar problems in the late 1990s, with board conflict becoming public followed by a dramatic decline in profits and share price.

The combination of an entrepreneur and a non-participating board is usually fatal in the longer term. Companies may have their powerful personalities or leaders, but to ensure continued success they must be supported by an experienced and competent team of managers.

It follows from the above that a company that seems to be overly dominated by one individual needs to be looked at carefully. The annual report may provide evidence of a personality cult, and the media often provide plenty of evidence of potentially dangerous large egos, the late Robert Maxwell being a case in point.

Non-executive directors

The role of non-executive directors is seen as increasingly important. They can provide a wealth of experience brought from other business sectors and companies, but their principal benefit should be independence of thought, view and personal income. This places them in a powerful position to reinforce the stewardship role of the board and to act on its various committees. A non-executive director who is a customer, a supplier or a friend of the family, or whose only source of income is the directorship, is unlikely to fulfil the independence requirement.

In much of Europe, however, there is a two-tier board structure. Large companies in the Netherlands and Germany usually have a supervisory board made up of representatives of shareholders and employees. France has some two-tier companies, but the majority have a single board with two-thirds of its members being non-executive. Best practice in the UK requires at least half of the board to be made up of non-executive directors to enable them to exert an independent influence on the direction of the company.

Audit committee

To comply with best practice, a listed company must have an audit committee made up of independent and reasonably financially acute non-executive directors. Details of its membership and duties will be found in the annual report.

The Sarbanes-Oxley Act in the United States emphasised the importance of the audit committee, expanding its role to include responsibility for not only the proper treatment of employees' whistle-blowing but also all other internal and external complaints concerning financial matters. The Public Company Accounting Oversight Board (PCAOB) was set up in 2003 to work with the SEC to oversee the auditing of all US listed companies and to support the development of auditing standards.

The main purpose of the audit committee is to ensure effective external auditors are employed and to assist them wherever necessary. The audit committee should oversee accounting policies and practices and the internal control and auditing function. Its members should have direct access at any time to the CEO and chairman. A report from the audit committee should be on the agenda of the AGM and appear in the annual report. If this is not the case, the company is not fully complying with best practice.

Most companies have their own internal audit function, linked to but separate from the work of the external auditors, which should report directly to the audit committee. Internal audit is to ensure that all employees maintain and follow company procedures and systems. Best practice in corporate governance places an obligation on directors to ensure that all appropriate internal controls are applied, all assets are safeguarded and accurate accounting records are maintained, and that company risk is at an acceptable level.

Remuneration committee

Every public company should have a committee to oversee the remuneration and terms and conditions for all executive directors, including the CEO and chairman. Best practice requires that its members are non-executive directors. The fact that directors' remuneration has been set by the committee should be recorded in the annual report. It is usual for the committee also to oversee the employment terms and remuneration of all senior staff, thus ensuring that these are not solely dependent on the whim of the CEO. The intention is to ensure a completely transparent and consistent remuneration policy.

Directors' remuneration
Although money is not everything, it is clear that remuneration plays a crucial role in the motivation and retention of high-performing directors.

Directors responsible for several billion pounds' worth of assets and thousands of jobs rightly expect substantial rewards. It is generally accepted that reward should be directly linked to performance, and that a significant proportion of a director's remuneration package should be performance related. The aim is to provide a match between directors' and shareholders' interests.

Managing an executive remuneration policy is a considerable undertaking. It is the acid test of the quality of the non-executive directors. The remuneration committee should make sure that there is a defensible policy, and where directors' remuneration is increasing out of step with company performance there should be an explanation.

When a company makes a loan to a director or executive (or any member of their close family) this should be disclosed in the annual report as a "related-party transaction" (IAS 24). The details should include not just the year-end balance but also the highest level of the loan during the year. This avoids the situation – sometimes referred to as "window dressing" – where a director borrows money from a company and, each year, repays it just for the balance sheet day – no loan appears in the financial statements. It is always worth reading the related-party transactions details provided in an annual report.

Are they worth it?

The annual report provides details of company policy on executive directors' remuneration and shows the total remuneration of the chairman and the CEO or, if they are not the highest paid, that of the highest paid director. The total remuneration and taxable benefits paid to all directors are disclosed, together with details of their service contracts with the company. In the UK, it is unacceptable for directors to have, without shareholders' agreement, service contracts of more than three years' duration.

These details can be compared with those of similar-sized companies to assess their generosity. Year-on-year changes can be set against the rate of inflation, the change in average wage rates, or growth in the company's turnover or profit to provide a benchmark to decide whether the cost of the board appears reasonable.

Changes on the board

To be effective, directors must develop a set of individual and group working relationships to support their function as the top management team. Changes in the team are inevitable through retirement, accident, illness or career opportunity. However, it is reasonable to expect that any company has a core of experienced directors continuing to run the business from year to year.

Changes on the board can be a direct signal of existing and potential problems. The annual report provides a complete listing of directors that can be compared with the previous year to see changes. Unfortunately, there is no requirement to provide the equivalent of comparative figures for directors, so it is often necessary to refer to the previous report. However, it is possible for someone to join and leave the board during the year and for this not to be noted in the annual report.

There should be a statement giving the reasons for board changes (most often these will be for retirement or career moves). A popular euphemism to disguise board conflict and disagreement is a director leaving "to pursue other interests". A continually changing board should be taken as an indicator that all is not well with the company. It can be assumed there are potentially destructive tensions at the top of the organisation that will not improve confidence in its future prospects.

A good warning sign is a continuing turnover in directors. As a general rule, where more than 20% of a board is seen to change in consecutive years, the company should be treated with additional caution. Particular significance should be attached to a group of directors all leaving at the same time; for example, all the non-executive directors resigning. Although the reasons may not be made public, history suggests it is prudent to assume the worst.

As a rough guide, the expected lifespan for the CEO of a major UK company appears to be about four years. The departure of the CEO is an important event for a company, and it should provide a quick and clear statement of the reasons for the CEO's departure. A warning signal flashed when the CEO of Enron resigned for "personal reasons" – although it was probably too late when Bernard Ebbers left WorldCom. If there is no statement, but there is adverse press comment on the CEO's departure, the apparent conflicting personal relationships of directors or the operation of the board, this should be taken as a convincing black mark against the company. If the directors cannot demonstrate that they are working as a team and are in control, you should sell.

Follow the finance director
The finance director, as head of the finance function, not only keeps the books but also plays a crucial role in ensuring good communications

with all investor groups. The finance director must keep them abreast of the business and maintain their confidence in it. In 2007 the UK finance director of a FTSE 100 company was, on average, male (only one woman had made it to this level), aged 49 and earned more than £1.1m in salary and bonus.

A sound working partnership between the CEO and the finance director or chief financial officer (CFO) is fundamental to the successful management of any company. The CEO of Enron pledged his "unequivocal trust" in his CFO the day before the collapse.

The departure of a finance director, other than for normal retirement or a non-contentious career move, is an extremely important event. The finance director of Northern Rock, a UK bank that had to be bailed out by the government following the 2007 credit crunch, retired in January 2007. Try to discover the reasons for the departure and details of who is going to take over the job. The sudden departure of a finance director with 3–5 years' service, to be replaced by either the chief accountant with 20 years' service or the auditor, has in the past proved a firm warning signal.

Relationship with the City

Successful companies in the UK may run into difficulties because they fail to establish a good relationship with the City. This is most often seen with small, rapid-growth companies in the years immediately following their listing on the stock exchange. A successful entrepreneur is not always best suited to dealing with institutional investors, who expect to be kept fully aware of what is going on.

The annual report lists a company's bankers and financial and legal advisers. Changes in the year of auditors, bankers, solicitors and advisers must be taken as negative indicators unless a clear and unambiguous explanation is given in the annual report.

Going for growth

Growth is often seen as a good measure of corporate success. A company growing at the rate of 15% per year is doubling in size every five years. Rapid-growth companies can be defined as those with annual growth rates of 20% or more, and supergrowth companies show a compound growth rate of around 40% per year.

Market share information can provide valuable support to the analysis and interpretation of changes in a company's turnover. The majority of companies display turnover growth details in their annual report, but few offer any details of market share. Where turnover is known for several firms competing in the same market, it is possible to devise a simple alternative to market share information. Four competing companies are shown here:

	A		B		C		D		Total	
Year	1	2	1	2	1	2	1	2	1	2
Sales ($m)	2,500	2,900	16,000	16,300	5,900	5,500	17,200	18,800	41,600	43,500
Share (%)	6	7	39	37	14	13	41	43	100	100

How their share of the joint total market changes can readily be seen. If this is done for a number of years the analysis can form the basis for a performance comparison.

A common view is that a rapid-growth company is a safe and sound investment. However, evidence suggests that rapid growth cannot always be sustained. There are of course exceptions, but it is probably safer to assume that rapid growth, particularly if associated with diversification, will not continue. If high compound growth rates are matched by increasing debt financing, extreme caution is called for.

For some companies, turnover growth is seen as the prime objective and measure of success, even when it is being achieved at the cost of profitability. In the late 1990s, e-business provided many extreme examples of this. Analysts decided to use a multiple of turnover as the basis for valuing internet companies. As soon as this became known, companies focused all their efforts on achieving the required numbers, and turnover growth became the only target. Inevitably, pressure to deliver turnover growth stimulated "creativity". If a big discount was offered to customers to get them to buy the product or service, the full price was taken into the income statement and the "discount" lost in marketing expenses. The provision for bad debts could be reduced. A company acting as an agent to sell holidays might take the full price of the holiday into the income statement rather than just the commission due on the sale. A single payment made by customers for the use of an internet site for a number of years might be taken into the current year's sales figure. These practices are contrary to GAAP, but they were adopted to boost apparent income growth.

Being pushed towards diversification to fuel continued growth is often the final challenge for the one-person company. Having proved itself in one business sector it moves into new areas, commonly through acquisition. More often than not its old skills prove not to be appropriate in the new business, attention is distracted from the core business, and it is viewed as having lost the golden touch. Its survival may depend on new management and financial restructuring.

When a one-person company's growth slows and criticism mounts, two scenarios may occur. In one, the individual running the company begins to take increasingly risky decisions in the hope of returning to previous levels of profit growth. In the other, recognising that there is little that can be done immediately to improve operating performance, the individual steps outside the law and accepted business practice to sustain his or her personal image and lifestyle. Often in these companies other executives are reluctant to "rock the boat" and go along with the deception – Cal Micro in 1997 was a good example of these problems.

Creative accounting and failure

All companies can be expected to apply creative accounting techniques to some degree. For most companies, all the necessary detail and support information is set out in the annual report, but it is unrealistic to expect attention to be drawn as clearly to problems as to good news items. To some extent annual reporting is an art form, but there are clear rules that must be followed. Breaking the rules is not an act of creativity but of misrepresentation and possibly fraud. The Treadway Commission defined fraud as "intentional or reckless conduct, whether by act or omission, that results in materially misleading financial statements". A creative finance director may be justly rewarded; a fraudulent finance director should be imprisoned.

Creative accounting is not a cause of corporate failure, but it makes it more difficult for users of a company's financial statements to appreciate the underlying performance or financial position of the business. The question then is why the company thinks it necessary to adopt this approach. If the operations and finances of a company are so complex you cannot fully understand them, walk away. If the terminology is incomprehensible, take this as a firm negative point.

Enron imploded with some $3 billion liabilities described as "special purpose entities", which enabled it to remove debt from its balance sheet and shuffle assets to create fictitious profits. Profits were overstated by £1 billion in 2001. A major frustration in the United States, resulting in the Sarbanes-Oxley Act, was that although much of Enron's accounting was aggressive or creative, it was not necessarily illegal.

Any changes in accounting policy should always be examined carefully; this is particularly important when warning signals relating to the company have been picked up elsewhere. Is the change appropriate and rational, or is it made in order to give the year's profit a boost? Changes in depreciation policy, inventory valuation, use of provisions, capitalising expenses, and treatment of extraordinary and exceptional events can all indicate a desperation to improve profits rather than provide a true and fair view (see Chapter 3).

Corporate strategy

Corporate strategy encompasses a planned approach to the achievement of defined objectives: knowing where you want to go and how to get there. The objectives or goals are the "ends" or the "where" and the strategy is the "means" or the "how" of successful implementation.

Every major company must have a strategy that is recognised and embraced by the board and ideally communicated to and accepted by all employees who are actively involved and participate in its development. The annual report should provide sufficient information to identify what the strategy is and how successfully it has been implemented. Where this proves impossible it must be assumed that the company has no strategy and so is rudderless and adrift; it will either hit the rocks or someone will take the helm.

A question central to company analysis is how to recognise a sound strategy. The answer is that it must be considered realistically capable of pursuit and that proof of positive progress towards its attainment can be found in the annual report year by year.

Single solution is no solution

If a company appears to have decided that it has found a single simple solution to its strategic problems, the likelihood is that it has not. Single solutions are often attractive, but they represent companies putting "all their eggs in one basket". If the single solution does not provide the answer, there is nowhere else to go.

Examples of potentially ambitious schemes which may take up valuable management time and attention with adverse effects on other areas of the business are those that involve product development, new technology, acquisitions, diversification and high-value contracts.

Acquisition is often seen as a good solution to company problems. However, when acquisitions are clearly outside a company's proven area of competence, bringing about rapid and major diversification, the problems are compounded. Managing businesses in new markets or overseas can speed decline, even though the acquisition may improve reported profitability in the year in which it takes place.

When a substantial acquisition represents a major diversification, experience in both the UK and the United States would probably support a view that the risk of the company failing has increased substantially. Diversification means new areas of activity which have to be experienced and mastered before positive returns are generated.

Mission and vision

Companies may include a mission or vision statement in the annual report which provides useful additional insight into its overall strategy and strategic management policy and practice. A mission statement normally defines a company's business, its objectives and how these will be attained. A vision statement is more concerned with defining the kind of company it wishes to be at some point in the future and the values needed to achieve its objectives and goals. However, the two terms are often combined or even used interchangeably.

Where to look for a strategy

It is reasonable to expect the annual report to provide sufficient information about a company's strategy and the success of its implementation to date. This information will not always be contained in a single section. It is usually necessary to study at least the chairman's statement, the directors' report, the review of operations and the financial review.

The information discussed below should appear, but not necessarily under the headings used here.

Chairman's statement

The main role of a company chairman is to run the board and its committees, allowing the CEO to concentrate on running the business. For this to work there must be a good working relationship with the CEO and executive and non-executive directors. The development of good two-way communication with all company stakeholders is also expected. The chairman oversees the composition of the board and succession planning is an important role, particularly as the lifespan of CEOs continues to reduce. The chairman is expected to provide good leadership in the process of achieving the company's objectives.

In their statements to shareholders, company chairmen are free to make any comments and take any view they wish. The statement is not constrained by legislation, auditing or accounting standards or even a code of best practice. It was originally developed as a personal comment on the year by the chairman to shareholders.

This section of the annual report is carefully read by typical investors. Indeed, it is often the only section they read, with perhaps a naive expectation of an objective overview of the company's performance and position. Chairmen are well aware of this, so it is not unusual to find that their statements concentrate on good news rather than less positive aspects of the business. Some are little more than public relations statements: high on presentation and low on content.

The quality of a chairman's statement is a useful guide to the quality of the individual charged with leading the company's strategic thinking and managing the workings of the board.

Directors' report

The directors' report was designed to assist in interpreting the financial statements and to provide additional non-financial information to users of the annual report. It provides an excellent basis for improving understanding of the operations of a company and its internal and external working relationships. The principal activities of the company are outlined with a broad description of the areas of business activity to be read in conjunction with the segmental notes. If you need to get a quick appreciation of the nature of the business, this is a good source.

The directors' report normally contains details of:

- principal activities;
- the review of the business and likely future developments;
- dividends;
- research and development activity;
- differences between market and balance sheet value of property;
- directors and their relationship with the company;
- employment policy;
- supplier payment policy;
- environmental issues;
- political and charitable contributions;
- purchase of own shares;
- major interests in the company's shares;
- post-balance-sheet events;
- auditors;
- compliance with the Combined Code.

The review of the business should give details of developments that are likely to affect future profitability, such as the launch of a new product, a major capital investment programme or planned acquisitions and disposals. However, sometimes the details given will be limited in order to avoid giving too much away to competitors.

A clear statement of directors' responsibilities towards the company, confirming that they have followed good accounting policies and practice and applied all appropriate accounting standards in the preparation of the financial statements, is normally provided here.

Details of anyone, excluding directors, owning more than 3% of a company's equity shares are provided and any transactions with a controlling shareholder described. It is not necessary to own 50% of the shares to control a company. Typically, the term "controlling shareholder" is used to refer to one owning more than 20% of a company's shares. US GAAP uses 20% equity ownership to measure a significant interest (see Chapter 2).

Social reporting

Companies have a corporate social responsibility (CSR) and can be expected to report on this. In the UK, 80% of FTSE 100 companies report on corporate responsibility in their annual reports, covering such areas as:

- the ethical behaviour of the company;
- how it treats employees
  - employee numbers and involvement;
  - sick leave, accidents, ethnic minorities, disabled employment;
  - involvement in local charities;
- human rights issues – child labour;
- relationships with society and local communities.

There are, as yet, no standards on social or environmental reporting. Sustainability is being given increasing attention by companies to make clear they are not endangering the future environment for short-term profit. The SEC requires companies to detail their environmental expenditure and the EU calls for a discussion of the environmental issues relevant to a company's operations.

Environmental reporting

Companies can now be expected to provide details of their environmental policies and activity. Typically this can be expected to provide information on:

- environmental policies;
- initiatives and improvements on previous years;
- key risks and how the company is responding;
- compliance with legislation;
- environmental expenditure;
- key performance indicators.

UK listed companies should disclose their key environmental performance indicators. Some 22 quantifiable performance measures have been made available for emissions into air, water and earth and the use of non-renewable resources.

Operating and financial review

The operating and financial review (OFR), management commentary (MC) or management discussion and analysis statement (MD&A) is where a company's strategy and its implementation together with the identification of key performance indicators (KPI) or targets should be spelled out. It should add to the amount of information available in the standard financial statements and, where things have changed, it should give the explanation (see Chapter 1). In 1998 the IOSCO published a set of recommendations as to the content of the OFR. Though these are not mandatory, they often provide the basis for the report.

The OFR is not meant to be just another set of complex numbers and diagrams – "accounting noise"; it may also contain relevant financial ratios. Any ratios should clearly relate to the published financial statements and/or be properly explained. The intention is to provide directors with the opportunity to use narrative to explain and expand on the information contained in the financial statements to shareholders. Directors are expected to indicate their views regarding the likely future prospects of the company and any significant changes expected in its operating environment.

There are normally two parts to the OFR. The first deals with a company's operating activities, often focusing on segmental analysis data, identifying any trends or events that may affect future performance. The second concentrates on a financial review covering dividends and EPS, capital expenditure and changes in equity and debt.

Typically, the OFR will cover:

- turnover trends and market share;
- analysis of changing market conditions;

- product development and new products;
- acquisitions, disposals and closures;
- financial structure changes;
- risk management;
- significant political, economic and environmental factors.

The OFR was introduced to the UK to encourage companies not only to report good news, but also to disclose:

> [The] principal risks and uncertainties in the main lines of business, together with a commentary on the approach to managing these risks and, in qualitative terms, the nature of the potential impact on results.

Some reference will hopefully be made to the key performance indicators used within the company. These will be either financial – for example, margins, earnings, or EPS – or non-financial – customer service and satisfaction, market share, new product development, productivity or employee turnover. Strategic Performance Measurement Systems (SMPS) have become popular in the past few years. These use a combination of financial and non-financial measures towards the achievement of a company's strategic objectives.

Risk disclosure

There should also be discussion of the major risks and uncertainties facing the company and how these are being dealt with. The 1999 Turnbull Report in the UK recommended that companies should disclose their risk management practices. IFRS 7 deals with the risks associated with financial instruments (see Chapter 2). The main classes of risk are identified as:

- market risk – exchange rate, interest rate, or other price movements;
- liquidity risk – possible problems in making cash available;
- credit risk – customers fail to pay.

The intention is that where a company has "obligations ... to transfer economic benefits as a result of past transactions or events" this is fully disclosed in the annual report. It does not matter how the obligation was incurred or whether it is wrapped up in a complex financial instrument or accounting jargon. If there is an existing or potential liability, you need to know about this in order to properly assess the company.

"New" measure of risk

An alternative approach to company risk assessment has been offered. It is suggested that if the number of times the word "new" appears in the annual report is counted this may provide a measure of risk.

Finance and investment

The OFR should give the current level of capital expenditure together with an indication of future intentions for non-current asset investment and, ideally, that allocated towards:

- marketing and advertising;
- employee training and development;
- research and new product development;
- maintenance programmes;
- technical support to customers.

This kind of detail can be helpful in assessing to what extent a company could, at least for a short time, reduce expenditure while maintaining the level of current operations. All the expenses listed might be cut for a short time without any immediate negative impact on profit.

One way of checking on the consistency of asset investment is to use the asset replacement rate and capital expenditure turnover ratios (see pages 186–7). The first provides an indication of the speed with which the company is replacing tangible assets, and the second links investment to turnover. Sudden shifts in these ratios can indicate a decision to reduce or halt investment in productive assets in an attempt to maintain liquidity or because finance has been refused.

The way in which capital investment projects are financed is worth investigation. The timescale of the planned investment should match that of the finance being applied. A company using short-term sources of finance to build a factory or make a long-term investment is more likely to run into difficulties than one using long-term finance.

You should expect finance for long-term assets to come from equity or long-term borrowings and for working capital to come from short-term loans or similar sources (see Figure 10.1 on the next page). The financial statements and the OFR should make clear the link between borrowing requirements and capital expenditure plans.

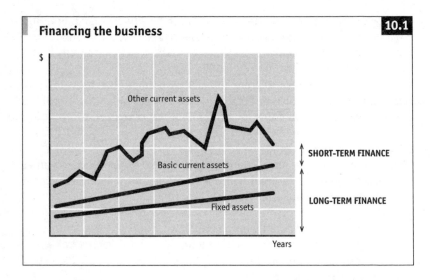

Financing the business 10.1

What you generally want to see is some consistency in the debt/equity balance and when finance is raised that it is being productively employed in the business. A simple source and application analysis of the balance sheet can give an insight into where funds are coming from and where they are employed in the business. A simple rule of financial management is that a company's long-term investment in assets should be financed from long-term sources. There should be a match between the length of time funds are being tied up in investment and their repayment terms.

The OFR should explain:

> The capital structure of the business, its treasury policy and the dynamics of its financial position – its sources of liquidity and their application, including the implications of the financing requirements arising from its capital expenditure plans.

Peak borrowings

The OFR should include some discussion on cash flow linked to the cash flow statement and liquidity disclosed in the balance sheet. This can prove particularly useful where the cash flow generated from business segments is different from the profit disclosed for them in the segmental analysis report.

The OFR should define the level of a company's borrowings throughout the year, not just those applicable at the balance sheet date. That a company may have approached, or indeed exceeded, its borrowing limits during the year is an important factor in the assessment of its current financial position and future viability.

Shareholder returns

The OFR should provide some information about dividend policy and shareholder returns. It must be accepted, however, that it is difficult for companies to commit themselves to a predetermined dividend level. Next year the profit may drop, and for a variety of reasons the company may wish to move away from its previous dividend cover or payout level (see pages 158–9 and 238). Many factors, other than profit, can influence the dividend decision, including the requirements of major institutional shareholders, how confident directors are that profit will improve quickly, general market expectations and what other companies are doing – if they are maintaining dividends it may be difficult for one company to break the trend.

Going concern

Directors must formally state that they are of the opinion that their company is a going concern. This statement most commonly appears in either the directors' report or the OFR. It is, however, normally hedged with reminders of the uncertainties of future events and the impossibility of guaranteeing continued operations.

Share price and balance sheet values

The OFR offers an opportunity for companies to comment on the "strengths and resources of the business whose value is not reflected in the balance sheet", including such items as brands and other intangibles. This can help in calculating the value of a company. More UK companies are now discussing their shareholders' equity with reference to share price and market capitalisation; this is normally included in the OFR.

Employee training and development

The annual report should contain an explanation of a company's policy in respect of the various statutory or other guidelines for the employment of minority groups and disabled people as well as equal opportunities. However, more important are details of the way in which employees are encouraged to participate in running the business and to continue their personal development and training. Companies treating investment in employees as seriously as their investment in capital assets appear to do better in improving shareholder value and long-term profitability.

The term intrapreneurship is often used to describe a positive approach to the working relationship with employees. New ideas are welcome and employees are encouraged and rewarded for taking decisions and using their initiative within their defined areas of responsibility. Flexible working hours, teams being used throughout the organisation, a fairly flat hierarchy and employee participation in performance through profit sharing can all be taken as indicating a sound employee working relationship.

Research and development

For many companies the amount invested in research and development (R&D) is directly related to their likely future performance. A useful measure of the R&D expense is to express it as a percentage of sales revenue.

Value added

Value added is an effective means of both measuring company performance and identifying the way in which the various interest groups involved share in the resources generated. If a value-added statement is not provided in the annual report, it is easy to develop one based on the income statement. Retained earnings can be defined as follows.

$$R = S - (B + Dp + W + I + Dd + T)$$

R = retained earnings
S = sales revenue
B = bought in materials and services
Dp = depreciation
W = wages
I = interest
Dd = dividends
T = tax

Value added is the difference between sales revenue and the amounts paid to external suppliers of goods and services (see page 169). This can be derived from the equation as follows.

$$S - B = W + I + Dd + T + Dp + R$$

Value added and shareholders

It can be argued that the prime objective of any company is to create value for its shareholders. Whether this should focus on maximising shareholder value or producing a balance between the interested parties (stakeholders) active in the company is open for discussion. During the 1990s companies increasingly focused on shareholder value, so much so that it almost became a mantra. Shareholder value is often mentioned in annual reports, but it is not so often or easily quantified.

Shareholders can gain value from two sources – an increase in share price or receipt of dividends. A company with high value added can decide either to reinvest funds in the business to provide continued growth or to give increased dividends to its shareholders. One simple measure of shareholder value is:

(Sale price of shares + dividends received) – purchase price of shares

Shareholder return can be calculated as:

(Dividend + (current share price − purchase share price)) ÷
purchase share price

If the dividend for the year is 10¢, the shares cost 100¢ to buy and the current price is 105¢, if the shares were sold, the shareholder return would be 15%:

$$(10 + (105 - 100)) \div 100 = 0.15 \ (15\%)$$

Such value measures can be readily understood by investors, but are not normally available from the financial figures found in the annual report.

Market value added

One way of calculating value added is to use market value added (MVA). This measures the net value of the company to shareholders – the "price-to-book" ratio. The total shareholders' equity (to which the market value of debt may be added) is deducted from the current market value (capitalisation) of the company (to which debt may be added). A positive figure means that value has been added to the shareholders' investment and a negative one means the investors have lost out. For example, if the capitalisation of a company is $100 and the shareholders equity in the balance sheet is $50, for every $1 of share-holders' equity the company has added $2.

Value based management

Value based management (VBM) is concerned with all aspects of a business, but particularly with the five "business drivers" from which shareholder value can be created:

- initial capital invested;
- rate of return on capital;
- rate of return required by investors;
- growth in capital invested;
- number of years involved.

Shareholder value analysis

Another means of quantifying shareholder value is through shareholder value analysis (SVA). This measure concentrates on seven value drivers:

- sales growth rate;
- operating profit margin;
- cash tax rate;
- fixed capital investment;
- working capital investment;
- the planning horizon;
- the cost of capital.

Free cash flow

An important factor in SVA analysis is the cash flow generating capability of a company. This is a specific measure of cash flow before taking account of the costs of shareholder or debt financing of the business. Referred to as the "free cash flow", it is normally calculated as follows:

> Operating profit
> *plus* depreciation
> *minus* cash tax paid
> = Cash profits
> *minus* investment in non-current assets and
> investment in working capital
> = Free cash flow

Free cash flow is useful in providing an indication of the level of a company's cash flow generation. It also measures the amount of cash potentially available to cover the financing costs of the business after all necessary investment has been made.

Economic value added

A popular approach is to use economic value added (EVA), which measures after-tax profit against the estimated cost of capital – normally taken as the weighted average cost of capital (WACC). Companies should be expected to produce not only an accounting profit but also one that more than covers the cost of capital. It is argued that EVA is better than earnings per share or price/earnings ratios as these do not take account of the real cost of capital.

A simple example of the calculation of EVA is shown below. After the charge of $10 ($100 × 10%) representing the estimated cost of capital, the company shows an EVA of $30 for the period.

			$
After-tax profit	$40	After-tax profit	40
Capital employed	$100	Cost of capital	10
Cost of capital	10%	Economic value added	30

A positive EVA indicates that a company is giving investors added value. A company with a consistent EVA should have an increasing MVA; it will be generating a rate of return above the cost of capital so the share price should rise. For example, the three companies in the following example are all generating a positive return on capital employed.

($)	A	B	C
After-tax profit	50	60	50
Capital employed	200	400	600
Cost of capital (10%)	20	40	60
Return on capital employed (%)	25	15	8
Economic value added ($)	30	20	−10

Although company C produces a positive 8% return on capital employed, it is actually destroying shareholder value with a negative $10 EVA. In practice, the calculation of EVA requires several adjustments – to allow for the treatment of R&D, goodwill and brand values, leases and depreciation – to be made to the after-tax profit figure. It is claimed that EVA, as a single monetary figure, is better at concentrating manage-ment attention on the "real" results of running the business than are standard performance ratios such as return on total assets (ROTA). EVA is often used as a basis for managers' performance-related incentives.

Success or failure?

Future profit overrides current liquidity

The various ways of measuring profitability and liquidity were dis-cussed in Chapters 6 and 9. Ideally, a company can be expected to focus on two principal objectives. The first is to provide an acceptable and continuing rate of return to investors, and the second is to maintain an adequate level of financial resources to support current and planned future operations and growth. A company can survive without profit as long as it has access to cash. A profitable company with no cash faces difficulties. No company can survive for more than a few days with nei-ther profit nor cash.

A truism is that a profitable company is less likely to fail than an unprofitable one. The overriding factor in deciding whether to allow a company to continue in business is its profit potential, which is more important than its current liquidity. A company with low liquidity and a high profit potential will almost certainly be helped to overcome what may be regarded as a temporary problem. A highly liquid company with declining or no profit potential is unlikely to survive for long. Why should investors leave their funds to dwindle? The only decision facing such a company is whether to end operations immediately or to continue and see liquidity and profitability decline until matters are taken out of management's hands.

Financial management indicators

The interest cover ratio neatly combines profitability and gearing; a low-profit company with high debt will have a low interest cover. Gearing is an important factor in survival assessment. A highly geared low-profit company is more at risk than a low-geared high-profit com-pany. A broad measure of the way in which the company is financed is provided by the debt/equity ratio. An alternative is the debt ratio, which expresses total debt as a percentage of total assets, allowing appreciation of the contributions by debt and equity (see page 225).

($)	A	B	C
Equity	250	500	1,000
Long-term loan	500	500	500
Current liabilities	250	250	250
	1,000	1,250	1,750
Total assets	1,000	1,250	1,750
Operating cash flow	300	200	500
Debt (%)	75	60	43
Equity (%)	25	40	57

The debt ratio measures the proportion of total assets financed by non-equity and gives an indication of short-term future viability. The higher the proportion of assets seen to be financed from outside borrowings rather than by shareholders, the higher is the gearing and the greater is the risk associated with the company. A general rule is that where the ratio is over 50% and there has been a steadily increasing trend over the last few years, this is an indication of imminent financial problems. For almost any type of business, a debt ratio of over 60% shows a potentially dangerous overreliance on external financing.

In the example, the highest geared company A with a debt/equity ratio of 200% has 75% of total assets financed by debt and 25% by equity, compared with C which has proportions of 43% and 57%. Another way of expressing this would be to use the asset gearing ratio. When equity is providing less than 50% of the total assets, the ratio moves to above 2. Company A has an asset gearing of 4 and C's is 1.75.

Cash flow indicators

Companies producing regular positive cash flow are better than those that "eat" cash flow. Operating cash flow is a crucial figure, representing the degree of success management has had in generating cash from running the business. It can be used in several illuminating measures of performance and position (see Chapter 8).

Operating cash flow ÷ interest
Operating cash flow ÷ dividend
Operating cash flow ÷ capital expenditure
Operating cash flow ÷ total debt

The first three ratios allow an appreciation of the proportion of a company's cash flow being allocated to pay for external finance, reward shareholders and reinvest in the fixed assets of the business.

For most companies, an operating cash flow ÷ interest of at least 2 or 200% is to be expected. Linking operating cash flow to dividend payments provides some assurance that sufficient cash was produced directly from the business in the year to cover the payment of dividends.

Companies cannot easily manipulate or disguise their cash flow or their financial structure. These can be combined in the cash flow/debt ratio. The higher the ratio the safer is the company. A minimum of 20% is often used as a guide level, indicating that it would take five years of operating cash flows to clear total debt. If the ratio were 10%, ten years' cash flows would be required. The cash flow from the business expressed as a percentage of the total of all non-shareholder liabilities indicates the strength of cash flow against external borrowings.

	A	B	C
Cash flow/debt (%)	40	27	67

The poor cash flow of B, the least profitable of the three companies, produces a cash flow/debt ratio of 27%. Another way of interpreting this ratio would be to say that it would take B 3.75 years ($750 ÷ $200) of current cash flow to repay its total debt. The period would be 2.5 years for A and 1.5 years for C.

To gain a better picture of the operating performance of a company, calculate the cash flow rate of return on assets (CFROA) or investment (CFROI) and treat in the manner described for ROTA analysis in Chapter 6.

100 x (operating cash flow/total assets)

A	B	C
30%	16%	29%

Working capital and liquidity

The management of working capital is critical to company survival. Continual and careful monitoring and control of inventory levels and cash payment and collection periods are essential. Working capital, particularly in connection with inventory, is also a popular focus for fraud and misrepresentation. Inventory can be overvalued or phantom inventory devised to indicate an apparent improvement in profit.

The best way to monitor working capital and cash position is to use the liquid ratio, which is calculated directly from the balance sheet, and the cash cycle, which effectively combines operating activity with year-end position (see pages 201–2 and 210–11). The liquid ratio assumes that any inventory held has no immediate value. These two ratios should then be compared with those of previous years to test for consistency and identify any trends and with appropriate benchmark companies to assess conformity with the business sector.

The ability of a company to react to unexpected threats or opportunities by adjusting the timing and level of cash flows, its financial adaptability, is an important consideration. One way of assessing this from a more pessimistic viewpoint is to use the defensive interval, which indicates how long the company might survive and continue operations if all cash inflows ceased (see page 216).

Credit rating assessment

It is better to have several compatible measures than to rely on a single one in the assessment of a company. An early approach was to select a set of ratios considered to be good indicators of financial position and weight each of them to produce an index that would act as an overall credit assessment rating.

Ratio	Weight
Liquid ratio	15
ROTA	15
Interest cover	30
Cash flow/debt	20
Sales/inventory	10
Equity/debt	10
	100

Each ratio was calculated and then multiplied by the assigned weight, the results totalled and the index for the company produced. This was then compared with an average or standard for the business sector or type of company to provide a comparative credit rating. The higher the score of the company the better was its credit rating.

This approach is still valid. It does not require substantial computer resources or a high degree of statistical competence; it can be completed on the basis of experience or personal view of a sector or type of company. It is a straightforward task to select a set of ratios that are

considered to be good indicators of performance or position for companies operating in the business sector, to weight them according to their
importance, to combine them and produce an overall index for each company.

It is recommended that the ratios are kept to a maximum of five or
six, and that each one can be directly and independently interpreted.
The simplest form of weighting is to allow a total of 100 points and allo-
cate these to each ratio according to its perceived importance. Each ratio
can be calculated as a percentage, multiplied by its assigned weight and
the results totalled to give an index. It is important to remember whether
a high percentage ratio represents a good or a bad position for a company. This will depend on the ratios incorporated in the analysis.

It is simplest to select ratios where a high percentage rather than a
low one indicates good performance or position; for this reason the
equity/debt ratio is to be preferred to the debt/equity ratio.

	Equity/debt	Weight	Index
A	0.33	10	3.3
B	0.67	10	6.7
C	1.33	10	13.3

The result is a simple composite or multivariate index that can be
used to compare companies. The benchmark index level can be that of
the sector leader or the average or median of the sample companies.

Predicting failure

Another truism is that it is inadvisable to lend money to a company that
is about to fail. The ability to predict corporate failure before the event
has been the holy grail of financial analysis for more than 50 years.
There is normally a few years' warning before a company fails; a
sudden and unexpected collapse is unusual.

Two major companies that were apparently healthy one day and
failed the next – Rolls-Royce in the UK and the Penn Central railway
company in the United States – stimulated research into whether it was
possible to predict corporate failure. The first moves away from hindsight analysis were made in the late 1960s, when work in the United
States broke new ground in the development of a multivariate approach
to failure prediction. It was similar to that described above for producing a credit rating index, but it made use of computer power and complex statistical analysis.

A set of ratios was selected and weights assigned to produce a Z score.

$$Z = 0.012A + 0.014B + 0.033C + 0.006D + 0.010E$$

A = Net current assets ÷ total assets
B = Retained earnings ÷ total assets
C = Profit before interest and tax ÷ total assets
D = Capitalisation ÷ total debt
E = Sales ÷ total assets

A Z score below 1.8 was an indicator of probable failure, and a score of over 3 was seen as a clean bill of health. The model proved capable, for the sample companies, of predicting with an accuracy of 95% failure within one year and with an accuracy of over 70% failure within two years.

An advantage of this approach is that using a combination of several financial ratios makes it less likely that the result will be affected by manipulation of the financial statements. Each ratio attempts to provide a relevant measure of company performance or position and can be used independently as an indicator of financial viability.

The greater the proportion of net current assets (working capital) compared with total assets the healthier is the short-term position. The retained earnings used in the second ratio is the figure in the balance sheet representing the amount ploughed back from earnings to provide finance for the assets employed. The higher the figure the greater is the extent of the company's self-financing. The profit before interest and tax in the third ratio indicates the contribution of a company's profitability towards the end index score, profitable companies being less likely to fail than non-profitable ones. The fourth ratio brings market value (capitalisation) into the equation. The investors' view of the future potential of the company is set against total debt. This ratio represents the only figure, capitalisation, that is not guaranteed to appear in the annual report. The last ratio shows the ability of the company to use its assets to generate sales revenue. The higher the asset turnover the greater is the number of times cash from sales can be assumed to pass through the business. The higher the ratio the more productive are the assets and the higher is the amount of cash passing through the business.

Since the 1970s, increasingly sophisticated and arcane models have been developed to aid the prediction of failure, and those undertaking the research have not always been prepared to share their findings or index weightings.

Thus the rule "keep it simple" has been neglected, and many failure prediction techniques are beyond the comprehension of the average user.

Tell-tale signs ...
There are several signs that a company may be heading for difficulties.

- It has only one product.
- It relies on a single customer or supplier.
- It is the only one in the sector showing profit improvement.
- It uses a small, unknown firm of auditors.
- The directors are selling shares.

... and fatal combinations
Identifying a number of uncomfortable factors in the annual report should be taken as a warning sign. A company may:

- be operating a depreciation policy that is out of line with other similar companies in order to produce a profit;
- have negative operating cash flow;
- have made a series of rights issues;
- have debt that is continually rising;
- have sale and lease-back agreements.

Combine these with:

- a low-quality board with little experience;
- weak non-executive directors;
- the ex-audit partner chairing the remuneration committee;
- one dominant personality as CEO and chairman;
- a newly appointed finance director.

The result will almost certainly be fatal.

Bill Mackey's list
A serious base to a light-hearted listing of possible indicators of corporate demise was provided by Bill Mackey, an insolvency expert working in the UK in the 1970s and 1980s.

- Rolls-Royces with personalised number plates
- Fish tank or fountain in the reception area

- Flag pole
- Queen's Award to Industry (UK only)
- Chairman honoured for services to industry
- Salesman or engineer as CEO
- Recently moved into new offices
- Unqualified or elderly accountant
- Products are market leaders
- Audit partner grew up with the company
- Chairman is a politician or well known for charitable works
- Recently announced a huge order in Afghanistan (or equivalent)
- Satisfied personnel with no strike records
- Recently announced a technical breakthrough

Yes to three or more? Call the creditors together, you're broke!

3
USEFUL BENCHMARKS

11 Practical examples of ratio analysis

The aim of this section is to provide useful examples of the application of ratio analysis. On pages 284–9 are a number of reasonably representative benchmarks for five sectors and six countries against which you can compare companies you are interested in. The ratios are, as far as possible, calculated from the 2006–07 financial statements of mature, quoted companies with a track record of consistent profitability in their sector.

	Retail	Food	Construction	Hotels	Pharmaceuticals
Operating profit (%)					
France	3.9	8.3	7.6	11.1	31.4
Germany	6.7	1.5	8.2	3.4	49.4
Italy	–	11.3	9.3	7.8	21.3
Netherlands	6.1	2.6	9.9	11.4	21.4
UK	7.9	7.8	7.8	11.0	26.6
US	4.9	12.3	8.5	11.4	24.8
Pre-tax profit (%)					
France	2.7	6.7	4.0	4.7	10.0
Germany	4.0	1.4	8.4	2.8	13.7
Italy	–	5.1	8.2	9.4	20.7
Netherlands	5.7	1.9	9.7	7.7	18.7
UK	7.4	6.6	10.0	26.0	25.4
US	4.2	9.6	6.4	9.3	26.8
Sales/total assets					
France	1.7	1.4	0.9	0.7	0.8
Germany	1.6	4.3	1.0	1.8	1.2
Italy	–	1.0	0.9	0.7	0.9
Netherlands	2.2	5.2	1.0	0.4	0.8
UK	1.5	1.1	1.8	0.4	0.7
US	2.3	0.8	1.4	1.1	0.9
Operating profit ROTA (%)					
France	6.0	9.0	6.3	7.5	25.1
Germany	10.7	6.6	5.9	4.5	40.9
Italy	–	11.8	9.0	4.2	19.6
Netherlands	13.5	5.2	9.3	4.8	23.0
UK	11.8	7.5	4.1	6.5	20.2
US	9.3	9.6	15.1	11.0	19.2
Pre-tax profit ROTA (%)					
France	4.4	6.8	3.2	10.4	8.1
Germany	6.2	5.9	5.7	5.3	17.1
Italy	–	5.1	8.2	7.1	19.3
Netherlands	12.6	4.1	8.9	3.2	18.2
UK	9.9	6.3	5.5	11.1	19.4
US	8.2	7.4	7.7	10.0	20.8

	Retail	Food	Construction	Hotels	Pharmaceuticals
Operating profit RONA (%)					
France	11.9	12.2	9.7	13.6	32.8
Germany	21.3	17.6	8.3	11.5	47.9
Italy	–	17.4	19.5	5.6	30.2
Netherlands	19.4	7.8	16.3	6.1	25.3
UK	12.3	11.1	20.2	9.6	28.4
US	13.1	13.3	16.9	15.3	32.6
Pre-tax profit RONA (%)					
France	8.6	9.2	4.9	5.1	10.2
Germany	12.1	15.8	7.4	8.9	12.5
Italy	–	8.0	18.1	8.9	29.8
Netherlands	18.1	6.4	14.1	4.1	23.9
UK	11.8	9.3	28.4	12.9	24.0
US	11.5	10.4	9.9	14.1	35.0
Pre-tax profit ROE (%)					
France	19.7	18.5	17.7	6.8	46.6
Germany	27.5	20.2	17.7	11.8	16.3
Italy	–	13.1	27.4	18.1	36.0
Netherlands	29.5	14.6	20.6	8.2	25.7
UK	25.1	18.4	32.2	19.2	49.9
US	21.2	26.7	31.3	47.2	25.0
After-tax profit ROE (%)					
France	18.6	6.7	14.1	5.2	29.9
Germany	15.1	12.8	12.3	9.6	11.2
Italy	–	9.0	16.4	13.0	21.5
Netherlands	23.6	10.7	16.9	6.7	9.5
UK	17.8	13.0	23.5	21.3	35.1
US	13.6	10.4	33.9	30.5	26.6
Liquid ratio					
France	0.5	0.6	1.0	0.9	1.3
Germany	0.5	0.7	1.0	0.6	2.7
Italy	–	1.4	1.0	1.2	1.3
Netherlands	0.6	1.0	1.7	0.6	1.5
UK	0.3	0.8	0.9	1.0	1.0
US	0.4	0.7	1.1	0.9	1.6

	Retail	Food	Construction	Hotels	Pharmaceuticals
Cash/current assets (%)					
France	21	57	20	37	18
Germany	24	11	20	31	14
Italy	–	15	19	35	23
Netherlands	5	8	40	11	25
UK	25	18	22	44	12
US	10	8	19	6	12
Defensive interval (days)					
France	29	19	32	70	37
Germany	42	7	23	48	103
Italy	–	43	94	115	146
Netherlands	5	12	233	16	82
UK	22	23	68	156	91
US	8	10	171	10	138
Current liquidity ratio (days)					
France	991	211	93	81	106
Germany	753	225	66	278	−105
Italy	–	−551	−85	−164	−57
Netherlands	246	35	244	130	−2
UK	308	376	226	25	48
US	704	289	−15	148	121
Sales/cash					
France	26	24	13	16	18
Germany	15	62	47	25	17
Italy	–	15	10	15	34
Netherlands	108	28	14	25	20
UK	29	18	7	20	28
US	117	94	11	57	29
Cash flow/sales (%)					
France	5.7	7.9	4.2	9.9	29.3
Germany	3.9	6.2	9.2	6.1	11.8
Italy	–	11.9	6.7	8.9	10.0
Netherlands	7.3	4.5	10.7	7.2	21.4
UK	4.4	7.5	7.8	22.1	25.2
US	5.7		8.1	7.8	20.2

	Retail	Food	Construction	Hotels	Pharmaceuticals
Net current assets/sales (%)					
France	−4.6	−1.4	5.8	−11.6	12.1
Germany	−2.7	−0.2	9.8	−4.6	55.1
Italy	−	31.1	16.4	1.5	21.1
Netherlands	8.2	4.7	30.2	−10.2	15.8
UK	−4.4	1.7	43.4	2.0	12.8
US	2.5	4.0	36.8	6.8	39.4
Days' inventory					
France	41	38	32	13	54
Germany	82	16	41	18	98
Italy	−	53	47	14	112
Netherlands	75	48	110	79	94
UK	50	43	253	4	112
US	58	61	27	48	81
Days' receivables					
France	21	25	104	39	80
Germany	8	30	58	69	72
Italy	−	68	77	42	68
Netherlands	16	31	63	42	65
UK	23	56	57	51	68
US	7	34	40	32	67
Days' payables					
France	79	60	54	25	57
Germany	80	28	65	70	132
Italy	−	81	145	22	121
Netherlands	15	40	33	157	142
UK	54	50	137	172	181
US	41	47	31	66	98
Cash cycle (days)					
France	−17	2	83	27	77
Germany	10	19	33	18	38
Italy	−	40	−22	34	59
Netherlands	77	39	140	−36	18
UK	19	49	172	−117	−1
US	23	47	37	14	50

	Retail	Food	Construction	Hotels	Pharmaceuticals
Equity/total assets (%)					
France	23	37	22	49	13
Germany	24	29	34	17	73
Italy	–	39	25	46	41
Netherlands	43	39	45	39	47
UK	43	38	33	61	52
US	42	34	25	23	56
Debt/total assets (%)					
France	28	37	43	14	56
Germany	25	8	26	42	13
Italy	–	31	16	19	26
Netherlands	27	30	21	40	28
UK	30	30	8	28	20
US	30	42	25	51	22
Current liabilities/total assets (%)					
France	49	26	35	36	31
Germany	51	62	41	41	14
Italy	–	30	59	35	33
Netherlands	30	31	35	21	25
UK	28	32	59	11	28
US	28	24	50	26	22
Interest cover					
France	6.1	3.0	3.3	12.2	16.3
Germany	6.3	7.7	9.1	3.2	19.8
Italy	–	5.5	11.9	12.2	30.4
Netherlands	10.3	2.9	8.2	2.5	21.9
UK	5.8	4.5	6.9	4.5	14.4
US	7.5	4.8	13.9	5.9	18.4
Sales/employee ($'000)					
France	400	316	460	254	270
Germany	463	360	426	181	277
Italy	–	302	311	284	489
Netherlands	562	418	403	222	403
UK	147	293	701	85	514
US	181	379	351	125	581

	Retail	Food	Construction	Hotels	Pharmaceuticals
Operating profit/employee ($'000)					
France	12	27	32	29	22
Germany	28	21	26	16	20
Italy	–	23	26	17	31
Netherlands	31	20	33	13	21
UK	11	23	98	18	43
US	10	46	39	13	30
Non-current assets/employee ($'000)					
France	161	247	386	244	166
Germany	160	121	258	193	199
Italy	–	217	165	255	191
Netherlands	138	221	229	221	172
UK	86	174	70	189	210
US	85	205	97	156	290

Glossary

English	French	German	Italian
assets	actif	Aktiva	attivitá
balance sheet	bilan	Bilanz	bilancio
cash and bank balances	trésorerie, disponibilités, caisse	Kassenbestand Liquide Mittel	cassa e banche
cost of sales	coût des ventes	Herstellungskoten	costo del venduto
current assets	actif circulant	Umlaufvermögen	attivitá correnti
current liabilities	dettes à court terme	Kurzfristige Verbinlichkeiten	passivitá correnti
depreciation	amortissement	Abschreibung	ammortamenti
earnings per share	bénéfice par action	Ergebnis je Aktie	utile per azione
going concern	continuité	Unternehmens- fortführung	continuitá operativa aziendale
goodwill	écart d'acquisition, survaleur	Geschäftswert	valore di avviamento
income statement	compte de résultat	Gewinn- und Verlustrechnung	conto economico, conto profitti e perdite
intangible assets	actif incorporel	immaterielles	attivitá immateriali
inventory	stocks	Vorräte	inventario
liabilities	passif, dettes	Passiva	passivitá
non-current assets	actifs non courants	Langfristige Vermögensgegenstände	attivitá non correnti
profit	bénéfice	Betriebsergebnis	utile
public company	Société Anonyme (SA)	Aktiengesellschaft (AG)	societa per azioni (SpA)
sales revenue	ventes, produits, chiffre d'affaires	Umsatzerlöse	vendite
shareholders' funds	capitaux propres	Eigenkapital	patrimonio netto
trade payables	dettes fournisseurs	Verbindlichkeiten	altri debiti, fornitori
trade receivables	créances	Forderungen	crediti

Abbreviations and acronyms

ADC	Average daily cost
ADS	Average daily sales
AICPA	American Institute of Certified Public Accountants
ARC	Accounting Regulation Committee (EU)
CAPM	Capital asset pricing model
CDO	Collateralised debt obligation
CFROA	Cash flow return on assets
CIFR	Committee on Improvement to Financial Reporting (advisory to SEC)
CON	Concept Statement (US GAAP)
CPA	Certified public accountant
CSR	Corporate social responsibility
DCF	Discounted cash flow
DPS	Dividend per share
EBITDA	Earnings before interest, taxation, depreciation and amortisation
ED	Exposure draft
EFRAG	European Financial Reporting Advisory Group (EU)
EPS	Earnings per share
EU	European Union
FAS	Financial Accounting Standard (US)
FASB	Financial Accounting Standards Board (US)
FRC	Financial Reporting Council (UK)
FTE	Full-time equivalent (employees)
FVTPL	Fair-value-through-profit-and-loss (financial instruments)
GAAP	Generally Accepted Accounting Principles
IAASB	International Auditing and Assurance Standards Board
IAPC	International Auditing Practices Committee
IAPS	International Auditing Practice Statement
IAS	International Accounting Standard
IASB	International Accounting Standards Board
ICAEW	Institute of Chartered Accountants in England and Wales
IFAC	International Federation of Accountants
IFRIC	International Financial Reporting Interpretations Committee (IASB)
IFRS	International Financial Reporting Standard

IOSCO	International Organisation of Securities Commissions
ISA	International Standard on Auditing
KPI	Key performance indicator
LLA	Limited liability agreement (auditors)
MC	Management commentary
MD&A	Management discussion and analysis
MOU	Memorandum of understanding (FASB and IASB)
MRP	Market risk premium
NCA	Net current assets
NOA	Net operating assets
NOCE	Net operating capital employed
OECD	Organisation for Economic Co-operation and Development
OFR	Operating and financial review
PBIT	Profit before interest and tax
PCAOB	Public Company Accounting Oversight Board
P/E	Price/earnings ratio
PEST	Political, economic, social and technological (market analysis)
Plc	Public limited company
PPE	Property, plant and equipment
PTP	Pre-tax profit
PV	Present value (discounted cash flows)
R&D	Research and development
ROA	Return on assets
ROCE	Return on capital employed
ROE	Return on equity
ROI	Return on investment
RONA	Return on net assets
RONOA	Return on net operating assets
ROSF	Return on shareholders' funds
ROTA	Return on total assets
ROTTA	Return on total tangible assets
SAC	Standards Advisory Council (IASB)
SBU	Strategic business unit
SEC	Securities and Exchange Commission
SIP	Stock incentive plan
SOCE	Statement of changes in equity
SORIE	Statement of recognised income and expense
SOX	Sarbanes-Oxley Act (US 2002)
SPE	Special purpose entity

SPMS   Strategic performance measurement system
SPV   Special purpose vehicle
SWOT   Strengths, weaknesses, opportunities and threats (analysis)
TA   Total assets
TSR   Total shareholder return
WACC   Weighted average cost of capital

Index